Shunryu Suzuki W

The Ease of Zen

Table of Contents

Acknowledgement and Note

I would like to thank all those individuals at the San Francisco Zen Center whose assistance has been invaluable in the preparation of this compilation of transcriptions.

Roshi's speaking style was such that, at times, following along could be a challenge. I have made my best efforts to clean up the texts herein to facilitate the ease of reading.

Brief Introduction

Shunryu Suzuki (1904–1971) was one of the most influential spiritual teachers of the twentieth century and is truly a founding father of Zen in America. A Japanese priest of the Soto lineage, he taught in the United States from 1959 until his death in December of 1971.

On May 23, 1959, Suzuki arrived in the U.S. to attend to Soko-ji, at that time the sole Soto Zen temple in San Francisco. Suzuki took over for the interim priest, Wako Kazumitsu Kato. Suzuki was shocked by the watered down Buddhism practiced there.

At the time, Zen had become a hot topic among intellectuals and pseudo-intellectuals alike. Suzuki began teaching and had the class do zazen for 20 minutes, sitting on the floor without a zafu and staring forward at the white wall. In each closing, Suzuki invited everyone to stop in at Soko-ji for morning zazen. Over time, more and more people would show up each week to sit zazen for 40 minutes with Suzuki in the morning.

The small group eventually formed the San Francisco Zen Center with Suzuki. Suzuki left his post at Soko-ji to become the first abbot of (one of ?) the first Buddhist training monasteries outside of Asia.

A collection of his teishos (Zen talks) appear in the books Zen Mind, Beginner's Mind and Not Always So: Practicing the True Spirit of Zen. His lectures on the Sandokai are collected in Branching Streams Flow in the Darkness and a biography of Suzuki, titled Crooked Cucumber, was written by David Chadwick in 1999.

Suzuki said "The most important thing is to find out what is the most important thing." It is to that end that this collection is offered for the first time.

The Attainment

The attainment….. here it means to resume to our true nature is actually attainments. To attain nirvana means to resume to our true nature. Our true nature is beyond our reasoning, beyond our sensory world. If.when we.when we are beyond our reasoning, or sensory world there is no problem, there is no fear. There is just our true nature itself. When we resume to our true nature we say we attained enlightenment. So actually there is nothing to attain; to resume to our true nature is our attainment. But from the viewpoint of intiate...initial awareness of the true nature it is attainment, because we will attain.we will resume to our true nature by going beyond our sensual world or sensory world, so step by step, one by one, to get rid of all the emotional functions and thinking.stop thinking we will attain enlightenment. So in this sense it is attainment. But, what we attain is not something quite different from our empirical world, so in this sense it is not attainment. So in this sutra it says "no attainment (or no dharma), no five senses or sense organs, or no world of five or six senses; no problem of birth and death, and old age and illness. Of course no self at all.

If there is no small self there is no problem. When we have no self there is nirvana. The realm where there is no problem is called nirvana. Nirvana...so...from the viewpoint of initial awareness, it is a state of no frame of mind; calmness of our mind is nirvana. This nirvana...from initial awareness.. .viewpoint of initial awareness of state.. .it is from negative viewpoint it is the calmness, but from positive viewpoint it is the origin of all our activities. All our activities is supported by this state of mind even though you are taking activity.strong activity.there must be calmness of your mind, or you will be lost in your activity.

If you have...if you obtain calmness even though you are in strong fierce activity, you will be lost if you have no calmness of your mind. So calmness should be found rather in zazen, rather in activity. You should find out the calmness in your activity rather than in your sitting posture.

And why we sit is because there is no other way to appease your innate nature. You think.perhaps you think when you are.it may be better to take some medicine, rather than to sit, but even though you take medicine, even though you obtain the calmness of your mind when you take some medicine, you will not be satisfied with it. You have deep, deep request. To appease that deep request the medicine is not strong enough or good enough. Even though you take medicine you want something more, you know.

Now my mind is very calm, but I want something more. Because you have inner, strong...some desire, you don't know how to appease it. It is just as you take food when you are hungry. Even though you take food, that is not enough. In America you have. in California you have various fruits which is very delicious and beautiful. So we Japanese think, "If I go to California I will take as much fruits as I can, best fruits" but we find out that even though we eat the best fruits in California, that is not enough and we are rather disappointed with myself or with fruits. I don't know which. The fruit is not good enough to appease my hunger. not hunger maybe. I don't know what it is but we have some inmost request. So actually something which appease your inmost request is not something which you eat, which you see, which you feel; or is not something which is called your desire or instinct. We don't know what it is, but we have some deep request, and this request is very, very deep and everyone has this kind of request. This is called our inmost nature- nature which will take various forms, which is the origin of all our activity - mental and physical.

The only way is to give up all the appeasement, all the medicine, all the way which is supposed to be effective, and to give up our desires even. When we give up everything, we will have direct insight of the hunger, direct insight of our instinct. When we know what is our inmost request, then all the things you eat, all the things you do, or see will serve as an appeasement. to appease your inmost request. That is why we sit.

Some people say, "My mind is not calm enough to sit this morning so I rather stay in bed." This is opposite. Even though you stay.. .if you are... desire is not so strong, it may be better to stay in bed. But if you find out what is our inmost request, you cannot stay in bed. You have to do something. Even though you do something it will not work. If you hit your head, or smash you hand and feet, it will not work. In this case, the best way is to sit. This is the best way.

And we should know that all those temporal means of appeasing our inmost request is not good enough. We should know that. That is why we sit, because we know it is all those temporal means of appeasing our request is not good enough.

So, when we sit, we have attainment. When we sit we have nirvana. All the Buddhas, past and present and future will attain supreme enlightenment by this practice, by this wisdom, wisdom what is the inmost nature of our selves. And they attained supreme enlightenment. A NOKU TA RA SAN MYAKU SAN BO DAI is perfect enlightenment. So, we know that, we learn that this wisdom of true nature is great, holy mantra; and great mantra and supreme mantra, and this is incomparable mantra; and this mantra will appease our request, and it will help our suffering, and it is true, and it is true it self, and it is not false, not fake, not temporal. It is true, and permanent way to attain nirvana. So we recite this sutra of wisdom, and . as follow: "Gone, gone to the other shore, gone, or reach enlightenment, and accomplish enlightenment."

This is supposed to be the meaning of this Sanskrit words; GYA TE GYA TE HA RA GYA TE HARA SO GYA TE BO DHI SO WA KA."

I don't know Sanskrit so. so much, so I will just explain this interpretation. this is "Gone, gone, to the other shore." To the other shore does not mean. figuratively speaking to the other shore. But the other. to go to the other shore means to resume to our true nature, or to find out. to realize our true nature. But this realization is not awareness or some experience by thinking, or by feeling, or by five or six sense organs. By direct experience we will know what it is. That direct, genuine experience is the experience before any thinking activity or feeling activity arises. In other words, when you just sit, you have this feeling.

True Religion

A talk is always—the conclusion of my talk is always why we should practice zazen. This is not—my talk is not just casual talk. And basically, my talk is based on Shobogenzo. And fortunately we have a system of— we have a complete system of how to understand true religion.

The true religion cannot be understood by philosophical way or scientific way. The only way to understand or to realize our true nature is just through practice. Without true practice it is impossible to realize our true nature. Of course, what we do, whether we are aware of it or not, what we do in our everyday life is based on true—our true nature. True nature drive us to do something, but if you do not understand, or if you do not realize your true—what is true nature, and if you have no system to know the actual meaning of your true nature, you will get into confusion.

There are many and many scientists who become interested in religion, it is true. Some of them are perhaps interested in true religion, but some of them will not have the true understanding of religion. As long as there are just—their understanding is just limited in scientific realm, it is impossible to know what is true religion because religion should be understood by religious way. Religion is not understood by philosophy or science.

And some philosophers, of course, may [be] interested in true religion, but it is impossible for philosophers—it is impossible to reach the complete understanding of religion through philosophical study, because in philosophical study the conclusion of philosophy will be different. The authority of Greek philosophy is still powerful in this age. So it is very difficult to understand—to reach the true understanding of religion which everyone will agree with it.

So—but Soto school has pretty deep philosophy, but as I said last night, the Shobogenzo, or the philosophy of Zen, is just a lid, just a cover of a pan, because people may interested in Zen, but it may be rather difficult for them to know what is true Zen. Without some intellectual understanding, it is difficult to figure out what is Zen. So that is why we have philosophy of Zen. But by philosophy you cannot have true understanding of Zen. Zen should be understood by Zen, by practice of Zen, not by philosophy—even by Shobogenzo, even reading—even by reading Shobogenzo, you cannot understand what—you cannot realize what it—actually realize what is Zen.

So only way is just practice Zen with right understanding. If you do not have right understanding, the—your practice will be mixed up with some other practice. And that is why, I think, in America there are so many misunderstanding of Zen.

So by Shobogenzo we have to polish our practice, and we have to keep various misunderstanding—keeps our practice [of] Zen from various misunderstanding. That is why we have Shobogenzo. That is why in sesshin I should talk. This kind of talk is not, you know—the purpose of my talk is not to give you some knowledge, but to—by my talk I want you to—I want to encourage your practice without being interested in philosophical depth of our system. In this point, if you make misunderstanding, result will be pretty serious.

And fortunately our system of encouraging people is the same—is the same as other schools—philosophy of other schools. So if you understand Shobogenzo, you will understand some other schools and why there are so many schools in Buddhism. If we do not have this system of various schools in Buddhism is quite different from other schools, and there will not be any connection with each other. With this system, we will —each schools—we will find out the meaning of existence—why Soto Zen exist, why Rinzai Zen exist, why Pure Land school exist, why Tendai school exist, why all those schools are important. Unfortunately, it is rather difficult to translate Shobogenzo in English, but we are making effort to do it. And many scholars has given some interpretation—some modern, or some up-to-date interpretation to it. So if we only have time, it is not impossible to give you complete system of our understanding of Buddhism.

We say we have two kinds of knowledge: intuitive knowledge and—and thinking, discriminating knowledge. The scientific knowledge and the philosophical knowledge is the dualistic thinking knowledge. As long as we use word and we think by words, it is impossible to reach the absolute conclusion. When we just resume to our own nature, which is universal to everyone, we can achieve—we can realize our true nature, which is universal to human being and even for animals, and plants, and everything—existence. And that is why in Zen practice we stop our mind. We do not put any consideration to our sensitivity or thinking. Whatever image come, you just accept it and let them go out. And whatever sound you hear, you let them come in and let them go out. When you do not pay any attention to outward object, you will find out your true nature.

This true nature, when you are healthy and practice zazen in this way, it— it is just calm and some inexplicable thing itself. But when you have some actual problem—when you have pain on your legs, you will have direct experience of your true nature. But, you know, don't [make the] mistake [that] that is true nature. That is true nature plus something—plus your painful legs. Something is added on true nature, and true nature takes the form of pain. This relationship is very important, and if you understand this relationship—your true nature and your pain—there is a key to solve all the problem of life. Through problem we will realize our nature—true nature. When we—when I am hungry, what I feel is what you will feel when you are hungry . There might be some difference, but not much difference.

And how you feel when you sit is how everyone feels when you sit. Strictly speaking, that is enough, even though you do not attain enlightenment . If everyone sit and find out how you feel when you sit, that's good enough. We will—in this point—we will reach some agreement. But if you are caught by some fancy idea of religion—there may be various religion—and you don't know what religion is yours —Buddhism, Christianity, or Indian religion, or some folk native religion—you don't know what to choose. Sometimes everyone—every religion looks like same. Sometime it doesn't look like same. But when religion is studied [in] the most simplest way, the most universal way, for an instance, want of sleep, or hunger, or pain, or—we will reach the universal religion—universal religion even to animals. Here we have common playground. Everyone will play in this common playground.

So you shouldn't have—according to Buddha, or our patriarchs, or founder of various religion—you should not have too fancy idea of religion. Religion should be understood [by] the most foolish man, not learned wise man. Wise man's religion is very complicated and very fancy. If he is s—too great, you will—you will be attached to his religion. That is good. If you really want to do it, that's good —but just because of the name or, you know, some gaining idea.

We should not attach to some particular religion. That is why we say don't study religion with gaining idea—gaining idea. Gaining idea is not— gaining idea is not based on your true nature. That's a very superficial desire—not so deep as your hunger. When we give up various gaining idea, we will find out our true nature. And this true nature is very primitive, of course. And at the same time it could be very, very refined and deep, lofty idea—desire. In this primitive, fundamental desire there are true strengths and various possibility. But if you start from fancy idea of religion, you will be confused, more confused. So to realize why we study—why we study religion is to find out the meaning of our fundamental desire—how important it is, and how miraculous it is, and how much possibility it has.

When we—all of us is concentrated on this point, there will not be any religious sectarianism. Because we start from some particular philosophy of religion, we have various sectarianism. When we have just one lid, just one cover which covers various pan and bowls , there will be no problem. Our cover, our philosophy, is not the same philosophy as usual philosophers will provide for us.

Today, I just gave you some general—general idea of our system. But this point, as a Soto student, this point should not be neglected. We should be—when we study Buddhism intellectually, we should be concentrated on this point and—as well as your practice. Just practice is not so good, because you may practice zazen for sake of something. You will abuse your Zen practice until you mix pure practice with various fancy or wrong practice.

In short, Soto way is to use everything in right purpose and to put everything [in] its own— its own place. What should be put on high place should be put on high place, and what should be put on floor should be on floor.In America, you know, you put scriptures on the floor where you walk. We don't, you know. But I don't know how to do it—how to treat those scriptures in your way of life. So until I find out some way, I don't say, "Don't put scriptures on the floor." But this is not supposed to be put on—supposed to be treated as a rubbish, you know— as rubbish. This is not rubbish. Scripture should be put on table, or altar, or in your hand. Those small things is very important.

And this idea—with this idea, we study science: What is science? What is religion? What is philosophy? There is the way to study philosophy. There is particular way to study science. There is particular way to study religion. Religion should be studied by religious way, not by science. Scientist cannot criticize what religion unless he become religious. But—and religious—religion gives—or give way [to] science and philosophy. The find—to find the meaning of science is religion. To find the meaning of philosophy is religion. But science or philosophy—in science or in philosophy, there is no religion. This relation—this relationship is very important. Dogen Zenji says, "Our ordinary way—although you know our ordinary way—in our ordinary worldly life there is no Buddha's way." People understand that or not, I don't know —may not understand it, but he says: "They may understand there is no—it is impossible to realize—to know what is religion in worldly way. But from viewpoint of religion, there is no worldly life. Everything what we do is religion.

This kind of system is very important for us. I shall be very glad if you find out why this kind of understanding is so necessary for us. It is very important because it is the only way to find out the harmony in various religion we have. When various religious people understand this secret— this system, the religion will be one: not Buddhism, not Christianity, not one school of Christianity or Buddhism. The one whole big family of religious people will be established. There is this possibility in his [Dogen's] understanding.

Right Way

For a long time after Renaissance, you have forgotten the value of religion. You try to exchange religion for, you know, science and philosophy. You—you are Christian , but actually what you have been doing is to replace science to religion—to exchange science. And you wanted to establish, you know, human culture, which is quite free from authority of religion. You have quite good reason in your effort to try to exchange or try to reform your culture before it is too dark . Now it is too bright . You went to the —too extreme, I think .

But recently, even though you have excellent—very advanced culture, but there is something—there is something which you don't know what to do— or that is your mind . You don't know what to do with this mind. You have various tools, but you have no mind to use it . That is your problem, I think. And we, you know, we Japanese people studied what is our mind , but we have enough tools , so we become attached to your civilization too much and almost forgetting what we have studied . That is our problem just now. So combination of the two will create something wonderful, I think.

If I say, "Treat everything in right way," it looks—it will—it looks like very rigid and formal, but it is not so. This secret of Dogen Zenji will work. Someone said Western people failed in creating their culture by ignoring true—ignoring religion. And Oriental people made a great mistake in abusing religion. The Buddhism is—was too handy, so they—we abused religion too much. So now we don't know what is true religion. Oriental religion is mixed up , you know. In— in India, in China, or in Korea, even in Japan, Buddhism is so handy that they use religion instead of medicine. They use religion instead of education, science, and every— our culture is based on Buddhism. That is too much for us . And you abused Buddhism—Oriental people abused Buddhism too much. When you abuse something, you know, the true original advantage will be lost. If you cut paper by razor, razor will—will be blunt? What do you say?

Dull—will not be sharp enough. So you should not use razor when you cut paper. That is why Dogen Zenji emphasized the purity of the Buddhism—the religion. Religion should be pure and sharp always so that it can serve its original purpose, its own purpose. Leave every— activity for some other people. We religious people should devote ourselves to the pure genuine religion. And we should keep religion always sharp enough to cut various entanglement completely.

This is why Dogen worked so hard. And this is why I came here and why you are studying Buddhism.

Way-Seeking Mind

In our way of Zen, we emphasize the way-seeking mind—way-seeking mind. This is, in another word, bodhisattva-mind or way-seeking mind. In Zen, people say "way it is" or "to observe everything as it is." But "the way as it is" or "to observe things as they are" will not be the same what you mean by that. I don't know what—how do you understand "to observe everything as it is." I find out there are big misunderstanding in your understanding of "way it is" or "to observe things as it is."

We mean—I think if I say "to see things as it is" means to observe things in rather scientific way or materialistic way. In your philosophy, there is two ways of—you say "things as it is" and "things as it should be." Now this is two contradictory—not "contradictory," but this is two antonymy. Things do not exist "as it should be." And you do not observe "things as it is." And you observe things your own way. You observe things "as it should —as it should not be" or, you know, you thinks "there is flower." But actual flower is changing. So—and yet you see the flower —"there is flower, and this flower is always like this." This is, perhaps, your understanding of flower. But actually the flower is changing. When you see something in scientific way, actually, you do not see "things as it is." And you knows—and yet you know what is true and what is not true. But you like—you [are] apt to—you [are] apt to see things as it—"as it should not be."

This—in this point, there is big mistake. So when we say "to observe things as it is" means "to see things as it should be" . For you, this is opposite, you know. For you, way should—we say—when we say "to observe things as it is" means "to observe things as it should be." Do you understand? In your—for you, "as it should be" and "as it is" is quite different. "As it should be" means "it is not so, but it should be so." It means some—in this case, you have some moral—morality, or you want to be religious, or you want to be moral. But human being is not so. We are not always moral. Or we are not always religious. So we should be more moral, or we should be more religious. "This is way it should be." And when you are not religious, when you are not good, that is how you are. So "way it should be" is—means morality or religion. And "way as it is" is science.

But for us, "things as it is" is morality, not science—is morality—"things as it is." So to observe "things as it is" means to—to be moral and to be religious. It's what I mean by "way it should be." So statement is same, but what we mean is opposite, not same.

When you take religious viewpoint, everything become opposite , you know. You are talking same thing from this scientific standpoint, and we are talking from religious standpoint. So same statements makes big difference. And this misunderstanding—the misunderstanding you have about Zen, I think—when we say:

Zen, oh, Zen is wonderful . Whatever you do, that is Zen . Even though you are doing something wrong, that is Zen. Whatever you do is Zen. That is why I like Zen.

This kind of misunderstanding I think you will have about Zen. But what we actually mean is quite opposite.

And way-seeking mind—what I'm going to talk just now is the problem of to choose one—one of the two: good or bad. Refrainings from bad to take good is way-seeking mind, not from moral viewpoint but from religious viewpoint. When we take religious viewpoint, there is no alternative way. We should choose good. And we should refrain from bad. There is no alternative way. But if you have no way-seeking mind, or if you have no idea of religion, you will wonder which to choose.

In morality, when you choose one of the two, you have freedom of choice; whatever you do it is up to you. You can take bad instead of good . But if—once you choose good, you have responsibility for taking good, that is, moral responsibility you have. But that is responsibility. But in religion we have, we—I said, no alternative way, but it is our choice, you know. Which way to go is our—up to us. And yet, for—for us there is no other way than to take good. This is way-seeking mind. So to pursue good and truth and beauty is also our way-seeking mind, although there is some difference from ethics. This mind is the mind—traditional mind transmitted from Buddha to us, and for Zen students this is most important spirit.

Enlightenment, so, is not only kind of state of mind, a kind of psychological state of mind. When the—some psychological state of mind is supported by right wisdom, we call it enlightenment. When it is supported by way-seeking mind, when you attain that state of mind by everyday practice, by way-seeking mind, that is called enlightenment. Even though you attain—or you have—you obtain the same psychological state of mind by LSD , if you lack the way-seeking mind, we do not call it enlightenment. That is quite different matter. It should be based on the way-seeking mind.

So Dogen Zenji said when you hit the mark, that is the same effort you have been doing. After trying ninety-nine times—suppose after trying ninety-nine times of failure, you hit the mark at the one-hundredth—one-hundredth time. That effort, that meaning of—meaning of "hit the mark" and the meaning of "losing the mark" should be the same. The difference is, now you hit the mark . You—from, you know, materialistic viewpoint, you know, to lose the mark is not good at all . You should hit the mark. But from the meaning of practice, actual practice, even though you lose it, the meaning of the practice is the same: to hit the mark or lose the mark is not different. That is our, you know, enlightenment.

So enlightenment only is—it is not only enlightenment that is valuable. The failure by true spirit is also valuable. It has same meaning. So even —so that is why even though your zazen is not perfect, it has same meaning if you have way-seeking mind. If you do not have way-seeking mind, even though you attain enlightenment, that enlightenment is so-called-it "dry enlightenment" . Dry enlightenment. No meaning in it.

This is bodhisattva-mind. So this mind is universal to everyone. There is no difference between priest or layman. There is no difference [between] wise man or for—when we have way-seeking mind we are all—all bodhisattva. This is so-called-it bodhisattva-mind.

Again, this bodhisattva-mind is impossible to—to value. It is "non-value" practice. And this bodhisattva-mind—if you have some question this— about this bodhisattva-mind, I think it may be interesting to discuss about this point. Enlightenment, or way-seeking mind, or to help others before we attain enlightenment is bodhisattva-mind—-spirit. Even though you— before you save yourself, you should save others. This is also bodhisattva-mind.

Non Dual Bodhisattva-Mind

Bodhisattva-mind, which is rather dualistic, but if you understand bodhisattva-mind in dualistic way, it is not right understanding. When you try to understand bodhisattva way by thinking or philosophical way, it is dualistic. Each school has its system of teaching, but Zen has no system of philosophy. Although we have—Soto school have—has Shobogenzo, that is not possible to understand [in] just [a] philosophical way. That is why when some scholar write something about Shobogenzo, he will submit what he wrote to some Zen master, you know. He does not announce, or he does not print before a Zen master check-up. This is—this point is pretty strict with our—in our schools because just philosophical understanding is not good enough as a work of Soto school. So we—we are pretty strict with this point.

Whenever you write something, strictly speaking, it should be checked up by some Zen master. And mutual understanding is wanted [between] scholar and Zen master. It is very difficult to tell just by reading. The mutual correspondence is wanted, or mutual, you know, "Hi, how are you?" . This kind of friendship is necessary between Zen master and scholars. We have many scholars and Zen masters. And Zen masters and Zen scholars should be always, you know—must be quite intimate, and mutual understanding is wanted.

You cannot be both scholar and Zen master . If it is possible it may be wonderful, but we are not so capable. It can't be helped. If you want to read or understand—because it is necessary for a scholar to understand Shobogenzo and other culture too, or else, you know, his teaching will not work. So for scholar it is necessary to read many and many books and to understand Eastern culture and Western culture. This is necessary for—for us. And Zen master should devote himself to our own teaching and practice. But as both scholars' and masters' understanding is based on Shobogenzo, the mutual understanding will be easily attained.

Bodhisattva's way in other school is rather philosophical, and that is why they have their own system. But for Zen school, bodhisattva's way is—our practice itself is bodhisattva's way. Not philosophy, but our actual practice is bodhisattva's way. Or management of the monastery is itself bodhisattva's way.

As someone asked me last night, how do—how is it possible to help others, or what is the right way to help others? To help others—the most important point in helping others [is] to actualize bodhisattva's way in its true sense. So you can actualize bodhisattva's way in your management of Zen Center, or in your management of a monastery or a temple. If you actualize his way, that is also dana-prajnaparamita.33 That is to help others, to give something, to give most valuable things to the society. If you actualize our way in your actual life, that is the most valuable contribution to the society. Even though you give something, if you give it, you know, something in wrong way it will create more trouble. So just to give something is not our way. It was given—everything was treated in right way in bodhisattva's way.

So bodhisattva's way of helping others is not some moral code or some written conditions. To help others does not mean actually to give something or to lead someone in special way. So if you want to understand what is actual bodhisattva's way, you should practice our way. That is why Dogen Zenji was particular to our everyday life. He was very, very particular because he thought it is impossible to express what does it mean by bodhisattva's way in word or in philosophy. Before he gave up philosophy, before he gave up art, or literature, or scientific approach, he had had pretty good understanding of science. Today we call it science, but at that time in Japan there is no idea of science. It was twelfth century. But he was—in this point he was wonderful person. He — he understood—in his mind—he was very scientific mind, and he was— he understood philosophy of history and history—philosophy itself. And he had good knowledge of philosophy of religion as you started at—by— after Kant.

By the way, when we say science or philosophy, we mean pure science, pure philosophy, not philosophy under the authority of God or some particular belief. It is the same philosophy after you have had—after— since Renaissance. This is good points—good point—one of the good points of Buddhism. We, you know, we treat human being as human being. Religion is not some particular thing. Religion is to find—to find true meaning of human nature. We do not try to change human being to God. From beginning to end, we are human being. We should be human being. There is no need to be God . Some religion, you know, treat us as a god.

Christian—in Christianity, I think it is impossible for you to be a god, the God. So for Christianity there is—Christian—there is no danger in this point . Human being is always human being. I don't know after you die what you will become. What will become of you I don't know. You go to heaven and you—will you become a god or what? I don't know exactly. Maybe even though you go to heaven, you are human being and simple person, maybe. Unless you cannot be a god. Which —which is it? Are you supposed to be a god when you go to heaven? Or still human being?

………But anyway, we have this kind of mind. And this mind is very important. And we call it buddha-mind, which is impossible to explain why. This mind was accepted by your philosophers. And this mind is called by Northrop "ideal," and this ideal means buddha-nature in ourselves.

But philosophers found out in logical or in philosophical way what was our true nature. But no one bring it—no one had brought it in our practice. So that is why Zen—we have in— Buddhism has practice of zazen. To bring something which is inexplicable to actual practice is Zen—Zen practice. This is one of the eight—eight noble truths. That is why Zen is so important in our—in Buddhism. Without Zen the teaching of Buddha cannot be understood by us.

So anyway, in East and in West, the truth is always same, and we are coming to the same conclusion, I think. Although the way is different, but more and more your philosophy will become like Shobogenzo, and our way will become more and more scientific. And in this way I hope we will achieve something very good.

Now here we are practicing a very rigid way after the example of Japanese way, but it does not mean we are forcing our way to you. It does not mean so. But it will give you some suggestion, and it takes, I think, pretty long time before you establish your own way. So for you, a pioneer of Buddhism, it may be pretty difficult . But if you have right understanding of our way, you can explain it, you know, why we have this kind of practice and why you should do this kind of practice. Then they will understand our way pretty well.

So the most important point is not to be one-sided. Practice and study is both important. But it is not possible for anyone to, you know, achieve many things. So, as I said, to have same cover, you know , is very important point. Cover should not be used. When you do something you should take off the cover . If you want to boil something by cover , you will get it—into confusion. Cover is, you know—for us, cover—the cover is the Shobogenzo. This is perfect understanding of our way. But perfect understanding will not work . It's too perfect . So—but it will keep dust from the pan, and if you put cover on your pan you can use it whenever you want to use your pan. So it is very important to have a cover to it.

Dogen thought that, as he wrote, it is not the time to make them understand what is Buddhism in Japan right now. It is not. It was not possible. So he trained several [of] his disciples, and he prepared perfect cover , so that some day people may use the pan of Soto school. Before they use Soto way, it is—it was necessary for him to put cover to it. That is Shobogenzo. That is why Soto school exist after seven hundred years later. Still exist—Soto school still exist because of the cover he made . If there is no—he—if he didn't prepare any cover to it, as we are human being, so it was impossible to keep his pure teaching always fresh and in use.

Everyone agreed in this point that his cover was the best cover, anyway. No dust can enter the pan, it was so perfect cover. Everyone agree with that. So we have to understand—we have to have some Soto priest who can understand what is Shobogenzo. And there must be many Zen masters who is actually practicing zazen. But those who practice zazen will some make—will make some mistake, you know . So we should, you know, have cover. Mistake, by "mistake" I mean dust, you know . Soon we will be dusty. There may be many and many misunderstanding of Zen. When we become— when we enter some astray or dead end , we should find out what we are doing. That is Shobogenzo

The Purpose of Practice

Purpose of practice is to have direct experience of buddha-nature. That is purpose of our practice. So whatever you do, it is—it should be the direct experience of buddha-nature.

We say—in fifth precept we say, "Don't—don't—don't be attached"—not "attached," but—"don't be—don't violate event the precepts which is not here." It is rather difficult to understand. In—in Japanese it is not so difficult, but in English it is rather difficult to understand. It means, anyway—we say when you sit, you say I have something—something occurred in your mind which is not so good. Some image come. Something covered your wisdom or buddha-nature. When you say so, you have the idea of clearness, you know, because you have—you think you have to clear up your mind from all images; you have to keep your mind clear from various images which will come to you, or which you have already—you have—which you have already should be cleared up. This —so far you understand it, but Dogen Zenji says:

Don't—don't even try to clear up your mind, even though you have something here. Don't want to be pure. If you want to be pure, it means you have attached in—to pureness—purity. That is also not so good. Don't attach to purity or impurity.

Do you understand? So when you [are] bothered by what you have done, it means you—you are attached to purity. This is not good.

Our buddha-nature should be beyond pure or impure. It means just to be aware—just to be aware of your true nature which is beyond pure or impure. Do you understand? Purity is not—to attach to purity is good, but buddha-nature is not pure or impure. Do you understand this point? If you understand this point, just to sit without thinking—without [being] bothered by something which will come, or even though you have something in your image, don't try to escape from it. Just sit. It will go. And you are beyond it. Those come and—come in and come out of the images. This is so-called-it—you have—you are beyond intoxicating liquor.

This is fifth precept. And interpretation to the fifth precept. In fifth precept we say, "Don't take, don't sell, or don't buy intoxicating liquor." Don't buy —don't buy some images, or don't sell some images, some intoxicating liquor, some attachment. Don't sell any attachment to anyone. Or don't buy any attachment from outside.

And to this precept he said, "Don't be attached even to the purity, even to the evil which—which is not here. To attach to the evil which is not here means purity." You know, if there is no evil here, you are pure. But don't be attached to even the state of mind you—you have in purity. And even though you are not pure, don't try to be—escape from it. If you try to escape from it, it means you are attached to the purity. A small ego is working still. Your small ego is trying to push out the evil thought. So still you are occupied by small ego as long as you are trying to get out of it.

So the most important point is to acknowledge exactly what is buddha-nature. The buddha-nature is not small ego; it is big ego which is observing what you do and accepting what you do always. Whatever you do, he will say, "Ah, that's good." "Nothing wrong with it," he —he may say.

So if you have—if you are always aware of the true nature, that is enlightenment. There is big misunderstanding in our practice, I think.

Most of people have this misunderstanding:

The practice is some—something which we try to get out of evil. This is our practice. If we by training—eventually we will attain enlightenment, and we would be completely free from evil. That is our practice.

This is usual understanding. But this practice is small practice, not big practice, not pure practice. That practice is your small practice. There is no big mind in your practice. So to be aware of—to—knowing what is true buddha-nature—what is true nature—being aware of it, and—and practice our practice as a practice of big mind is our true practice.

So in our practice there is no evil or no good. It is not matter of evil or good. Both is good. There is no need to fight with it. Just let them come and let them go out. So-called-it evil or good are something which your small mind created. In—for your true nature there is no good or bad. Your true nature is something which is beyond good or bad. It is valuable because it is beyond good and bad. It is valuable—it is—because you cannot figure out what it is.

If you cannot accept something intelligible, you are still pursuing good or bad in worldly sense, scientific way, philosophical way, or ethical way. You are not pursuing religious practice.

Ryokan—do you know Ryokan? A famous Soto priest. He didn't mind "nothing bad"—the secret of the Soto way. Concerning Soto practice, he was very strict, but he didn't—he didn't mind whatever they say or whatever he himself feel. He doesn't mind—he didn't mind at all. Even though he is sick, he didn't mind. Even though people did not understand him, he did not mind at all. But if someone ask seriously—seriously, if he is not serious he didn't mind, but when he thought someone was quite serious or sincere, he mind very much. And if he—if someone ask him what is Soto way, he was very serious. While he has strict sense of buddha-nature, his buddha-nature is very very sharp and strict. Because of that strictness, he can accept whatever life he had —he could accept his life—his poor and humble and unfortunate life. But he didn't mind at all because he had, you know, strict sense of buddha-nature.

So our practice is the practice to accept everything as it is and to do things as much as you can. Don't be greedy about your progress in your practice. If you can make progress, little by little, as much as you can, that is enough. But concerning to the sense of buddha-nature, it should be very clear and strict.

We say you cannot plant any plants on the stone . You should be like a stone. You cannot plant anything on it. Any good or evil cannot grow on the buddha-nature. It is so hard and so strict. Good and bad is delusion. Any delusion can cannot grow on your spirit. Or we say shinsatsu— when you—this is Chinese word. You cannot—any needle can—cannot thrust into—thrust into a stone. Shinsatsu—when you—it is impossible to thrust a needle into a iron. This kind of spirit is wanted when you practice our practice. Then you will make—little by little you will make progress.

So Dogen Zenji says our practice is like to go through the fog. It is not like to go out in thunderstorm . If you go out in heavy rain, your clothes will be all-at-once wet. You will be soaked in water, but sudden rainstorm will not penetrate in your, you know, underwear. It will be like when you walk through the thick fog for a long time, even though you don't know —realize your clothing is wet, it is wet, and it will penetrate into your underwear. This is the true practice. You don't think you made some progress, but you did a remarkable progress if someone who knows what is real practice will acknowledge it.

Some people asked Ryokan, "Do you have—do you have—in—do you have Daihannya-kyo—Great Wisdom Scripture? We have 600 volume of scriptures about the wisdom. Do you have Great Wisdom—Scripture of Great Wisdom—600 volumes in your temple?" someone asked. And he asked him to write Daihannya-kyo in Chinese character on his back. "You—please write down Daihannya-kyo—Lo-pya-kan—here on his back. Thank you very much." "Here we have Great Wisdom Scripture—Scripture of Great Wisdom, and today I—I want to dry those 600 volumes of scriptures in the sun so that no worm can eat it. So he write down in the sunshine. Now today we have mushiboshi. Mushiboshi means, in Japan, once a year we spread all the scriptures in the sunshine when it is—when it is fine and dry. "So tonight we will have party, so please join us," he said . It means if you cannot acknowledge, you know, my practice, may be better to write down big Prajnaparamita Sutra. "I am the big Prajnaparamita Sutra," you know. "If you don't acknowledge me, please write down on your back so that you can acknowledge it."

People who has no understanding of true practice cannot acknowledge who is good or who is bad. That is true. He himself—even for he himself [it] may be difficult to know how much progress he made. But for him this is obvious. For him each day is—is good day, and each day is day of enlightenment. Enlightenment is on each day, on each practice you do, as long as you have clear understanding of buddha-nature.

Dogen Zenji looks like giving his work for us [in a] rather philosophical way. But it is not so. It is not philosophy at all. That is why it is difficult to understand in philosophical way or to translate it in English. In English you have—you haven't enough vocabulary to express it. Chinese or—for him Chinese or Japanese was not perfect. So he made many words for himself to express his idea. That is why it is difficult to translate it.

But here what we are discussing about is not philosophy at all. What I am saying is not philosophy. So if you understand what I say, it is possible to know what I mean by buddha-nature, I think. It is possible because although my English is not good but I think I can express myself about buddha-nature in my poor English . That is why I repeat same thing over and over again. When I think you don't understand, I will repeat it until you understand it. If my words is not good enough, I will hit you . Then you will understand what I mean. As long as I understand it, you will understand what I mean—someday . If you—if you don't understand me just now, some day you will understand. Someday someone will understand. This is great patience. I think I will wait for a island to go to Seattle from Los Angeles . They say it—it is moving from Los Angeles to Seattle like a boat in millions of millions of years. By the time it will reach to Seattle , someone will understand it.

So if you don't understand it, I don't mind at all . Buddha said whether you take my medicine or not is not my responsibility. Just to talk about it—just to try to help people is my way. Whether or not you take it, that is not—it can't be helped if you don't take it. That is true. But he said:

I left—I prepare—I—I prepared everything [for those] who will understand me. And I saved people—all the people which is possible to save. And I prepared to save all people when the time come. So I saved all the human being in my eighty years of age.

That is true. So I don't think—he wouldn't mind—if one of his disciple understand him, it's good enough. There is possibility to save all human being if one of the—his disciple understand him. In this way, Buddhism was spread, one by one, little by little.

When we become lazy, Buddhism looks like no more. But when we have to be sincere, Buddhism will come out. Buddhism will be understood. You may say there is no more Buddhism in India or China or even in Japan, but Buddhism is eternal teaching.

Don't be Bothered by Your Mind.

The science or philosophy is like a dissection. It is possible to analyze what we did after we did something. But it is already dead corpse —dead corpse of our practice. So even though you analyze what you have done, it will not work. It will not help you so much. It is nearly the same as to count your lost child's age . So we cannot help counting our lost boy's age. It is our nature, but actually it will not help us so much.

So the most important thing is to understand our true mind or inmost nature in our practice. How we understand our actual mind is the most important point—should be the most important point. That is why Zen emphasize to live on each moment.

Bodhidharma said—Bodhidharma, the First Patriarch of Chinese patriarch —he is 28th patriarch from Buddha, and in China he is the First Patriarch —and he said, "If you want to see a fish—if you want to see a fish, before you see a fish, you have to watch water." Do you understand? If you want to see a fish, you have to watch water before you see the fish. If you want to see the buddha-nature, you have to see your small mind before you see buddha-nature. Actually, when you see water, there is true fish. Don't you think so? Here, by "fish" he meant "true nature." If you want to see the true nature, when you see the water, there is true nature. The true nature is watching water. You are watching water. At the same time, true nature is watching water.

As Decartes says, "I think, therefore I am." What does it mean? Here, "therefore I am": I— that "I" is not just small mind. He could not deny that "I" which thinks, which watch water. That someone, who is watching—you —who is watching water is true nature itself. You think fish is true nature , but it is not true nature. You—you are watching water. And that "you" cannot be denied. That is ultimate existence. And at the same time, that is universal existence. That is your "I" and at the same time it include everything.

Anyway, when you watch water, there is actually—actual fish is in the water. Before you see the water, there is fish. Before you see the buddha-nature, you see your mind. You watch your mind. When you watch your mind, when you say, "My zazen is very poor zazen" , here you have true nature. But you, you know, fail to realize—do not realize that is true nature. You ignore it on purpose. This is a silly mistake. There is immense importance in the "I" when you watch your mind. That "I" is not big "I." That "I" is always incessant activity. That "I" is always acting. That "I" is always swimming. That "I" is always flying through the vast air with wing. Here I mean by "wing," thinking and various activity. That "I' is flying through the vast sky.

In this case, the vast sky is his home—is my home. There is no bird or no air. Air and bird is one. So Dogen Zenji says, "Fly—bird flies like a bird; fish swims like a fish. Water is his home. And when she swims—when it swims in the water, it is water and a fish are—a fish—there is nothing but fish. The all the water belongs to him. And when he can swim everywhere, it means he can think. That thinking is right thinking. Logical thinking, after you did something, or analytical thinking is not true thinking.

So in your practice, whether or not that practice is good or bad, perfect or imperfect, when this kind of mind is at work, your practice is practice of enlightenment. Your practice include everything, within and without. Whole world is your home, and everything belongs to you.

So that you can understand this short statement: "Fish swims like a fish, water—bird flies like a bird," I—not denied, but I explained what is logic, what is philosophy, what is science. Because you are firmly believing scientific truth, and you are caught by scientific way of life, you have no idea of what is true mind. You are always watching shadow of the— chasing after the shadow of the mind. Philosophical interpretation or psychological interpretation of your mind is just a shadow of the mind, and you are firmly believe in it. So you mistake enlightenment for drugs, LSD . If the Sixth Patriarch is here, what he will say ? "With such a people I cannot talk," he may say.

We have shadow. It is inevitable to have shadow for us. But to try to step on your shadow is impossible. How can you catch your shadow? If you goes—if you try to step [on] your shadow, shadow will be ahead of you . If you go one step behind , shadow will be one step behind of you. It is impossible. It is foolish to think "future" or "past." Why don't you catch yourself in this moment? When you are doing something, you are there. You are too much attached to visible things.

So when the Second Chinese Patriarch see Bodhidharma, and confessed his shameful mind, he said, "Bring me a shameful mind . Catch the shameful mind." He [Eka] said that— he said, "I cannot catch it." Of course , no one can catch it. If you try to catch it, that is shadow, you know. How can—can you catch the shadow of your hand ? So you [he] said, "I cannot catch it." And Bodhidharma said, "The confession is over."

So accurate—what they point out is so accurate, you cannot move back and forth. There is no need even to read one page of a book. There is no need even to listen to it. It is here. Before fish comes, there is fish . Sandokai said, "Before the night is here— when—even—before night has not gone, the dawn is here." When you watch—when you waiting for dawn, dawn is here; you are there, right there. Your true mind is that right there. When you wondering, the true mind is right there. When you are suffering, the true mind is right there, with suffering.

Science cannot solve this problem. The true activity will stop—true activity of your life is no more. So if you do not catch it, when you are active, how can you catch it? And there is a way to catch it. That is our practice. That is sesshin. Shin is mind. To catch our true mind is sesshin. This mind cannot be caught by thinking—thinking mind, or feeling. It is too late. So moment after moment, to watch your breathing, to watch your posture is to dwell on your true nature. There is no secret beside this point.

Straightforwardness

Japan and America are not so far away today, although the ways of life are quite different from each other. I have studied many things in America which I could not study in Japan. And I think that you will study many things from us which you cannot study in America. In this way our effort will bring some result if we keep our straightforward way in practice.

In zazen practice, the most important point is straightforwardness, as the Sixth Patriarch emphasized. According to him, if we always remain in straightforwardness we have our Way and we are expressing our true nature. But this straightforwardness does not mean to remain lazy without making any effort to improve yourself. When your true nature is covered or bound by something, even though you try to express your straightforward nature, it is impossible. So, for the beginner, it may be necessary to know what is the straightforwardness meant by the Sixth Patriarch.

If you always remain straightforward, you will have some confidence within the straightforwardness. Whatever comes to us, whatever we face, we should accept and respond to without fear, without being caught by anything-any idea of fear. It is not easy to be straightforward. If you realize this, you will accept pretty hard discipline to keep your true nature.

What I want to talk about now is how to orient your mind in practice. For the beginner it is inevitable that there will be hard discipline, the observation of some rules. The observation of rigid rules is not our point. But if you want to acquire vital freedom, it is necessary to have some strength, or to have some discipline, in order to be free from one-sided dualistic ideas. So our training begins in the realm of duality or rules: what we should or should not do. These kinds of rules are necessary because before you start practice or realize the necessity of religious life, before you adore something holy; you are bound in the realm of necessity, you are controlled completely by your surroundings. When you see something beautiful you will stay there as much as possible. When you are tired of it you will go to another place. You may think that is freedom, but it is not freedom. You are enslaved by your surroundings, that is all! Not at all free. That kind of life is just material and superficial.

Because we have some idea of freedom, because of our true nature which wants to be free from our surroundings; we start to study something and we choose between good and bad, right and wrong. This will be a new kind of life called life seeking for freedom, which is not realized in a true sense. Some people may think: if we were like cats and dogs there would be real freedom. But this kind of desire will not satisfy our true nature or inmost desire. After striving and seeking freedom you will realize you cannot attain freedom by searching for it.

Of course, if you keep up this kind of effort for a long time, you will develop a kind of intuition so that you will know what you should do without thinking and wandering so much. This is like the expert who can tell how much a package weighs without using a scale. From his experience he will know. In this way you will have a certain ability to know or intuition about what is good and what is bad. But this kind of ability based on experience is not religious experience. Religious experience is not only intuition about what is good or bad, but also joy, happiness and composure.

Even though you continue a certain discipline, it may be difficult to attain enlightenment if you do not know what is true religious experience, or how you should concentrate your effort. But for the beginner, it is the same whether you understand this or not. Anyway it is difficult. Just to practice zazen in certain posture is enough for a while. After you are used to a certain posture, it is necessary to know in what way your practice should be oriented.

Dogen Zenji said that Bodhisattva Kannon (Avalokiteshvara) changed the direction of a sound by hearing it. Usually sound comes from a bell and you hear it. You think, "There is a bell, it's a wonderful sound," and you are listening to it. That experience is quite usual. But when Avalokiteshvara heard the sound, he made the sound at the same time . Do you understand? He made sound, not the bell—you made the sound. You practice zazen, zazen is there. You practice zazen in Zen Center.

"In Zen Center they are rigid" —"they insist on rigid forms." So long as you want to study Zen, you should practice in that way. That is your understanding of our practice. It is true but it is not perfect. At first it should be like that, but at the same time, when you practice zazen there is no other zazen than your practice. The practice that you are doing is zazen. None can force you to practice our way. Because you practice zazen there is zazen, and that zazen is your zazen, as sounds come from some temple and go back to that temple from you. When you realize this fact there is no duality or dualistic ideas, no need to choose between two, for you there is only one way.

In naive, childish, animal, or inanimate life there is no freedom; in human or moral life there is freedom; but when we enter religious life there is no longer freedom. Religious life is moved by necessity like animal life. The way we take is the way we should take. In this realm we become one with human beings and one with all the rest of existence, animate and inanimate; we can accept scientific truth and mechanical civilization.

Our vital freedom will be like running water originating from a mountain and passing through valleys and fields, reaching the sea. There is no freedom for the water to return to the mountain. But at the same time there is vital freedom. This kind of life is called religious life. To attain it is to practice zazen without the idea of gaining. To expect some result from your practice is like trying to hear the bell from outside yourself. To expect something from outside, to try to achieve something, is to try to hear the bell from the outside only.

If you do not have the faintest idea of gaining, the sound will arise from you. When the bell is sounding, you are sounding. Stop your gaining idea and keep alert and ready to accept—ready to respond to the slightest sound which will come. When you have no pain in your legs, if you can keep your posture right, if you can practice zazen without difficulty, what you should work on is to stop your ideas of gaining by your practice and concentrate on making yourself alert enough to respond to activity and ready to express yourself in your own way. This is the ability which you will gain by practice. No one has this ability without practice. we should not mix up animal life, the life of a cat or a dog, with the life of an enlightened person.

We are now studying, practicing zazen in one room. Some of you have practiced zazen for a long time. Some of you started just now. But each should have his own way, even though we practice in the same way. This is very important in our practice, but it is not difficult. It should not be very difficult for you to understand what I am talking about right now. Just practice zazen until you get accustomed to right posture and when you get tired of it you should conquer the tiredness. You should make yourself alert; you should try to respond in the right way; and you should try to express yourself in the right way. This is how we practice zazen.

Benefits of This Practice

Someone may ask us how this kind of practice will benefit our everyday life. The answer may be no benefit, as Bodhidharma said, "no merit." But we mean by merit: merit and no merit. Beneficial and not beneficial. Mahayana Buddhists emphasize the saving of others and the saving of ourselves. To save others is to save ourselves. It does not mean to save others after we save ourselves, or to save others before we save ourselves. Our way is "to save others is to save ourselves." To hear a sound is for the sound to arise. It is one activity. We practice this kind of practice because for us there is no other way to appease our inmost desire. Until we attain this way of life, our inmost desire will not be appeased.

So Dogen Zenji always emphasized "beginner's mind." We should always remain in beginner's mind. It means our experience should always be refreshed and renewed. It means always have the joy of discovering something. The same joy as children discovering something new. This kind of experience is not possible to attain just by training through which you expect some result.

Dogen Zenji said Avalokiteshvara Bodhisattva's hundreds of arms are like seeking for something, for our pillow in complete darkness. Because the darkness is complete, we stretch our arms in no particular direction. Although we are seeking for something, we cannot say we are seeking for something. His hand is not his hand, his hand is always, as are also his eyes and his mind. This kind of activity is true activity, which is based directly on our inmost nature.

Seeking for something in the dark is no usual activity based on an idea of gaining. He cannot say he is seeking for the pillow with an idea of gaining. He cannot say he is acting with an idea of gaining. He may not even know what he is doing. So Nangaku said to Baso: "If you practice zazen to try to attain Buddhahood, there is no Buddhahood." You think you are practicing zazen in that way, but Zen is not some particular form. Whatever you do, that is Zen. Everyone is Buddha. There is no particular person who is called Buddha. The to practice zazen is just to practice, without any idea of attaining Enlightenment or Buddhahood through zazen. To take some activity that appeases our inmost desire, that is our way.

As you know, Nangaku picked up a tile and started to polish it. Baso asked his master what he was doing? "I want to make a mirror," he said. Mirror (laughing). "How is it possible to make a tile a mirror?" the disciple said. Nangaku answered, "When a cart does not go, which do you hit, the cart or the horse?" Which do you hit, the cart or the horse (laughing). Baso could not answer. If Baso had known the true practice, he would have said: "I will hit a horse!" The answer is quite simple (laughing), but he started to intellectualize, so he couldn't answer his master's question. So Nangaku kindly said to him, "If you want to acquired Buddhahood, there is no Buddhahood. If you want to practice zazen, just to sit on a cushion is not zazen." Baso hearing this instruction felt as if he was drinking ambrosia. He appreciated and was able to understand his master's remark.

Shobogenzo

Buddhism is very philosophical, and sometimes intellectual and logical. It is necessary to be logical and philosophical to believe in the teaching completely. If it is not logical and philosophical, you cannot believe in it. Our teaching should not be doubtful. Although intellectual and philosophical understanding of the teaching is not enough, it should be at least be logical and philosophical.

Sometimes a student of Buddhism will become proud of the lofty, profound philosophical teaching. This is wrong. The philosophy is for the believer himself, not for others. Because it is difficult for us to believe in the teaching, we should enter it from an intellectual approach. However, there is no need to be proud of the profundity of it. It is just for the student, not for others. If it is possible to believe in Buddha's teaching without philosophical understanding it may be all the better. For most of us it is quite difficult to believe in it without intellectual understanding. So philosophy is just for ourselves.

We of the Soto School have the Shobogenzo, which, as you know, is very very philosophical, deep, and lofty. It takes a pretty long time to understand the teaching, even philosophically, and there are not so many people who understand Shobogenzo completely. A man may study Shobogenzo intensively and even become quite famous as a result; but by the time he understands it completely he will likely not be a religious leader any longer, but just a scholar, proud of his understanding of Shobogenzo. In the Soto School this is quite possible, so we usually do not talk about the Shobogenzo so much. Rather, we practice Dogen's way whether we have a deep understanding of our practice or not.

The Soto way may seem formal and rigid, if you do not know the background of the rituals. If you want to study it is necessary to have a strong, constant, way seeking mind. Sincerity to accept rituals, to accept the teaching without any discussion. So Dogen Zenji emphasized the straight-forward attitude which accepts the teaching as it is. Just say "Hai (yes), I will do it." That is all. That is our way. If there is some doubt in our way, you may make a philosophical or intellectual study of Shobogenzo. But we should know that Dogen's way is the result of a long intellectual effort based on his pure way-seeking mind. Buddha's teaching has two faces. One is practical and the other is philosophical. The Four Noble truths and the Eightfold Holy Path are practical teaching. The teaching of interdependence and transiency are the philosophical side. The practical side of the teaching is for human beings, you may say, or the teaching based on value. For human beings the teaching has some value, you now: that is the practical side of the teaching. But the teaching that everything changes and is independent is not just for human beings, it is the teaching for everything.

According to the teaching of transiency or interdependency, there is no difference between human beings and other animate or inanimate beings. It is universal for everything. However, the Eightfold Holy Path and the Four Noble truths are for humans and the teaching we should practice. The teaching of interdependency or the teaching that everything changes gives human beings a strong faith in the Four Noble truths and the Eightfold Holy Path. It gives us the reason why we should practice Zen or why we should behave.

These teachings are not just Buddha's invention. The teachings are based on eternal and universal truth. Buddhism has its validity or universality in the scientific world, that is why people like Buddhism. For a Buddhist there is no reason to be proud of the teaching because of its universality. But there is a danger for Buddhism in its universality and profundity. Buddhism, at the same time, is a very practical, vital, and active teaching. A Buddhist should be concentrated on his practice, rather than on philosophical study. Buddhism should not disappear into the realm of science or philosophy. This is a pretty important point in studying Buddhism and we should always be concentrated on our sincere effort and practice.

That is why we reject the idea of gaining from our practice. Gaining ideas belong to our visible world, whereas sincerity belongs to our inmost nature. Buddha's teaching is based on his inmost nature, which is called Buddha Nature. To realize our inmost nature or appease our inner most request is how we practice Buddhism. It may be difficult for a beginner to realize the inner most request, but by your practice you will realize your inmost, deeper nature and this deeper nature will encourage your practice.

Before Zen Buddhism was established, there was no idea of the pure practice of Zen. The Hinayana school classified Zen in four ways excluding any idea of gaining. The practice which was based on gaining was called "desire practice" (desire world practice: yokukkai-jo). When you practice Zen in order to prepare for true Zen, that is of course practice based on the idea of gaining. For example, before you begin zazen, you swing right and left centering yourself, or you rub your muscles. These actions are done from a gaining idea in order to prepare for practice.

The Hinayana school made provision for this kind of practice based on desire. It was not part of the four stages of pure Zen. Desire-world Zen is not Buddhist, is not our Zen. You may call it preparatory Zen which belongs to the world of desire, but not to the world of form or the world of non-form.

This early Hinayana distinction of pure-Zen and desire-Zen is why it is not correct to say that Zen Buddhism was established only after Bodhidharma came from the west. Although there was no specific Zen school by that name, Zen ideas were clearly pointed out in the Hinayana way. If we miss this point the Zen school will become one of the many schools of Buddhism. Every school should be only Buddhism. A Buddhist should not have sectarian ideas, and there should not be sectarianism in Buddhism. If we understand this point we will be concentrated on the practice itself without any idea of gaining.

Practice without an idea of gaining is called Buddha's practice. If we become attached to enlightenment or to the profundity of the teaching, we will lose the point. When we just practice zazen as a human being without any idea of gaining we have the universality of the teaching, and also its individuality and validity. If we attach to some idea of perfection, we will lose the validity of the teaching, although we may have its universality. But this is no longer religion: it is philosophy or science. So the point is to practice our pure way as human beings with sincerity and without an idea of gaining. That is pure practice. It is not important whether it is the first stage or the second stage or the third one, that is not the point. Just to practice with a pure-way seeking mind, that is true Zen and true Buddhism.

If you practice zazen for one or two years or more your Zen will become part of your life and you may feel as if there is no need even to practice Zen. At this stage you understand Zen properly. When you have some joy or ecstasy in your practice, that will be encouraging; but it is not good enough. This encouragement helps you to reach the realm where you do not have joy in your practice. On the other hand, if you come to think that you understand Zen and that there is no need for you to study or practice Zen any longer, that is a big misunderstanding. Zen should be our whole day and whole life work. We should follow this way without any idea of gaining. It does not mean to ignore the encouragement and joy in your practice; but true practice is beyond our joy or understanding.

Samapati

Almost all of you have not practiced Zen so long, but I think you have made great progress. This result is more than we expected. As I always say, for the beginner the most important point is posture. While you are working hard on your posture you will study many things besides your physical training. Physical training always follows mental training, even though you do not try to train your mentality. To put your mind in the right way is one interpretation of Zen. Or to resume your right mind is called Zen. Samapati means to resort to the right state of mind. Another interpretation is to put our mind in the right place. Physical training will result from the right orientation of your mind. If you are determined to overcome your pain your mind will follow your pain. But if your determination is not strong enough your mind will be in agitation. Zen is not struggling. When you practice Zen your mind should be calm-even though you fight with your pain your mind should always be calm. It means your mind follows your pain like water, as water always follows the lower place. If your determination is strong enough, your mind becomes clam: following your physical condition and finding out many things. As long as you are struggling with your physical condition your mind will not find anything; your mind is shut; your mind is occupied so it will not be anything. When your mind is calm enough, even in your pain, you will find out many things. When your mind is in this state it is called a "well-oriented" mind. To put your mind in the right way is Zen.

When it is completely calm you will find various tastes, whatever you eat. So your mind will change according to circumstances, that is why old Zen masters were quite strict with disciples. If he was very strong and strict they would surrender-their minds would surrender. So you will find out many things in this kind of situation. You have to do many things which you do not like. That is a quite usual routine for us. As long as we want to stay sitting we have to find out some way to control ourselves, and soon we will find out how to control our mind.

Pickles are not something to boil. You eat pickles without boiling them. When I was a boy our master did not like to throw away any food, not even pickles which became moldy. So we boiled the pickles and ate them. We tried them and said, "This is not too bad. This is how to eat old moldy pickles." It was pretty good, so we served a boiled pickle to our master. He said, "What is it?" He did not know. We usually did extraordinary things so he thought, "They must have done some extraordinary cooking." Anyway he did eat them. If we have surrendered to our master, we employ all our effort to control our mind so that we may exist under all conditions, extraordinary and ordinary.

This kind of training is necessary. For some of you it is time to just practice your breathing. In this activity your mind should follow your breathing in and out. We should not try to control our breathing with our mind, the mind follows the breathing. If you try to control your breathing with your mind, your mind will not be alert enough or soft enough to follow the subtle activity of your inhaling and exhaling. If your mind is soft enough to follow the subtle, delicate breathing, then you forget yourself in your breathing. So, that which exists is just your breathing. Your mind has completely become the breathing exercise. If you wish to attain this feeling, just to follow your inhaling and exhaling is the way. This is the way to do things according to our way. Follow the wave and drive the wave; follow the breathing and drive the breathing. It means to become one activity. On the other hand, if you try to make your breathing become smooth, your breathing will not become smooth. If you just follow your breathing, your breathing will become more and more smooth, without trying to make it smooth. If you have this secret in your everyday life, you will find out many things which you did not notice before. This kind of activity will take place only with strong determination, or a strong way-seeking mind. As long as you are trying to do something, you cannot do it. However, if you are determined to do it, you can do it. That determination is not working on your activity, but rather on your physical and mental existence. "I will not move whatever happens to me"- this kind of determination will work on every activity you do, and because of that determination your mind will become quite flexible. In Buddhism a flexible well trained mind is always appreciated.

This kind of training is called samadhi, or samapati in Sanskrit. In Chinese we call it dhyana or chan, or toji. Toji is a well-balanced mind, like water, it gets through the smallest holes imaginable. So before you start practice, it is necessary to make some firm decision, by yourself. No one can force you to make this kind of decision.

As you have made pretty good progress, I want you to make this decision in your practice. It is not just for the practice of Zen, but also for enjoying your life. Without this kind of decision you cannot have a rich life. Your life will be rough and coarse if your mind is not flexible enough to accept things. We are lucky to be able to come together and practice Zen with so many persons. It is not so easy to practice with people in this way. Even though you want to do so, it is not always possible. Today we did it, but we do not know about tomorrow. If only we can make this decision there is no difficulty in our life, there is no problem. Because your determination is not strong enough you have a problem. Actually there is no problem or difficulty whatsoever in the world.

Beginner's Mind

People say to study zen is difficult but there is some misunderstanding why it is difficult. It is not difficult because to sit in cross legged position is hard or to attain enlightenment is hard, but it is hard to keep our mind pure and to keep our practice pure in original way. Zen become more and more impure and after zen school established in China it is development of zen but at the same time it is.it become impure. But I don't want to talk about Chinese zen or history of zen this morning. But why I say I want to talk about why it is difficult is because just you came here this morning, getting up early is very valuable experience for you. Just you wanted to come is very valuable. We say 'sho shin'. Sho shin means beginner's mind. If we can keep beginner's mind always that is the goal of our practice. We recited Prajna Paramita Sutra this morning only once. I think we recited very well, but what will happen to us if we recite it twice, three times, four times and more? Then we will easily lose our attitude in reciting - original attitude in reciting- the sutra. Same thing will happen to us.

In beginner's mind we have many possibilities, but in expert mind there is not much possibility. So in our practice it is important to resume to our original mind or inmost mind which we, ourselves, even we ourselves do not know what it is. This is the most important thing for us. The founder of our school emphasized this point. We have to remain always beginners mind. This is the secret of zen and secret of various practices....practice of flower arrangement, practice of Japanese singing and various art. If we keep our beginner's mind, we keep our precepts. When we lose our beginner's mind we will lose all the precepts and for zen students the most important thing is not to be dualistic or not. we should not lose our self-satisfied state of mind. We should not be too demanding, or we should not be too greedy. Our mind should always be rich and self-satisfied. When our mind become demanding....when we become longing for something, we will violate our precepts not to kill, not to be immoral, not to steal, or not to tell lie and so on. Those are based on our greedy mind. When our mind is self-satisfied we keep our precepts. When we ourselves is always self-satisfied, we have our original mind and we can practice good and we are always true to ourselves. So the most difficult thing is to keep our beginner's mind in our practice. So if you can keep your beginner's mind forever, you are Buddha. In this point, our practice should be constant. We should practice our way with beginner's mind always. There is no need to have deep understanding about zen. Even though you read zen literature you have to keep this beginner's mind. You have to read it with fresh mind. We shouldn't say, "I know what is zen" or "I have attained enlightenment.". We should be always big enough. This is very important. And we should be very very careful about this point.

I was very much impressed by your practice this morning. Although your posture was not perfect, but the feeling you have here is wonderful. There is no comparison to it. At the same time we should make our effort to keep this feeling forever in your practice. This is very very important. In Japanese art, when you master some art..when you become successor of your master, you will receive some paper on which something is written.

No one knows what it is. It is very difficult to figure out what it is....to explain what it is.

But if you have beginner's mind, it's all right. If you can say, "Thank you very much" from the bottom of your heart, that's all right. If you say "What it is?" you have no secret....you can say "Thank you very much". That's enough. But this is very difficult. So by your practice we must make our beginner's mind more and more....we should appreciate beginner's mind. This is the secret of practice....zen pratice.

The Secret of Practice

Most of you are beginners, so it may be rather difficult for you to understand why we practice zazen or meditation in this way. We always say "just to sit." And if you do, you will find out that Zen practice—just to sit—is not easy. Just to sit may be the most difficult thing. To work on something is not difficult; how to not work on anything is rather difficult. When we have the idea of "self," we want some reason why we work on something. But if you do not have the idea of self, you can remain silent and calm whether or not you work on something. You will not lose your composure. So to remain silent and calm is a kind of test we receive. If you can do it, it means you have no idea of self. If your life is based on the usual idea of self, what you will do will not be successful in its true sense. There will be success in one way, but in another you are digging your own grave. So to work without the idea of self, is a very, very important point. It is much more important than making a good decision. Even a good decision based on a one-sided idea of self will create difficulties for yourself and others.

So for students of Zen, to work on something or to help others is to do things with our single mind. Our effort is concentrated within ourselves. This is the activity of our essence of mind, according to the Sixth Patriarch. He said that in the realm of our essence of mind, we do not do things outside of mind. All that we do is the activity of our essence of mind which is not dualistic. By essence of mind he means the Big-Mind and not the selfish mind. Of course there is dualistic activity, but it takes place within the big mind. This kind of single-minded activity is distinguished from ordinary dualistic activity.

When you practice zazen you will of course have physical pain in your legs and mentally you will have some difficulty. You will find it difficult to be concentrated on your breathing. One after another images will come into your mind. Or your mind will go out for a walk and wander about. I have many difficulties in my practice, so I think you, too, will find it very difficult to sit in good zazen.

All the difficulties you have in zazen should not take place outside your mind. Your efforts should be kept within your mind. In other words you have to accept the difficulty as not being other than what you are. You should not try to make some tentative particular effort based on your small mind like, "my practice should be better." My practice you say, but zazen is not your practice, it is Buddha's practice. Your effort is based on big mind which cannot get out of. If your small self begins to act without the care of big mind, that is not Zen. What you do should be well taken care of by big mind. Our practice should be based on mind or original way-seeking mind which works on and on continuously.

The secret of practice is also true in observation of Buddhist precepts. The dualistic idea of whether to observe or not observe the precepts takes place within your mind when you practice Zen. There are no precepts to break and there is no one who is violating the precepts. To make up your mind to make the very best effort to observe the precepts constantly, forever, whether your effort is complete or not, is Buddha's—Buddha-Mind's effort. But if you put yourself outside the precepts or Buddha-Mind then there is no time to observe them completely. If your activity is involved in Buddha's activity, whatever you do is Buddha's effort. The even if it is not perfect, you are manifesting Buddha's mercy and activity.

Dogen Zenji was enlightened when he heard his master strike and say to the disciple sitting next to Dogen, "What are you doing? You have to make a hard effort. What are you doing?" That effort is Zen.

That effort is to observe the precepts. If we make our best effort on each moment with confidence, that is enlightenment. When you ask whether your way is perfect or not, there is an insidious idea of self. When you do your best to observe the precepts, to practice Zen, within the Big Mind then there is enlightenment. There is no special way to attain enlightenment. Enlightenment is not some certain stage. Enlightenment is everywhere. Wherever you are, enlightenment is there. Whenever you do with best effort enlightenment follows. This is very important for our Zen practice and our everyday life. We should make our effort in our everyday as well as in practice of Zen.

In order to have this kind of practice in everyday life, you want your friend, you want your master, you want the precepts we have. Some form is necessary because it is not possible to be concentrated on an uncertain way. There must be strict rules to observe. Because of the rules, of the way of sitting, of the way of practice, it is possible to be concentrated. It is the same thing in your everyday life. Without purpose or aim you cannot organize your life.

My master Kishizawa Roshi used to say that we had to have a vow or aim to accomplish. The aim we have may not be prefect in its strict sense, but even so it is necessary for us to have it. It is like the precepts. Even though it is almost impossible to observe them, we must have them.

Without an aim in our life and the precepts we cannot be a good Buddhist, we cannot actualize our way.

We should be very grateful to the rigid formal way of practicing Zen and Zen precepts. You may think these precepts are useless if we cannot observe them perfectly. But they are the traces of human efforts based on the great mercy of Buddha. The life we have now is the result of such useless effort. From one-celled animals to monkeys. I do not know how long, but we wasted much time, many efforts until we came to this human life. The giant redwood trees of Muir Woods have annual rings or layers and we have these annual layers in our human life too, I think. That is precepts in its wide sense. You say we don't want them, but you have them. As long as you do, you should sit, and thus you have to know how to continue your effort to have another annual ring. In this way we will develop Buddhism more and more forever.

Strictly speaking we must have more precepts in America. You think 250 precepts for men and 500 for women is awful and that it should be made simpler. But I think you have to add some more to the precepts we have in Japan. Actually, I think you will have more difficulty in practicing zazen in America than we do in Japan. This kind of difficulty should be continued forever or we will not have peace in our world. Without the precepts there can be no congenial life for human beings. By reflecting on our human life and by respecting the precepts and rules of humanity, we will know the direction in which to make an effort and we will have the right orientation in our life. This is how we practice Zen and how Buddhism has been developed.

Believing in Nothing

I found out that it is necessary absolutely necessary to believe in nothing. We have to believe in something which has no form or no color_ something which exists before every form and colors appear. This is very important point. Whatever we believe in whatever god we believe in_ .when we become attached to it, it means our belief is based on, more or less, self-centered idea. If so, it is_.it takes time to acquire_.to attain perfect belief or perfect faith in it. But if you always prepared for accepting which we see. _is appear from nothing, and we think there is some reason why some form or color or phenomenal existence appear, then, at that moment we have perfect composure. When I have headache, there is some reason why I have headache. If I know why I have headache I feel better, but if you don't know why, you may say, "Oh, it's terrible I have always headache-- maybe because of bad practice. If I_if my meditation or zen practice is better, I wouldn't have this kind of trouble." If you accept things_.understand things like this. It takes time. You will not have perfect faith in yourself, or in your practice until you attain perfection (and there's no_I'm afraid you have no time to have perfect practice) so you have to have headache all the time. This is rather silly practice. This kind of practice will not work. But if you believe in something which various... .which exist before we have headache and if we know just reason why we have headache, then we feel better, naturally. To have headache is all right because I am healthy_healthy enough to have headache. If you have stomach ache your tummy is healthy enough to have pain, but if your tummy get accustomed to the poor condition of your tummy, you will have no pain. That's awful. You are coming to the end of your life from your tummy trouble.

So it is absolutely necessary for everyone to believe in nothing, but I don't mean voidness. There's something, but that something is always_is something which is always prepared for taking some particular form and it has some rules or theory or truth in its activity. That is so-called Buddha nature or Buddha himself. When we understand what him.....rather when we personify this existence we call it Buddha, or when we understand it as the ultimate truth we call it Dharma, and when we accept the truth, and when we act as a part of the Buddha, or according to the theory we call ourselves Sangha. But, in short, even though we have three Buddha form, in short it is one existence_.some existence which has no form or color, and always prepared for_.ready for taking forms and colors. This is not just theory. This is not just teaching of Buddhism. This is absolutely necessary understanding of our life and this kind of understanding is_ .without this understanding religion will not help us. By religion we will be bound by it and we will have more trouble_.because of the religion. If you become victim of the religion_.victim of Buddhism, I shall be very happy, but you will not be so happy. So, this kind of understanding is very, very important_I found out. Before, I talked about Dharmakaya

Buddha, or Sambhogakaya Buddha, or Nirmanakaya Buddha, and I explained what the three bodies of Buddha are and what is emptiness but I didn't realize that this understanding of Buddha was so important for us....for everyone.

You know, while we are practicing zazen we heard rain dropping from the roof..in the dark. I think soon we will see the wonderful mist coming thru the big trees, and later, before when the people start to work, we will see the bright sunshine rising from the easr, and we will see the beautiful mountains, but for some people, if they hear rain drop, in their bed, they will be annoyed, you know, without knowing, later he will see the beautiful sun rising from the east. If our mind is concentrated on our selves we will have this kind of worry, but if we accept ourselves as embodiment of the truth.....temporal embodiment of the truth we have no worry. Now, it is raining, but....you will think, but we don't know what will happen next moment. By time I go out it will be beautiful day, or stormy day.....we don't know.. .so let's appreciate the sound of the rain now. This kind of attitude is the right attitude, but if our activity is concentrated, or if you think you act something, you have always difficulty, but if you understand yourself as a temporal embodiment of the truth, you have no difficulty whatsoever. And we can appreciate our surrounding, and we can appreciate ourselves, as a part of...a wonderful part of activity.

Even we are in difficulty_____thru difficulties we will acquire some experience. This is our way of life.

Having the Buddhist terminology we should start from enlightenment to practice, and thinking. Thinking is rather self-centered, but sometime it is not, but almost.in everyday life, our thinking is ninety-nine percent self-centered. "Why I have to suffer? Why I have trouble?" This kind of thinking is ninety-nine percent of our thinking. When we study science. .start to study science we become sleepy or drowsy quite soon, but we are very much interested in self-centered thinking. So, the enlightenment is first....enlightenment, I mean....by enlightenment to believe in nothing is enlightenment. To believe in something which has no form or no color and ready to take form or color by some immutable truth that is our enlightenment. So enlightenment, our activity and our thinking and our practice, and then thinking...if it is necessary. If you are not interested in it, that is our way.

Cultivate Your Own Spirit

The message for us for today was 'cultivate your own spirit'. It says there on the calendar.'Cultivate your own spirit. This is very important point and this is how we practice zen. When.for us to hear lecture, to give lecture or to recite sutra, or to sit, of course, is zen. Each of those activities should be zen, but if you do not...if your effort or practice is not... does not have right orientation it does not work at all. not only it does not work.it may spoil your pure nature. The more you know something about it the more you will get spoiled.you will have just stains on your mind, and your mind will be filled with rubbish. That is not.that is quite usual for us.gathering various information from various source, and you think you know many things, but you don't know anything at all. That is quite usual. So we should not be.our understanding of Buddhism should not be just gathering many information and knowledge. Instead of gathering various knowledge we should accept it as you listen to something which you have already known, or you have already knew. This is so-called emptiness or you may say omnificent self.you know everything. You are like a dark sky_some time a flashing come through the dark sky and you forget all about it. After flashing gets through it there is nothing, but the sky will not be surprised even though thunderbolt break out all of a sudden. It does not make_it will not cause any surprise for the sky. But when the lightening hits though we will see the wonderful sight of it, but we do not_we are not_we are always prepared for watching the flashing.

People may be interested in various sights and they may go for sight seeing tour, but some Chinese said, "Rosan is a famous place for its misty scenery". I haven't been to China yet but there must be beautiful mountains, and white clouds or mist may come and go through the mountains. It must be very wonderful sight. Although it is wonderful sight, he says, "Rosan is famous for its hazy sight on a rainy day. Seko, the great river, is famous for its tide coming and going." That's all. That's all but splendid. This is how we appreciate things. We should not expect various information, just_on the other hand we should not accept various information just as the (echo?) of ourself. But we should not be surprised at seeing something and hearing something. If you accept things as an echo of yourself it does not make any sense. So, "Rosan is famous for its misty sight" does not mean to see the mountain_to appreciate the mountain recollecting some scenery you have seen before. "It is not so wonderful. I have seen that sight before" or, "I have painted much more beautiful paintings. Rosan is nothing". This is not our way. We appreciate with quite new feeling. We do not accept it as an echo of ourselves. Even though you have various knowledge, if you accept the knowledge as if you collect something familiar to you only. For collection it will be very good but that is not our way. Or we will not try to surprise people by some wonderful treasures. That is not our way at all. We should not be interested in something special but we should appreciate_if you want to appreciate something fully you should forget yourself even, and you should accept it as utter darkness of the sky_accept lightning.

Sometime we think it is impossible for us to understand something_ something unfamiliar to us. Some people may say, "It is almost impossible to understand what is Buddhism as our cultural background is quite different from Oriental cultural background. How is it possible to understand Oriental thought?" But this is wrong. Although the background of the_of course Buddhism in our heritage cannot be separated from the cultural background. It is true, but if Buddhism_if a Buddhist come to the United States, I am not already a Japanese. I am living in your cultural background. I am taking nearly the same food as you take and I am communicating with you. So for the people who have some narrow-minded people may say it is impossible, but it is possible. Even though you do not understand me so well it_I want to understand what you are talking about. I can understand - maybe more than many people who can speak and understand English. That is true. If we could.if I can understand several words in long sentence it is all the better, but even though I cannot understand English at all I think I can communicate with you. So in this way there is possibility as long as we exist in utter darkness of the sky.world.as long as we live in emptiness. I always say we must be very patient if we want to understand Buddhism. But I think.I was seeking for some good word for patience. And I think it's better to say.to translate it as 'constancy'. 'Constancy' is better than 'patience'. 'Patience' means to force something on...to be forced for some time.that is 'patience'. But 'constancy' means constant facility or ability, or possibility to accept things. There is no particular effort, but constant ability or facility we have to know.to accept. For people who has no idea of emptiness it may be all what they practice should be.may be patience, but for the people who know, even just intuitively what is emptiness, all what we do, even though it is very difficult you can resolve the problem by constant ability or facility.

So that is what we mean by (ning?) in Chinese (or Japanese). So I think it's better to interpret ning constancy. This is our way of practice, and continuous practice. If so, even after you attain enlightenment it is necessary for us to have another enlightenment, and one after another we have to have enlightenment. If possible.. .moment after moment we have to have enlightenment. That is enlightenment before you attain enlightenment, and after you attain enlightenment.

The Joy of Giving

Everything is something which was given; every existence in nature, every existence in human world, every cultural work we do is something which was given to us or which is being given to us, relatively speaking. But actually everything is originally one. So it may be better to say we are giving out everything. It is the same thing. Relatively speaking everything is something given to us but actually we are giving everything.giving out or expressing out moment after moment we are creating something, moment after moment. This is the joy of our life.

This 'I' which is always giving out something is not small 'I'. It is big 'I'. Big 'I' is big self is giving out various things. This is actually our joy when we become one with big mind even though you do not realize the oneness of the big mind. When we give something we feel good because we.first of all, at that time we are one with it.that may be. We don't know. anyway, when we give something we feel very good rather than to take something. So give and take is not different. To take something when we.relatively speaking to take something, but originally it is actually giving. We say, "Dana prajna paramita". To give is one of the six ways living. Dana prajna paramita.this is to give, and sila, and endurance. endurance prajna paramita and zeal prajna paramita or constant effort, and wisdom and dhayana or zen prajna.those are six ways of living. But actually those six prajna paramita is one, but we observe it from various sides. So we count six prajna paramita.

Dogen zenji says "To give is non-attachment". To give is not to attach to anything.is to give. Although things we have is not originally ours but there is the truth to give. To give the treasure of penny or a piece of leaf is dana prajna paramita. To give out the teaching_one line of teaching or one word of teaching is dana prajna paramita. The material of offering and teaching dana offering is one_not different. And he says to produce something and to participate in human activity is also prajna paramita. To provide a ferry boat for people, to make a bridge for people is dana prajna paramita. In creating something_of course every existence in nature is something which is created, according to Christianity. Something which was created or given to us - that is perfect giving_.but, according to Christianity we are also created by Him and so the created thing_we create_we have some ability to create something which was not given. For instance, we create airplane and freeways and many things. We create many things but when we repeat, 'I create, I create, I create', soon we will forget who is 'I' which create various things. We will soon forget about our God. This is danger of our human culture. So to give to create is actually to give. To provide something for us all is to give.

It is not actually to create and own something; it is actually to provide something for people, to create something for people_as everything was created by him. This point should not be forgotten but because we forgot all about who is creating something and what for, so when we become attached to material value, or exchanging value, this kind of material value is no value_absolutely no value in comparison to the absolute value which was created by God_no value at all. When you are dying it doesn't make any value to us_no value at all but even though it has no value to each one of the small individuals it is_it has absolute value in itself. So we say 'valueless value".

When we realize that valueless value we say non-attachment; non-attachment to exchange_to material value, but to be aware of absolute value what we do should be based on the awareness of absolute value... not material, or not selfish, self-centered idea of value. This is dana prajna paramital (to give).

When we sit in cross-legged posture we resume our fundamental activity of creating. There is, maybe, three steps. The first step of creation is to be aware of ourselves after we finish zazen. When we sit we are nothing. We are 'just sit'; we do not even realize what we are. We just sit; but when we stand up, you are there. That is the first creativity. You are there. When you are there everything is there. Everything is created all at once. When you act you give. When you create something_food, or tea, or coffee (which we will take soon) this is secondary creativity. The third one is to create something within ourselves; that will be education or culture creativity or artistic creativity, or to give_to provide some system to our society. Those cultural creativity. So there are three steps but if you forget most important one, (holding up three fingers and then hiding thumb) those are children (the two fingers remaining) who lost their parents. It means nothing.

But usually all of us forget zazen. They don't practice zazen. They forget all about what was God. The God is someone who helps those (two children). Yes, they are helping but the God does not help the activity. How is it possible for him to help when he does not realize who he is? That is the problem. That is why we have so many problems in this world. It is exactly the same as the children who do not know what to do when they lost their parents. So those three steps.all those three steps is said to be done by dana prajna paramita, to give, or to create.perfect creation. Through and through those dana prajna paramita must be in full (work?) but what we are doing is very very .based on some idea which is very very (fashion?) and limited and ignorant of what we are. So if you understand what is dana prajna paramita you will understand how we should live in this world and how we create for ourselves many problems.

Of course to live is to make some problem. That we came to this world is enough, you know. We create...that is the first step. If you do not appear in this world your parents have no difficulty. Because you appear in this world you create some problems for your parents. So that is all right. That is all right. Everyone is creating some problems; so that is quite all right. But that problem should be solved or resolved. When we die everything is over. Even though we do not die, day by day we should forget what we did. That is non-attachment. And we should do something new. To do something new we should know our past and future. This is all right but we should not have something, you know, something...you should not have something in your mind you did. We do not have anything what we did but we reflect on what we did. That's all, and we must have some idea of what we should do in future. But future is future, past is past. Now we should work on something new. This is our attitude and this is how we should live in this world and this is dana prajna paramita, to give something or to create something for ourselves.

So to do something through and through we resume our true activity of creation or to give up. This is why we sit. If we do not forget this point everything will be carried on beautifully. But once you forget this point all the confusion...this world will be filled with confusion.

Way Seeking Mind II

When we feel the evanescence of life, or when we have problems for ourselves, and direct feeling of the problems—of the fact you have to face —is how you arise the way-seeking mind.

Usually when we set ourselves to studying something, we put our everyday problems aside, concentrating our attention for a time on something of particular interest. That is how we study generally. On Sunday you may go to church, but to you going to church and your everyday life are two completely different activities. Eventually, however, you will feel some contradiction in your everyday life, and some uneasiness, feeling you have nothing to rely on. It is this feeling which gives rise to the way-seeking mind.

When you are young, young enough to act as you want, you can choose something good, ignoring something bad, and by working on something good, you may feel good enough to spend your early life. But some uneasiness, some dark feeling will follow in your life. Even though you try to appease your conscience by working hard and exhausting yourself on what you are doing, this kind of effort will not give you any conviction. Jumping around in this world without conviction may be the pitiful life. You will be pitied by someone who has strong conviction and deep wisdom concerning our life. Thus we should be ashamed of doing something proudly, vigorously, with some ecstasy even, ignoring the other side of the world, the dark side of our life.

By nature human beings have good and bad sides, half and half. When you want to do something good, at the same time you don't want to do something good. If you want to get up early, at the same time you say, "I will stay in bed five more minutes. It is too early!" At the same time you want to get up, you will say to yourself, "No, yes, no!" "Yes" is fifty percent; "no" is fifty percent ... or more! Bad things sixty percent; good, forty percent."

The more you reflect on yourself, however, the more conscientious you become. Because you become more and more conscientious, you feel as if you are doing ninety-nine percent bad things! That is actually human nature. It is not a matter of what is good and what is bad. It is a matter of our human nature. When you realize this fact in your everyday life, you have to wonder what we should do. If you realize this fact, you will not be fooled by anyone. You may take some pleasure in entertainments, but you cannot fool yourself completely. You cannot deceive yourself when you realize the true state of our human nature.

Some people say, "If we have a perfect social construction, we will not have these difficulties." But as long as there is human nature, nothing will help us. On the contrary, the more human culture advances, the more difficulties we will have in our life. The advancement of civilization will accelerate this contradiction in our nature. When we realize the absolute presence of our contradictory nature, the way-seeking mind arises, and we begin to work on ourselves instead of the material world. Most people who are interested in Buddhism are more or less critical of our social condition, expecting a better social framework. Some people have become disgusted with our human life. We cannot approve of these criticisms fully, however, because they do not rest on the full understanding of our human nature.

Human nature is always the same. Some people may say our spiritual culture will progress when our material civilization progresses. Strictly speaking, however, as long as we have human nature, it is impossible to obtain a perfect idealistic spiritual culture in our human world. We should fully realized this point. Because of our uneasiness, we are too anxious to achieve something perfect in our spiritual life. Here we have some danger. Our spiritual life cannot be regarded as we have come to regard our material life. You cannot work on your spiritual life as you do your materialistic life. Even though you talk about our spiritual life thousands of times, it will not help you. It is necessary to know actually what is our human world, or what is our human nature. This is a very important point. If you fail to observe our human nature fully, even though you study Buddhism, what you acquire is not what Buddha meant.

For many years we have been practicing zazen here at Zen Center. And we think it is time we made some progress. I think so. You think so as well. But when we feel in this way, we should be careful not to mistake our way. We should know what is the way-seeking mind, what is human nature.

Some people may say, if human nature is always the same, then it is useless to practice zazen, to study Buddhism. But our study is based on this fact. Our study is not to improve upon the actual fact that we have good and bad, half and half, as our human nature. We should not try to improve upon this actual fact. Even Buddha accepted this truth ... he started Buddhism based on this fact. He accepted this truth. If you try to change this truth, you are no longer a Buddhist.

Buddha said our human life is a life of suffering. This is a fundamental truth. Knowing this fact, having this deep understanding of human nature, we may continue our life step by step helping each other. Because we have good and bad, half and half, we can help. If all of us (laughing) were good, it would be impossible to help one another. It is a good thing that we have good nature and bad nature ... we are able to feel the improvement, however slightly we may change. It would be wonderful if we could help another even by a hair's breadth. It makes no difference what sort of problems or situation in life we have. If we have something to work on, it is enough. Because we have good and bad, half and half, because we can find some way to help others, if only by the width of a sheet of paper, by a few words, we can enjoy our life.

The way-seeking mind should be realized in our actual world, which includes flowers and stones, and stars and moon. The true way-seeking mind can only be actualized in full scale. Where there are human beings, there is the sun and stars, land and ocean, fish and grass and birds. Without this vast area to live in, where we can have our various problems, we cannot survive in this world. But forgetting this vast realm where we have absolute freedom, we seek for something merely for the sake of ourselves, just for human beings. Thus we have to suffer our nature, which has good and bad, fifty-fifty. When we become aware of this big realm, which includes everything, then we have big, big mind and big, big trust. We have perfect eternal freedom within this big realm.

Actually the way-seeking mind is the conviction to fly as a bird that flies in the air, to enjoy our being in this vast world of freedom. Enjoying our nature as a part of this vast world, we have no uncertainty because we don't know there is nowhere to go. Life and death is not our problem anymore. We attain enlightenment in this big realm. We suffer in this big realm. We are ignorant of the limit of the world. Here we don't have even the problem of attaining enlightenment. Ignorance is good, enlightenment is good; zazen is good, to stay at home is good. Every activity will take place in this big realm. Our human effort, our human culture should be based on this kind of imperturbable conviction. Our effort should not be limited to ourselves. That is what I mean by the way-seeking mind.

When Dogen Zenji attained enlightenment, he said he forgot all about his body and mind. This means he found himself in this big world. So our activity should be limitlessly small and at the same time should be limitlessly great. There is no difference in the greatness of our activity, and what may seem a trivial small activity. They have the same value. Our pleasure and conscience will be fully supported by this big, big realm. In this way we practice zazen. We should strive for enlightenment, of course. We should try to calm down our mind. But it is impossible to obtain enlightenment or to calm down your mind without realizing the fact of this big realm which supports us. If you don't realize this fact, trying to calm your mind is the same as arguing which came first, the chicken or the egg. The moment you say the hen came first, the egg is already there as her mother. There is no end to the argument.

That we appear in this world means we should disappear from this world . If you were not born in this world, there would be no need to die. To be born in this world is to die, to disappear. That we can do something good means that we can do something bad. It is true. Do not be fooled by this kind of contradiction, home-made contradiction! You made some contradiction in your life.

Our study, our effort or practice, should be firmly supported by Buddha's wisdom. You may come to realize how true Buddha's teaching is to the circumstances under which we suffer. When you realize how this teaching is true to us, you will begin your practice. But when you are jumping from one place to another, it is difficult to teach you how to practice Buddhism. Anyway, for the beginner, it is difficult to sit. However, if you continue your practice you will discover your own posture, good or bad. Then you can say it may be better to put some more strength in your abdomen, make your posture straighter; or you may find that you are leaning forward or backward. That you have some posture, your own posture, is at the same time to have some bad habits. Without bad habits you cannot improve your posture! It is good for us to have bad habits!

But you ask me what is right posture. That is also a mistake. Whatever you do is right. Nothing is wrong with what you do. But some improvement is necessary. Something should be done with what you have attained. Even though you attain enlightenment like Buddha, something should be done with it. That is his enlightenment. So the point is not whether your posture is right or wrong. The point is constant effort or way-seeking mind.

I think I should not talk too much. The more you practice zazen, the more you find out the true, deeper meaning of our practice. Anyway, we should be more friendly and frank and straightforward, and we should be more free, and we should accept the instruction. This is our way.

The Secret of Buddhism

The secret of the entire teaching of Buddhism is how to live each moment. Moment after moment we have to obtain absolute freedom, and moment after moment we exist interdependent with the past, future, and other existences. In short, if you practice zazen concentrating on your breathing moment after moment that is how to keep the precepts, to have an actual understanding of Buddhist teaching, to help others, yourself, and to attain liberation.

In India there wan an Indian way of life, in China a Chinese, and in Japan a Japanese. To keep the precepts is not to keep an Indian way of life. When you are here, you should eat here. You cannot eat in India all the time. If you want to keep the precepts literally you have to go to India. There is a story about an Indian monk who came to China, but who had to return because he could not keep the Indian precepts in China where the customs were different. If you know how to keep the precepts, Buddhism will continue to develop as Zen develop in China.

Time is originally one with being. Twelve hours is the duration from sunrise to sunset. The sun needs twelve ours for its rising from the east and setting in the west. When your mind follows your breathing, it means your mind drives your breathing as water follows waves. Your breathing and mind are one. Here we have absolute freedom. We become one independent being. We should not say firewood becomes ash. Ash is ash, firewood is firewood. But ash includes firewood with everything and firewood includes ash with everything. So one breath after another you attain absolute freedom when you practice, when you are concentrated on each exhale and inhale.

When Dogen speaks about the evanescence of life, he speaks of exhaling and inhaling. After all what is inhaling and exhaling? When you are completely absorbed in your breathing there is no self. What is your breathing? That breathing is not you, nor air. What is it? It is not self at all. When there is no self you have absolute freedom. Because you have a silly idea of self you have a lot of problems. So I say your problems are homemade. It may be very delicious. That is why you like them On the other hand, if you like them, as long as you like them, it is all right.

Dogen Zenji says, "It is specifically taught in Buddhism that life does not become death. For this reason life is called no-life. It is also taught that death does not become life. Therefore death is called no-death." It is not a matter of life or death. When death is accepted through and through, it is no death anymore. Because you compare death with life it is something. But when death is understood completely as death, it is no death anymore; life is not life anymore. Dogen Zenji says, "Flowers fall with our attachment and weeds grow with our detachment."

In the Genjo Koan Dogen says, "When we first seek the truth we are far away from its environs. When we discover that truth has already been correctly transmitted to us, we are ourselves at that moment. If we watch the shore from the boat, it seems that the shore is moving. But when we watch the boat itself directly, we know that it is the boat that was moving. If we examine all things with a confused body and mind, we will suppose that our self is permanent. But if we practice closely and return to our present location, it will be clear that nothing at all is permanent. Life is a period of itself and each is a period of itself. It is like winter and spring. We do not call winter the future spring, nor spring the future of summer." So when you practice zazen even for a moment, the whole universe is reflected in you as the moon in a drop of dew in the grass. This is a fact you may say. The period of reflection long or short will prove the vastness of the dewdrop and the vastness of the moonlit sky. Dogen says, "When the truth fills our body and mind, we know that something is missing. For example, when we view the world from a boat on the ocean it looks circular and nothing else. But the ocean is neither round nor square, and its features are infinite in variety. It is like a palace. It is like a jewel."

You say you attained some stage in your practice. But that is just trivial event in your long life. It is like saying the ocean is round, or like a jewel or palace. For a hungry ghost the ocean is a pool of blood; for a dragon the ocean is a palace; for a fish it is his house; for a human being it is water. There must e various understandings. When the ocean is a palace it is a palace. You cannot say it is not a palace. For a dragon it is actually a palace. If you laugh at a fish who says it is a palace, Buddha will laugh at you who say it is two o'clock, three o'clock. It is the same thing.

Eternity is in mortality. When you become a mortal being through and through you will acquire immortality. When you are absorbed in sheer ignorant practice, you have enlightenment. So in order to be a true Buddhist, you must find the meaning of life in your limited activity. There is no need for you to be a great man. In your limited activity you should find out the true meaning of yourself. If you pick up even a small stone you have the whole universe. But if you try to pick up the tail of a comet you will be crazy. People will sympathize with you.

For this limited activity we need such precepts as: "Do not kill. Do not steal. Do not commit adultery. Do not lie. Do not sell liquor. Do not bring up the faults of others. Do not boast and blame others. Do not withhold material and spiritual possessions. Do not become angry. Do not debase the Triple Treasure."

I cannot explain them all at this time, but I will explain a few.

Do not kill means to realize our true nature. It does not mean just to have mercy. It is deeper than that. Of course it does mean we should not kill even an insect or an ant, but that is not the real meaning.

Do not steal. When we think we do not possess something, then we want to steal. But actually everything in the world belong to us so there is no need to steal. For example my glasses. They are just glasses. They do not belong to me or to you, or they belong to all of us. But you know about my tired old eyes and so you let me use them.

Do not commit adultery means not to be attached. The precept emphasizes especially our attachment to particular things as we attach to a woman or man.

Do not sell liquor means not to boast or emphasize the advantages of things. Liquor may be medicine if taken in the right way, but we should take into consideration that by nature we are very susceptible to temptation. If you boast about he profundity of Buddhist teaching, you are selling liquor to the people. Any spiritual teaching by which we are intoxicated is liquor. Do not sell liquor means absolute freedom from all teachings. We should keep the precepts and yet not be bound by them. That is our way.

"When a fish swims in the water there is no end," says Dogen Zenji. It is very interesting that there is no end. Because there is no end to our practice is good. Don't you think so? Usually you expect our practice to be effective enough to put an end to our hard practice. If I say you have to practice hard for two years, then you will be interested in our practice. If I say you have to practice your whole lifetime then you will be disappointed. You will say, "Oh, Zen is not for me." But if you understand that the reasons you are interested in this practice is because our practice is endless, that is true understanding. That is why I am interested in Buddhism. There is no end. If there were an end, I would not think Buddhism was so good. Even if human beings vanish from this earth, Buddhism exists. Buddhism is always imperfect. Because it is not perfect, I like it. If it were perfect someone would do it. Many people will be interested and there would be no need for me to work on it. Because people are very much discouraged with Buddhism, I feel someone must practice Buddhism.

A while ago when we had Wesak service with all the Buddhists in the First Unitarian Church I thought it might be better to bow in the way we usually do at Zen Center. But someone said if we bow in that way people may be discouraged. It is true, very true. I know people will be discouraged. I know we are causing a lot of discouragement for American people when we bow nine times, when they bow only three times in Japan. I know that very well. So I bow nine times here in America. Buddhism needs our continual effort eternally. Until you are interested in this point you cannot understand Buddhism.

Mortality makes eternity, eternity makes mortality. Enlightenment makes practice, practice makes enlightenment. Dogen Zenji says, "Birds make the sky, and the sky makes the birds. Fish make birds, birds make fish. In this way there must be further and further analogies to illustrate our practice." In short, if you do one thing with sincerity that is enough. There is no need to try to know the vastness of the sky or the depth of the sea.

You may say, now realization of the truth takes place through my activity. But it is not so. Or you may say it is a process of self-realization. It is not so. For you, the realization of the truth you have now is the absolute realization of truth. You cannot compare your realization with other things. Each one who realizes this fact and who practices in his own way has absolute freedom. This is how we live each moment, moment after moment. Thus all things are made possible: the observation of the precepts, the attainment of enlightenment, freedom from the various sects, and perfect satisfaction in our life. Your realization of the truth is the same as Buddha's realization of the truth. There is no difference at all.

Studying Ourselves

To study ourselves is to go beyond ourselves. To go beyond ourselves is to be enlightened by all things.

So enlightenment comes from all things to us. And when we attain enlightenment, everything comes, you know—enlightenment comes from all things. You may say enlightenment. "They made me enlightened," or "I attained enlightenment." That is same thing in direct experience, but in intellectual understanding it is not same. I understand something. But in direct experience, "I understand something" means a truth came to me, although I didn't expect to—I didn't try to understand it , but they made me understand.

So, to study ourselves is—to go beyond ourselves is to be enlightened by all things. To be enlightened by all things is to free our body and mind, and to free our body—bodies and minds of others.

So no trace of enlightenment remains because there is no subjectivity or objectivity in our enlightenment. So, "There is no trace of enlightenment, and this no-trace continues endlessly."

When first we seek the truth, we are far away from its environs.

When you say, you know, "I attained enlightenment," that—you are far away from the direct experience of enlightenment.

When we discover the truth is already being correctly [inherently] transmitted to us, we are ourselves at the moment of enlightenment.

It is not, you know, matter of effort or practice anymore. Our practice is not just effort or —our practice is—should I say?—you know, you —you—you come here and study or practice zazen so that you understand what is Buddhism, I think so . And I —I'm making effort to give you some understanding of Zen. That is true. That is actually what we are doing here . But until—I shall be very much disappointed if you do not come when you think, "I know what is— now I know what is Buddhism." So there will not be no need to —to practice zazen, to study Zen. That is, you know, I shall be very disappointed. I want you to come here even though you understand what is Buddhism . I am not selling you something , you know, but I want you to be my customer . And I want to live with your support, and I think I shall be very glad if you have some joy in practicing with us here. That is actually Buddhism. It is not matter of enlightenment or understanding.

And why we are continuing this kind of practice—we will—what should I say?—we will be a perfect, you know, character, we say. The character-building is—we cannot force anything, you know, to others. But it is necessary for everyone to do things over and over again until the— you acquire some acquisition—perfect acquisition which will—which will not vanish from you. It is like a to—like to press your dress, you know, trousers. It is—you want iron, you know. Just to fold your trousers is not good enough. You should press. If possible you should put something on it, you know, after—even after you put iron. This kind of effort is necessary, but this effort is—

when this kind of effort is forced on you, that does not work . That kind of effort should be continued without effort, with mutual encouragement. In this way, our practice will be continued.

So when we—when we know—when we think we know what is truth, that is not enough, and that is "far away from its environs. When we discover that the truth has already been correctly or—correctly transmitted to us, we are ourselves at the moment." When we find our true nature or our way of life as the most suitable way to our inherent nature, that is enlightenment.

At first it looks like, you know, you are trying to do something, but when you understand what is the purpose of practice, you will understand that that was my nature but I didn't know. I feel someone is always mean to us, and someone is forcing his—the practice to us. Or you may think, "I practice for a long time. It may be enough for me. And it doesn't looks like I made any progress" . So that may be not, or if you go to Eiheiji, you may say, "I have been Eiheiji for one year . I cannot speak any Japanese, and intellectually I don't," you know, "I cannot study anything here. Just what we are doing is eat and work and recite sutra and practice zazen in the same way always . What does it mean? I know everything already, quite well." That is what you may say.

But he says, when you say so it is "far away from its environs." When you discover that the truth has been transmitted to us inherently long before, and now I have find—found it. That is true understanding. You have to continue it until you find your true nature in your practice. That is realization of the truth. What you study is, as he says, what—"to study Buddhism is to study yourself"—ourselves, you know. When we find out ourselves in our study, in our practice, that is realization of the truth.

So as long as you try to find out your true nature by practice, you know, you cannot find out. But if you find out your true nature in practice, or if you think the practice itself is your true nature, that is enlightenment. And our past sages found out their true nature in our practice. So—so we should find out our true nature in the same practice. That is true realization.

The practice is not something—some means to attain enlightenment. In— in practice, you should find out your true nature. Before you attain enlightenment, you are just ordinary people. After you attain enlightenment, you are sage . Before—so he says—he says, "That we move ourselves and understand all things is ignorance." You know, when we try to attain enlightenment by practice, we are ignorant. But things—when things come to us and understanding themselves, including us, that is enlightenment. So even truth will come by itself, and we will find ourselves in the truth, in the practice. That is enlightenment.

So practice is first, enlightenment is second . Next. So we— anyway, we should be absorbed in practice until you become one with practice, until you build up your character by practice, you—until you become Zen itself—Zen practice itself. Like a rock . That is enlightenment. A rock doesn't know who he is .

"When we discover that the truth has been transmitted inherently," even before we are born , that is true enlightenment. And we find ourselves in transmitted, inherent buddha-nature in our practice. That is enlightenment. So, "When we discover that the truth has already been inherently—correctly—"inherently" is better. Correctly, you know, is not strong enough. Inherently is better. "Inherently transmitted to us" before —before—even before we are born, it was transmitted to us, and when we realize that true nature in our practice, that is enlightenment. "We [are] ourselves at the moment." The moment we practice our practice with our utmost—utmost effort, that is enlightenment.

If we watch the shore from a boat, it seems that the shore is moving. But when we watch the boat, we know that it is the boat that moves. If we examine all things with a confused body and mind, we will suppose that our self is permanent. But if we practice closely and return to our present place, it will be clear that nothing at all is permanent.

We are caught by some ideas—some permanent or impermanent or ourselves or others. As long as we practice our practice in this way, we cannot realize what is true. Just when we do it, we will understand what is our true nature.

And here the second paragraph on Page 2:

Firewood turns into ash, and it does not turn into firewood again. But do not suppose that ash is after and the firewood before. We must understand that firewood is at the stage of firewood, and there we find its before and past.

And yet with its own past and future, its present is independent of others— of other. Ash is at the stage of ash, and there we have—we find its before and after. Just [as] firewood does not become firewood again after it's—it is ash, so man does not return to life after his death.

We say we attain enlightenment—we ordinary people attain enlightenment, just as—just like firewood become ash. But this is mistake, he says. We cannot suppose—we cannot—we should not think in that way. You say, "I attained—I will attain enlightenment tomorrow." And ordinary people become sage, like firewood become ash. But he says, ordinary people is ordinary people . Ash is—sage is sage, and ash is ash, and firewood is firewood. Firewood has its own past and future, and ash has its own past and future. So ordinary people has its own past and future. Future will be a sage , and sage has also its own past and future. In past, he is ordinary person . What is the difference ? The same thing. So we should not say fire—we should not say ordinary people become—became a sage, as we shouldn't say firewood become ash. What—that is what he says.

So when you practice it, that is it. Don't say, "By practice I shall be buddha tomorrow." That is what he—he said. So when you just practice it, you are at the moment a buddha. That is true . Don't you think so? You are buddha anyway . You cannot escape from it . But you make some excuse why you are not buddha , that's all. Maybe it is convenient for you . But because you are actually buddha, you do not feel so good when you make some excuse . That is what he is—what he says here.

Now it is specifically taught in Buddhism that life does not become death.

Ordinary people does not become sage.

For this reason, life is called "no-life."

For this reason, ordinary people called no ordinary people .

It is specifically taught in Buddhism that death does not become life.

Sage does not come back to ordinary people.

Therefore, the death is called "no-death."

Therefore, sage is called "no-sage". Ordinary people , no difference. When we practice in this hall, there is no teacher or no student. We are all sage . Even though your practice is not good enough, we cannot say your practice is not good enough. It is good anyway. You have your own past and future. You have future—bright future to be a sage . Don't worry .

Life is a period of itself; death is period of itself. They are like winter and spring. We do not call winter the future spring, nor the spring the future summer.

"Life is a period of itself." Enlightenment—sage is a period of itself, and ordinary people are—they are like winter and spring. We do not call winter the father of spring. We do not call ourselves—so we shouldn't call ourselves future sage . You are sage, not future sage. "Nor spring the future summer." You are sage.

We gain enlightenment like the moon reflecting in the water. The moon does not get wet, nor is the water broken.

If you practice it by yourself without any aid, you are sage. Even though you are sage, you do not lose your nature or form or character.

We gain enlightenment like the moon reflecting in the water. Even though your practice is not good enough, you may say—

The moon does not get wet— The moon itself in your practice no—nor the— nor is the water broken.

You will not broken. You are just as you are. And when you are just as you are, through and through, there is enlightenment.

Although its light is wide and great—

Although enlightenment is—truth is wide and great—the moon is reflected—reflected even in a puddle in—one inch wide. The whole moon and the whole sky are reflect—reflected in a drop of dew in the grass.

So in your practice there is enlightenment. And he continues:

Enlightenment does not destroy the man just as the moon does not break the water. Man does hinder enlightenment, just as a drop of dew does not hinder the moon in the sky. The depth of the drop is the height of the moon. The period of the reflection, long or short, will prove the vastness of the dewdrop and the vastness of the moonlit sky.

And here he emphasize oneness of the practice and enlightenment from various viewpoint.

And next paragraph I already explained. This is—in next paragraph, he emphasized you should not think enlightenment is some state of mind or some intellectual understanding. It is beyond our consciousness, or it is— enlightenment is there before you become conscience of it.

The Need for Training in Buddhism without Self-Seeking Mind

In Buddhist training we always received the true Key handed down by our predecessors. How can we use our selfish mind for this? We cannot gain Buddhism with mind or without mind. Just remember that if the training will—will—training will and the Buddhist way to do—Buddhist way do not combine, our body and mind are not calm. If not calm, our body and mind are not comfortable.

If we have gaining idea, we cannot practice Buddhism, which is something beyond our ordinary purpose of life. Usually our conscious activity is directed towards some merit or some result. We are expecting result, whatever we do. But there may be difference—there may be two cases: one you expect result after doing something, and you expect the result within your activity. There is—there may be two cases. The—to practice zazen because of the interest in practicing zazen is also, strictly speaking, a gaining idea. Of course, to expect something after your practice, this is of course gaining idea. "If you practice zazen you will be healthy," or "You will have some mystic power like some magic." This is, of course, is not Zen.

Maybe you will attain some result. But we do not practice it for sake of the wonderful result we will have. But it—but it does—it does not mean that zazen has—zazen practice has no advantage. It has some—it will result [in] something good for you, actually. But we do not practice it for sake of the result we will have. And we should be ashamed of to practice Zen which is to practice religious practice with gaining idea.

Gaining idea usually limits our meaning of practice. Our practice is not— our practice has the limitless meaning in it. So that is why Zen has eternal life in it. Because if Zen is some practice directed towards some result— some particular result, it will not—it will be the practice which you have in your everyday life. And why Zen help us in its true sense is because it will cut off the root of the problems we have. If you know how to practice zazen, you will know how to cut off your root of suffering—root of trouble. That is why our practice is valuable.

So the most important thing is to practice zazen in its true sense, in the transmitted way from Buddha to us. In Buddhism or in Zen, we have had various problems to discuss. But after all, we came to the conclusion that this practice is the most fundamental practice for understanding of profound meaning of Buddhism.

In Buddhist training we always received the true Key handed down by our patriarchs. How can we use our selfish mind for this? We cannot gain Buddhism with mind or without mind.

"With mind" means—"with mind or without mind" means you say—even though you say "without mind," still you have gaining idea. So he says "with mind or without mind." It is not matter of how to gain—how to understand Buddhism by mind, or if it is without mind, by what mind we can gain. This kind of question will follow one after the other.

So the purpose—so our way is to practice zazen as a—as our way transmitted from Buddha. Here we want absolute surrender. Before this surrender—absolute surrender come to you, it is not possible to practice zazen in its true sense. We do not ask why. We do not wonder the result of the practice. Whether we have the result or not is out of question. But the most obvious thing—the ultimate part is that you are here as a follower of Buddhist. So as a follower of Buddhist, you should practice the zazen, that's all. There is no reason.

If you are not a Buddhist, maybe you—there will be no need for you to practice zazen. Because you are here you have to do it, that's all . Quite simple. Even though you are very tired, you are right here. So as long as you are here, you should listen to me. "Oh, you should practice zazen. That's all."

So if tea come, you should drink tea. If you have cake, you should eat cake. That's all. That is exactly how we exist in this world. This is the way how everything exist here. This is zazen. So even though you do not enjoy the experience of Zen, Zen is Zen. So to practice zazen is also the goal of practice, whether it is, you know, joyous nor not joyous. It is the goal of practice. There is no other goal.

So our way is—our goal is—is not somewhere within or—within reach or beyond our reach. Or our goal does not—does not exist in our practice. You—you think you will—you sit because you will have some joy in your practice. That is why you sit, you may say. And actually, because you have some joy, you sit . But even though you do not feel any joy, you have to sit . That is what he is saying. So there is no problem . This is how to cut off the root of the problem.

You may say, then, whatever you do, that may be Zen, you know . So there will be no need for you to sit. Even though you do not sit, to have breakfast, to sleep, to go to bed is also zazen. If so, there will be no need for you to sit in cross-legged position all day long."It may be waste of time"—you may say so. But actually, fortunately or unfortunately you are here. It is too late to say so.

And if you sit and—our practice is not—moreover, our practice is not just to sit. Whatever you do, that is zazen. Why? Because you know what is true meaning of Zen. So for you, whatever you do, that is zazen . But for people who do not know what is zazen, you know, even though it is actually zazen, but for—for the people who do not know what is zazen, that is not Zen for him only. But for—for us, you know, whatever they do, that is zazen. I understand that, as you understand whatever you do that is zazen. So whatever others do, that is also zazen. This is our understanding of zazen.

So by selfish mind, or with mind or without mind, we cannot gain our way.

Just remember that if the training will—training will and Buddhist way do not combine, our body and mind are not calm.

If you do not practice with this understanding, your mind will not be calm.

If not calm, our body and mind are not comfortable.

So when you have some doubt or problem, you should consider whether your understanding of life is right or wrong. The absolute—ultimate teaching is always like this. For an instance, everyone has buddha-nature, we say. But you cannot say because everyone has buddha-nature, or therefore you—everyone has buddha-nature, therefore or because. If you, you know, limit the meaning of the statement, putting "therefore" or "because" , that is not the ultimate truth. But when you understand it, you put "because" or "therefore." You know, you say "everyone has buddha-nature. Therefore there will not be no difference whether we practice zazen or not, you know. You limit the meaning of the—original meaning of the statement by putting "therefore." You use the statement for your own excuse .

We—everyone has buddha-nature. Period. That is how to listen to the ultimate truth. There is no room for the statement to accept your reasoning. Then your body—your being and your mind will combine. It does not mean to force something on you. To see you yourself as you are —that is perfect combination of body and mind. This is the perfect calmness of your mind.

What should we do to couple the training will—training will with the Buddhist way? Our mind neither clings nor forsakes. The mind is free from fame and profit.

"Training will with Buddhist way." Our training will must not be the usual training will which you do by some purpose—which you do by means of something.

Our mind neither clings nor forsaken—forsakes. The mind is free from fame and profit.

We do not train in Buddhism for others. Like most people these days, the mind of the Buddhist trainee is quite far from the way. He practices what others praise although he knows that it is false. He does not practice what others scorn although he knows that it is the true way. This is indeed a cause of—cause for regret.

Usually people practice it for sake of profit or fame, even though he himself knows that isn't right. He emphasize this point very much.

When viewed objectively, this hardly seems the proper use of the true Buddhist mind. The penetrating eyes of Buddhas and patriarchs illuminate—illuminated egolessness—egolessly. We should emulate them.

This kind of way of practice is not right—is not proper, they know. But because they do not know what is Buddhism or because they do—they do not even expect something better way, and they are doomed in those useless way. So they [are] just caught by the fame and profit and practice zazen.

Buddhist trainee do very little for themselves. How can they do anything for fame and profit? They must train in Buddhist—Buddhism only for Buddhism. The various Buddhas, feeling deep compassion for all beings, do nothing for themselves or for others. They merely act for Buddhism. This is the Buddhist tradition.

Buddhist trainee usually do not very little—oh—do very little for themselves. How can they do anything for fame and profit?

They do not know how to save themselves, and so they do very little for themselves.

How can they do anything for fame and profit?

They say "fame and profit," but how can they do it? They are just trying to do so, but it will not work.

They must train in Buddhism only for Buddhism.

Buddhism is for sake of Buddhism, not for others or not for themselves: just to follow our way is our traditional way.

The various Buddhas, feeling deep compassion for all beings, do nothing for themselves or for others. They merely act for Buddhism.

This is the Buddhist tradition.

In Buddhism, in our practice, there is no idea—no different idea, or no dualistic idea for ourselves or for others. Just we do it—practice it for sake of Buddhism.

They merely act for Buddhism. This is the Buddhist tradition.

Observe how even insects and animals nurse their young and bear hardship to bring them up. When the young—when the young reach maturity, the parents seek no profit.

This is our way.

Compassion for the young is strong even among tiny living creatures. Likewise, the various Buddha have a natural compassion for living beings.

The [superb] teaching of the Buddhas are not limited to compassion. They are expressed universally in many facet—facets. This is the basic spirit of Buddhism.

So we say "compassion" or "Buddhism," but actually in true—for true Buddhism there is no name—no name of Buddha or no name or compassion or mercy. By those names we just limit the true meaning of compassion or Buddha. If so, the only way to grasp the true meaning of the word is just practice it without any gaining idea before we know what it is, just [as] a bird or animal raise their babies up. This is how to study Buddhism in its true—strict sense.

Today I think our practice may not be so good because I myself could not devote myself to the practice thoroughly. But I think we are reached in— we have reached to some stage—reached to some—reached some stage where we can practice the true way. At least even though quite a few— some of us understand this is the true way, and this is how to live in this world in its true sense. Even though it looks like strange way to understand our meaning of life, but it is not so.

We have had very difficult time before we reach this understanding: the understanding where there is no problem of attainment, there is—where there is no problem of distinction between religion in its true sense, where we can find the advantage—various advantage of—in various religion. And people say nowadays we are busy, but to have fine chance to sit here in this way is very valuable. This is very rare opportunity. We should not neglect—we should not waste this rare opportunity to practice zazen.

Mistakes in Zazen

There may be various kinds of practice, or ways of practice, or understanding of practice. Mostly when you practice zazen you become very idealistic with some notion or ideal set up by yourself and you strive for attaining or fulfilling that notion or goal. But as I always say this is very absurd because when you become idealistic in your practice you have gaining idea within yourself, so by the time you attain some stage your gaining idea will create another ideal. So, as long as your practice is based on gaining idea, and you practice zazen in an idealistic way, you will have no time to attain it. Moreover you are sacrificing the meat of practice, set up for the future attainment, which is not possible to attain. Because your attainment is always ahead of you, you are always sacrificing yourself for some ideal. So this is very absurd. It is not so bad, rather not adequate.

It is much better than to practice zazen involved in some competition—competing your practice with someone. This is very bad shape. This is rather ridiculous and shabby-- poor practice much better that that, but not so good. We emphasize shi kan taza. This is.We do not call our practice shi kan taza, or we have no particular name for our practice, but when we practice zazen we just practice it, whether we find joy of practice or not, we just do it. Even though we are sleepy, and we are very tired of practicing zazen, repeating the same thing day after day, even so we continue our practice. Whether or not someone encourages your practice we just do it. Here, I think there is some, especially when you practice zazen alone, without teacher, I think you will find out some way to find out whether your practice is right or wrong. When you are tired of sitting, or when especially I mean when you are disgusted with your practice, or when you are discouraged with your practice there you should think that is warning. Why you are discouraged with your practice is because your practice has been very much or somewhat idealistic. Because you have had gaining idea in your practice, and your practice was not pure enough, or your practice is rather greedy practice, you become discouraged.you are discouraged with your practice. So you should be grateful that you noticed or that you have a sign or suggestion to find out your weak point of practice. At that time, forgetting all about your mistake, and renewing your way of practice and you resume your original practice. This is very important point.

So long as you are continuing your practice you are quite safe, but as it is very difficult to continue it there must.you must find some way to encourage yourself. But the way you encourage yourself is not adequate. Your practice will be involved in some other practice, or some poor, shabby practice so without being involved in some poor practice, to continue our pure practice is rather difficult. Maybe pretty difficult. This is why we have teacher. With your teacher you will be correct.. .correct your practice. Of course you will have a very hard time with him, but even though you find it hard, you are always safe from wrong practice.

We are.we have had pretty difficult time with our teacher. When we talk about the difficulties we have had you may think without this kind of hardship you cannot practice zazen or you cannot attain some stage. But this is not true. Whether you have difficulties in your practice or not, as long as you keep continuous practice you will have our pure practice in its true sense. Even when you are not aware of it you have it. So Dogen-zenji said, "Don't think you will be aware of your own enlightenment. Whether or not you are aware of it, you have your own True Enlightenment within your practice." While you are.. .if you see people involved in various practices, you can compare your practice with the other's practice and you will.then you will feel true gratitude for our way.

The other mistake will be to practice it with some joy in it. But this is not very good shape, you know. This is pretty good, of course, not bad, but if you compare it to the true practice it is not so good. In Hinayana Buddhism they classify our practice in four ways. The best way is just to do it without having any joy (even spiritual joy) in it. Just do it, forgetting our physical and mental feeling.. Just do it and forget all about yourself in your practice. This is the fourth, highest stage. The next one is just to have physical joy. This stage.. .you can compare this stage to the stage your find some pleasure in practice because you like it you practice it. In this stage you have still physical joy. And the second stage is the stage you have mental joy and physical joy. But in the third stage you have just physical feeling, physical good feeling. In the second stage you have mental and physical good feeling. In the second stage you have mental and physical good feeling. So, those two stages are the stages, because you feel good, you practice zazen. So this stage is the best stage, the second and third one. The first stage is the stage you have no thinking, you have no curiosity in your practice. This is the first stage. When you stop your thinking you have the first one. This is also true with our Mahayana practice. The highest stage is just to practice it, and if you find some difficulty in it that is the warning that you have some wrong idea in your practice, so you have to be careful but don't give up your practice; continue it knowing that.. .knowing your weakness of your practice. Here we have no gaining idea in our practice. Here we have no fixed idea of attainment. You don't say 'This is enlightenment' or 'That is not right practice'. Even in wrong practice, when you realize it, and continue it, that is right practice. Our practice cannot be perfect. But without being discouraged by it to continue it.. .in short, is the secret of practice.

And if you want to find out some encouragement in your discouragement, when you get tired of, that is the encouragement. You encourage yourself when you get tired of it, or when you don't want to do it, that is the warning. Like when you have a tooth ache when your teeth are not good. When you feel some pain in your teeth you go to the dentist. That is our way.

The other day someone whom I met in New York came yesterday he came to San Francisco and I saw him and he is working with U Thant for eighteen years and he is from the same country with U Thant. And he practiced various ways and he told me what kind of experience he had and he asked me, "Which is your practice?" He had many experiences of practice. And when I said, "This is our practice", he was very glad to hear that. He said. "I thought this was the best practice." And we talked about when we have conflict in our world. The cause of the conflict is some fixed idea or one-sided idea. So when everyone knows the value of pure practice we will have no conflict in our world and he was so glad. And he agreed with me and I thought this is my secret of practice and Dogen-zenji's way. He repeats in his Shobogenzo this point. If you have this point you can practice various ways and you can find out the meaning of the various practices without being caught by it. If you do not realize this point you will be

easily caught by some particular practice and you will say, 'This is enlightenment. This is perfect practice. This is our way. The rest of the ways are not perfect. This is the best way.' This is big, big mistake. There is no particular way in our true practice. This.in this understanding you should find out your.and you should know what is your practice you have now. Then you will now, knowing the advantage and disadvantage of the practice, some special practice, you can practice it. If you do not know this practice you will ignore the disadvantage of the practice, and you will emphasize good part of it but eventually you will find out the worst side of the practice and you will be discouraged when it is too late. This is very silly. This is why we are very grateful for the ancient teachers to point out strictly this point.

Right Effort

The most important point in our practice is to have right effort. The right effort which is directed to right direction is necessary. Usually our effort is making towards wrong direction. Especially, if your effort is making.. .your effort is directed towards wrong direction without knowing it means so-called deluded effort. Our effort in our practice should be directed from being to non-being, from achievement to non-achievement. Usually when you do something you want to achieve something but in our practice from achievement to non-achievement means to get rid of some evil result of the effort. Whether or not whether you make your effort you have good quality. So if you do something that is enough but when you make some special effort to achieve something, some excessive quality or element is involved in it. So you should get rid of some excessive things. If you.. .when your practice is good, without being aware of it you will become proud of it. That is something extra. Pride is extra. What you do is good but something more is added to it. So you should get rid of that something which is extra. This point is very, very important. But usually we are not subtle enough to realize that. And you are going to wrong direction. So this kind of effort to get rid of something extra is very important point and that is the effort we make.

As all of us are making same mistake, or same.. .doing something in the same way. We do not realize it. So without realizing it we are making many mistakes. And we create problems between us. This kind of bad effort is called 'dharma-ridden, practice-ridden'. You are involved in something big and you cannot get out of it. When you are involved in some dualistic idea it means your idea is not pure. The purity means just things as they are. When something is added that is impure. When something becomes dualistic that is not pure. So purity does not mean to polish something, to make some impure thing pure. Purity.by purity we mean just things as it is. So we say there is enlightenment and practice but we should not be caught by it. You should not be tainted by it. Of course we practice zazen. Practice is necessary but we should not attach to the attainment. Because even you are not aware of it you have the quality so forget all about what you gained from it. Just do it. Then you will have it. If you think if you practice zazen you will get something, that is already.. .you are involved in some impure practice. Just do it then you have it. Even though you do not know.that is pure practice and there you have enlightenment.

People may ask you if you practice.what do you mean to practice zazen with gaining idea? What kind of effort is necessary in your practice.. .if you have no gaining idea? The answer is to get rid of something extra from our practice. So if some extra idea comes over you, you should try to stop it.you should remain in pure practice. That is the point our effort is directed to.

...........You are living on this world as one individual, but before you take your form of human being you are there.. .always there. We are always there. Do you understand. We are always here, but you think before you were born you were not here. But how is it possible for you to appear in this world when there is not you. Because you are there, so you can appear in this world. You may say, if we disappear nothing exists, but how is it possible to vanish something which does not exist? Because something is there, that something can vanish. Even though it vanished something which is existent cannot be non-existent. That is the magic. We cannot spell any magic on this world. There is some reason why we vanish from our sight, but from our sight can vanish, but if we do not try to see it that something cannot vanish. Because you see it you are watching it, it can vanish from yourself, but if no one is seeing it how is it possible for something to vanish? If you are.. .if someone is watching you, you can escape from him, but if no one is watching you, you cannot escape from yourself. So try not to see it; try not

to achieve it. Because you have it. If you understand this ultimate fact there is no fear. There may be some difficulty, of course, but there is no fear.

When you have pain, you have headache, it is not intolerable, but when you become feverish and become dizzy, and when you feel.standing on your head, that is awful. So even though you have difficulty, that is not so bad, but if people have difficulty without being aware of the difficulty, that is true difficulty. You don't know what to do. We should not be like that. We should be always.have some basic understanding of our life. Then there is not much intolerable difficulty.

Naturalness

There is big misunderstanding about the idea of naturalness. Most people who come to us believe in some freedom or naturalness, but their understanding of naturalness is so-called heretic naturalness. Heresy.. .a kind of heresy. We call it (ji neng den getto)? In Japanese. (Jin eng den getto ?) means something which.some idea that there is no need to be formal or to be rigid, just a kind of 'let-alone-policy', or sloppiness. That is naturalness for most people. But that is not the naturalness we mean. It is rather difficult to explain what it is, but naturalness is, I think, some feeling which is independent from everything. That is naturalness. Or some activity which is based on nothingness. Something which comes out of nothing is naturalness. Like a seed or plant comes out from the ground. When you see it that is naturalness. The seed has no idea of being some particular plant, but it has its own form and it is in perfect harmony with the ground, with the surrounding, and while it is growing, in course of time it has its.. .it expresses its nature. So any plants.. .anything do not exist in no form or no color. Whatever it is it has some form and color, and that form and color is in perfect harmony with other beings. And there is no trouble. That is so-called naturalness.

For a plant or stone to be natural is.. .has no problem.. .there is no problem. But for us there is some problem, or big problem even. So to be natural is pretty.. .a kind of problem which we must work on. Some feeling.. .some quite new feeling.when you have.when you just come out from nothingness.for instance when you are quite hungry, to take some food is naturalness. You feel natural. But when you are expecting too much, to have some food is not natural. You have no new feeling. You have no appreciation for it. So zazen practice is. we practice zazen as if when we take of water when we are thirsty. That is true practice. There we have naturalness. It is quite natural for us to take a cup of water when we are thirsty. So when you are very, very sleepy, to take a nap is natural. Even though you are not sleepy, to take a nap just because you are lazy, as if it is the privilege for human being to take a nap.. ..My friends.. .all of them...the rest of the people.. ..when others take a nap, why shouldn't I take a nap. I must also take a nap. That is not naturalness. When we have this kind of idea or feeling.when everyone is not working why should I work so hard? We should.. ..I must take a rest too. When they have a lot of money, why don't I have some money. This is not naturalness. Our mind is entangled with some other idea. When you do not.. ..when it is not necessary to be bound by some other's idea, that is not naturalness.

So even you practice zazen, if your zazen is not natural it is not true practice. If you have true joy in it that is not true zazen. Even though you force yourself to practice zazen, if you feel something good in your practice that is zazen. It is not a matter of forcing something on you or not is not the point. Even though you have some difficulty, when you want to have it that is naturalness.

This naturalness is very difficult to explain. But if you can just sit and have the nothingness in your practice, whatever you do, coming out of the nothingness, that is the naturalness.and that is true activity, because you have true joy of practice, true joy of life in it. Everyone comes out from nothingness, moment after moment, comes out from nothingness. So moment after moment we have true joy of life. Here we have true joy. So we say, "True nothingness, true emptiness.from true emptiness the wondrous being appears (shin ku myo mu)". Shin is true, ku is emptiness, myo is wondrous, mu is being. From true emptiness wondrous being.shin ku myo mu.

So without nothingness there is no naturalness.no true being. True being comes out from nothingness, moment after moment. So nothingness is always there. From nothingness everything comes out. But usually, forgetting all about nothingness, as if you have something always, and behave with the idea based on some possessive idea or some concrete idea.that is not natural. For instance, when you listen to a lecture, you should not have any idea of yourself. You shouldn't compare.. .you should not have your own idea when you listen to others. You have to forget all what you have in your mind and listen to it. You have nothing in your mind and listen to it. Then you will understand what he says. That is naturalness. But if you have some idea to compare with what he says, that is not naturalness. So when you listen to it you just listen to it with empty mind. When you do something you should be completely involved in it.

You should devote yourself completely. Then you have nothing. So true emptiness... if there is no true emptiness in your activity, that is not natural.

Some people insist on some idea. Recently the young generation talks about love. Love! Love! Love! Their minds are full of love. And when they study Zen, if what I say does not accord with the idea of love that they have, they will not accept it. They are quite stubborn headed, you know. They are pretty stubborn. You may be amazed. That is not.. .some of them, of course, not all of them. Some of them have very, very hard attitude. That is not naturalness at all. Even though they talk about love, and freedom or naturalness, that is not naturalness. They cannot practice Zen in that way. They cannot understand what is Zen in that way. So if you want to study Zen you should just practice zazen. That is naturalness. And see what kind of experience you have in your practice. That is naturalness. Whatever you do this attitude is necessary. So sometimes we say 'soft mind'. Soft mind. Soft mind is nyu nan shin. Nyu is soft feeling. Nan is not hard. Something which is not hard is nan. Nyu is smooth, natural.. .mind. When you have that mind you have the joy of life. When you lose it you lose everything. You have nothing. Although you think you have, or because you think you have.you have nothing. When you think you have nothing you have nothing. Do you understand? That is what we mean by naturalness.

Three Treasures

Today I will explain Buddha, Dharma, and Sangha. Originally, Buddha is, of course, the one who attained enlightenment under the Bodhi tree and became a teacher of all the teachers. Dharma is the teaching which was told by Buddha, and Sangha is the group who studied under Buddha. This way of understanding Buddha, Dharma, and Sangha is called the "manifested three treasures," or as we say in Japanese, Genzen sanbo. Genzen is "to appear." Of course, whether Buddha appeared or not, there is truth. But if there is no one who realizes the truth, the truth means nothing to us. So in this sense we say the manifestation of truth: the manifestation of truth is Sangha.

People who join the practice with harmony and unity are called Sangha. So Sangha means not only his group, but also the state of harmony or unity. Also truth itself is Dharma, and the truth which is not divided into various forms is called Buddha, which is another interpretation of the three treasures. That kind of understanding is called "one body/three treasures." Although there are three treasures, it is an interpretation of the one reality. So we call this kind of interpretation, "one body/three treasures," ittai sanbo. Ittai: ichi is "one"; ittai is "body"; sanbo is "three treasures." Ittai sanbo.

But within the social framework of culture we have Buddhist culture. That culture consists of Buddha and his teaching, and the priests or followers of Buddhism. So, this understanding of three treasures in Japanese is called juji sanbo. Juji actually means cultural sanbo. Existing sanbo is what exists in society or within cultural framework. So, beautiful buildings and Buddhist art or Buddha's image are, perhaps, Buddha. Scriptures in beautiful design and literature are Dharma.

And priests in robes are maybe Sangha. Juji sanbo, or cultural sanbo, is closely related to society. The Buddhist organization is also Sangha. So there are three ways of understanding the three treasures, but actually the three are not different. It is one and it is three. This is a very old way of oriental thinking, even before Buddha. Buddha applied this interpretation to our framework of teaching. I think Christianity has the idea of trinity. This is the universal framework of religion. But in Buddhism there are many sects, so Buddhism does not combine many ways of understanding in one school.

Each school is based on some particular understanding or some standpoint. We do not take many standpoints in one school. In Japan, especially, we emphasize this point. This is not sectarianism. Once we take a standpoint, we should develop that standpoint through and through until we can understand various standpoints. At first, each way of understanding has its own insight. But if your understanding becomes higher and higher, you can see other standpoints with understanding at the same time.

This is how we establish various schools in Buddhism. The Nichiren school takes the standpoint of Dharma. Dharma includes the other two, Buddha and Sangha. So their object of worship is the Lotus Sutra, and they repeat nam myo ho renge kyo. Myo ho ren ge kyo is the Lotus

Sutra. Nam is scripture. Nam myo ho ren ge kyo is the title of the Lotus Scripture. The Shin school repeats Amida Buddha's name: namu Amida Butsu, namu Amida Butsu, namu Amida Butsu.

The Zen school repeats Buddha's name, but the emphasis is on Sangha, and they are not so concerned about the intellectual viewpoint or understanding. So we just repeat the founder's name and say namu Shakyamuni Butsu. When we say namu Shakyamuni Butsu, his scripture is included and his Sangha is also included; and we are a part of the Sangha. And even though we members of the Sangha are not direct disciples of Buddha, we are the descendants of Buddha.

We are successors of Buddha. So, because we emphasize the practice of attaining enlightenment as Buddha did, we naturally put emphasis also on Sangha. By practice we will build our character as Buddha did. So that is why we call Shakyamuni Buddha's name. For us it is natural to repeat Shakyamuni Buddha's name rather than Amida Buddha's name or the name of a scripture. If you repeat the name of some scripture, you are liable to be bound by some teaching which was told by Buddha. But actually, it is impossible to authorize some teaching as the absolute teaching because something which is told by some particular person could not be absolute, even though it was told by Buddha. It may be impossible to authorize the teaching for human beings.

You may say that, if it is impossible to authorize even the teaching told by Buddha, then how is it possible to authorize some person as a Buddha . This is the point we are studying. This is why we emphasize our practice. And we have a particular understanding of practice. The practice of other schools, for instance the Nichiren school or the Shin school, is quite different from how we need to understand our practice.

This practice is called practice based on original enlightenment. It may look quite unusual to authorize Buddha's Sangha, but this is more adequate and understandable. I'm not trying to explain this point today because I repeat it over and over. So Soto Zen emphasizes transmission from Buddha to us, and we emphasize Sangha, those who have transmission and who are disciples of Buddha. What I have talked about up to now is, in short, about the three ways of understanding the three treasures. The first is the manifested three treasures. The next is one body/three treasures, or philosophical understanding of the oneness of the three treasures. It is necessary to be concentrated on one thing. If we have three objects of worship, it is difficult to be concentrated; so we have to have some philosophical or intellectual understanding. But, in fact, what exists here is the actual activity of Buddha. Therefore we emphasize the Sangha. So the third one is the understanding of our daily activity. That is the traditional three treasures or cultural three treasures. But the cultural three treasures are supported by philosophy and Buddha's teaching and Buddha's character. So the cultural three treasures cannot be separated from the other two. When understanding those three treasures, each one will complement the other two and make our understanding complete. This is the Soto way of understanding the three treasures. We have the three treasures and what we do is practice zazen; that is our way. So, our understanding of practice is very different from that of other schools.

Each school has its own particular understanding of the three treasures. If you study each school's understanding of the three treasures, you will have perfect understanding. And you will find out that even though there are many schools, actually what each one means is the same. It must be so because religious life is the expression of our inmost nature which is universal to everybody. So, as Buddha attained enlightenment, we will attain enlightenment. What Buddha was striving for is the same thing we are striving for because we have the same inmost nature as a human being.

When we project our inmost nature into the objective world as Buddha, Dharma, or Sangha, it is nothing but our inmost desire to want to be someone whom you can accept. You strive for something acceptable in its true sense. So it is the same thing. You create God, and you strive for God. It means you are striving for yourself. And as we have the same human nature, your understanding of it must be the same. But if the standpoint is different, the way of explanation should be different, that's all.

Tentatively, I am giving you some explanation of the three treasures. It may be necessary to explain it more, but as we have no time, I will explain the next paragraph.

We should revere the three treasures and make offerings to them. Veneration of the Buddha, the law and the priesthood is in accordance with a precept handed down from the Lord Buddha in India to the patriarchs of China. These are the most important precepts handed down from Buddha to us. We should not worship a genie of the mountains, or call upon the spirit of death for any reason whatsoever, nor should we pay homage to any heretical religion or religious edifice. Such worship does not lead to emancipation. The Three Treasures are not just an idea invented by someone. They are the universal framework of all the advanced religions, not just the framework of the Buddhist religion. But some hasty person, who usually does not pay any attention to religion, finding himself in some difficulty, may worship something like the god of fire, or god of water or some powerful natural spirit without any idea of what the teaching is, what god is, or true practice.

It is quite easy to know our inmost nature if it is related to the right way. And if we express that inmost nature in an appropriate way, it will develop. But if our inmost nature is misled by a hasty idea, a person may go astray and even destroy himself. That is why he says you should not worship the Genie of the mountains or call upon the spirit of death for any reason whatsoever. This is too simple.

Nor should we pay homage to any hereticaL.here it says heretical, but heretical is not an adequate translation. I don't know if you have an appropriate word for this. We say gedo. Gedo is "outer way." "Outer way" is just a classification. We call Buddhist scripture "inner scripture," and other, non-Buddhist literature is called "outer." Whether inner or outer, it is the same thing; inside and outside. Outside does not mean bad, and inside is not always good; inside, outside. Gedo means outer religion while Buddhists call our way or our scriptures nai ten.

So, as Buddhists, we should not take absolute refuge in outer religious scriptures or organizations. It is not because they are bad, but because we should not mix up our viewpoint. If you try to discover something good, like a monkey in a cage, you will not find out anything. All you will find is radishes. And your stomach will be hurt. That is not our way. We should make some human effort always. That is why he says we should not pay homage to outer religious edifices. Such worship does not lead to emancipation. If we have only an idea of the Three

Treasures, the Three Treasures will be the goal. If you just have an idea of God without a teaching of the way to God, you will be lost. You will be discouraged. If there is a God, there should be a way to God. But God is the absolute one. So it is a perpetual idea we have which cannot be attained. This point should be understood by people.

It is necessary to have some way to enjoy Buddhahood. Someone who enjoys or rejoices in Buddha nature is the perfect one, or Buddha. This kind of framework is very important. And there must be some practice. There must be some understanding of life. For us, our everyday life is practice itself. So in our everyday life we have religion, if you understand Buddhism. Of course, you will reach Buddhahood through your activity in everyday life. But if you worship some god just because of fear, in what way can you appeal to your inmost request? You will be lost. You will not be lead to emancipation.

Before Buddhism became popular in Japan, Prince Shotoku set up our Constitution for the Japanese people. In the second chapter he said, "Respect the Three Treasures." He said that to follow the Three Treasures is the supreme way of attaining liberation for everyone. Because we use the terminology of Buddhism, it looks like what we are talking about is just Buddhism, but it is not actually so. That is why he says that if you worship some immature religion you will not attain enlightenment. To take refuge in the Triple Treasure it is necessary to have a pure faith. Whether it be at the time of the Tathagata or after his disappearance from the world, we should repeat his formula with clasped hands and bowed head: I take refuge in the Buddha. I take refuge in the Dharma. I take refuge in the Sangha.

Pure faith includes our mental, physical and verbal effort. It is not enough to just think something or say something superficial. So pure faith means, not just faith in something, but real action, reality, realized action. It is necessary to have real practice.

You should take refuge in the Triple Treasure with real effort, not false effort. And it doesn't matter whether it is in the time of the Buddha Tathagata or not. In Dogen's time, almost everyone believed in the Three Periods of Buddhism. They said that in the last period the people will not believe in him and Buddhism will fade away into some other religion. But Dogen did not believe in it. So there is no difference in our practice, whether Buddha is here or not. This was his belief.

We take refuge in the Buddha because he is the great teacher. We take refuge in the Law because it is our medicine and points the way. We take refuge in the Sangha because the members are our wise friends. Although the Three Treasures are one, the understanding, or the way they help us is different. It is through this triple adoration that we become the disciples of Buddha. Without the Triple Treasure, or if one of them is missing, we cannot be a disciple of the Buddha. It is on the basis of this adoration that all the moral precepts of Buddhism rest.

We say "adoration," but just to adore Buddha is like a dream. It means nothing. So adoration should follow some actual practice or guidance. Without guidance, God means nothing. Even though you believe in a God, it will not help you, actually, if your everyday life is cut off from God. In that way God means nothing. So all the great religions have their teachings and followers. And where there are followers, there should be a way to attain enlightenment. Not in the next life, but in this moment. This is Buddhism.

To take refuge in the Triple Treasure it is necessary to have pure faith, whether it be in the time of the Tathagata or after his disappearance from the world. We should repeat this formula with clasped hands and bowed head. D. T. Suzuki's translation is: "I take refuge in the Buddha, the incomparable honored one. I take refuge in the Dharma, honorable for its purity. I take refuge in the Sangha, honorable for its harmonious life. I have finished taking refuge in the Buddha. I have finished taking refuge in the Dharma. I have finished taking refuge in the Sangha."

In Japanese it is simpler:

Namu kie Butsu, namu kie Ho, namu kie So.

Kie Butsu myo sam, kie Ho rijin sam, kie So wago som.

Kie Bu kyo, kie Ho kyo, kie So kyo.

But if we translate it into English, we cannot arrange the words in this way. Anyway, whether in English or Japanese, we have to repeat those precepts.

Buddha is said to be the supreme world honored one. There are many names for him. We have ten names for Buddha. By Buddha we do not mean just Shakyamuni Buddha. At the same time we mean various Buddhas. So sometimes we say the Buddhas in the three periods of time: past, future and present. Namu sanze sho Butsu, we say: I take refuge in all Buddhas in the three worlds. Namu is to take refuge. Sanze means the three worlds. Shobutsu means all the Buddhas, or we say, Ji ho san shi i shi hu. Ji ho means ten directions. San shi means three worlds. I shi means all. Hu means Buddha. Ji ho san shi i shi hu, shi son bu sa mo ko sa means: Shi san is the supreme one, bu sa is Bosatsu, that's bodhisattva. Mo ko sa is great Bodhisattvas. That is actually Buddha, Dharma, and Sangha. Dharma is mo ko ho ja ho ro mi. Moko is maha or moka: great. Ho ja ho ro mi is Prajna Paramita. That is the teaching. So when we say ji ho san shi i shi hu, shi son bu sa mo ko sa, mo ko ho ja ho ro mi, that means that we are taking refuge in Buddha, Dharma, and Sangha. That is why we say: Ji ho san shi i shi hu. That is the old Chinese pronunciation, but the meaning is the same.

The Buddha is supposed to be the supreme one. The Dharma is called Dharma because it is truth itself. It is impersonal so it is pure. There is no dust on it . If there is any dust on the law, you will be put in jail, rules or Dharma should always be clean. So Dharma is something which is honored for its purity. I take refuge in the Sangha which is honored for its harmonious life.

You know, we human beings should be always harmonious and we should work in unity. So we call a Buddhist group "harmonious Sangha." Sangha means sang or so gya in Japanese. So means priest and ga is plural; so sangha means priest group, or group of followers.

Here he says, "We take refuge in the Buddha because he is the great teacher. We take refuge in the Law because it is our medicine and points the way. It is law or rule. We take refuge in the priesthood because its members are our wise friends. It is through this triple adoration that we become disciples of Buddha. We should respect the Three Treasures before we receive any further precepts. This is the fundamental precept, since it is on the basis of this adoration that all the moral precepts of Buddhism rest, from beginning to end. Buddhism starts from these three refuges and ends with these three refuges.

"A responsive communication between the refugee and the preceptor makes the maturity of the merit of the triple refuges." "Responsive communication" is the translation of kan no do ko. This is a very difficult work to translate. Kan no means to respond to each other. And do ko means true relationship. Do is dao. Ko is inter-relationship. Here we say Kan no do ko. In terms of consciousness it happens in this way to us: we feel some coherence, or interrelationship, or correspondence between Buddha and us. But, originally, there is no difference between Buddha nature and human nature. So this is more than responsive communication or relationship. But it happens in this way, so "a responsive communion between the refugee and the preceptor," or "protector" (not "protector," okay, maybe "Buddha") "marks the maturity of the merit of the triple treasure."

When we become one with Buddha, it means the Triple Treasure, or refuge, is completed. So, to take refuge in Buddha means to become one with Buddha or to find our true nature which is not different from Buddha. "Be he a devil or man, dwell in the lower regions, demon or animal; whoever experiences the responsive communion is sure to take refuge in the Triple Treasure." By nature, everything has Buddha nature. So when beings have this experience, they can attain the perfection and they can take the Triple Treasure. "The merit of having taken the three refuges continually increases through the various stages of existence and ultimately calls forth the highest right universal enlightenment." "Highest right universal enlightenment" is Buddhahood. If you repeat this experience, you will attain the highest Buddhahood. "This excellent and inconceivably deep merit has been proved by the Tathagata himself; therefore, all living beings should take this refuge."

Buddha himself experienced it and Buddha has the same nature that we have. This means it is possible to have the same experience.

This is not some particular experience when we realize our true nature or some occasion. So here we emphasize the universality of the three refuges. Here he just emphasizes the precepts, but precepts and Zen are not different. Both Zen and precepts are the expression of our true nature; the experience of finding or realizing our true nature. In this sense there is no difference. So the way to practice Zen is the way we take refuge in the precepts.

So, by mutual communion, or kan no do ko, we mean the true experience of Zen. It is not some ecstasy or some mysterious state of mind, but it is a deep joy that is even more than joy. You may have this true experience through some change in your mental state. But a change of mental state is not, strictly speaking, enlightenment. Enlightenment is more than that. That comes with it, but it is more than that. What we experience is joy or mysterious experience, but something follows. That something which follows, besides this experience, is true enlightenment. So we should not suppose that enlightenment will always be experienced in terms of consciousness. Even though you don't know, you know, that enlightenment is there. And by repeating various activities with this subtle caution, the experience becomes deeper and your consciousness will become more and more mature and smooth. So you may say that enlightenment is the maturity of your experience of everyday life. When enlightenment does not follow, your experience is black and white. But when true experience follows your conscious activity or conscious experience, the way you accept it is more natural, smooth, and deep.

It is not just joy. It is something more than joy. It may not be possible to experience enlightenment just in terms of consciousness. But what you do experience is much deeper. This point should always be remembered. If you remember this point, all the precepts are there. You will not be attached to some particular experience; you will not be caught by the dualistic experience of good or bad, or myself or others. When we violate the precepts, we attach to some particular experience.

When you have something, you will have some joy of possession. To do that is, you know, to break the precept of not stealing, (laughs) or not being greedy about giving either spiritual or material help to others. So when those three precepts are kept in the right way, all the precepts will be kept. In short, when you do everything as you do zazen, then all the precepts will be there. We say that we have to just sit. Our mind is clear. You have no experience whatsoever. Maybe the only experience you will have is sleepiness or pain in your legs . No particular experience.

But when you attain enlightenment, when some sudden change of mental state comes to you—happens to you—even that experience is not true enlightenment. You will see something, or realize something, in terms of consciousness, but that means you saw something, that's all. It may not be yours. You saw something there, something beautiful. That is the experience, that's all. It is a true experience, but that is not enough. We should obtain the truth. We should become one with the truth. That is taking refuge in Buddha or Truth. When we become one with it, there is no communion or interrelationship because it is just one. That is completely taking refuge in its true sense. That is the experience we have in our practice.

Namu in Japanese means "to plunge into something." We say, "you cannot skim over the water in a basket." But if you dip the basket in it, the basket will be full of water. That is the way. As long as you are making (laughter) a dualistic effort, you cannot do anything because you are a basket. You are full of holes. Holes are you. We say, muro-chi. Muro-chi means "no-hole wisdom." Our wisdom is hole wisdom. Wisdom with holes. Muro-chi means "no-holes wisdom." But for us, no holes wisdom is just dipping a basket in the water. Then there is no hole. That is taking refuge, and that is how we practice zazen. This is the interpretation of precepts and the understanding of our zazen.

"The Mind Itself is Buddha."

Usually when you study something, and even when you are listening to our lecture, I think that what you understand will be an echo of yourself. You think you are listening to me, but actually you are listening to yourself, so no progress will result. You always understand our lecture in your own way. Your understanding is always based on your way of thinking. So I think that you hear my voice and see my face, but actually you see yourself, and what you hear is nothing but an echo of yourself.

My study was like that for a long time. I think this is often the case when we study Buddhism. If you want to study Buddhism, you have to clear your mind. You should not have any prejudice. You should forget all you have learned before.

You say, "Speak up." "Speak up" is to speak up to here. We say, "Talk out." We do not talk in the realm of reasoning or thinking. We talk out, we get out of our talk. When you hear our lecture, you should not hear my voice or what I say. You should understand what I "talk out." Do you understand? It is rather difficult to express. Not up to here. You should understand something more than what I say in terms of reasoning or logic. That is how you study Buddhism and how to talk about Buddhism.

As you know, the teaching is, as we say, a finger pointing at the moon. You should not see the finger, you should see the moon. But usually your understanding of what I say and your questions are always in the realm of your thinking or conscious understanding. That is not the purpose of the study of Buddhism.

In "Sokushin-zebutsu," one of the important fascicles of the Shobogenzo, Dogen Zenji emphasizes this point. Although this is a very brief fascicle, what he talks about in this small fascicle is very deep and very wide. So I want to talk about it now. For a while my talk will be concentrated on verbal understanding. So now you have to listen very little, but later you should know what you have studied.

When we talk about Buddhism, it is liable to be a strained application of our teaching. You know we have certain faults of teaching and logic, so our talk is liable to be a strained application of Buddhist logic. This means a little, but it doesn't help so much. So we have to destroy the logic, and we should feel what we say, or we should have some intuition to grasp the teaching.

I think most of you have studied the five sense organs and mind. We call them the six sense organs, including the mind. Mostly our study will be limited to the six consciousnesses: eyes, nose, tongue, body, ears, and mind. The mind controls various senses, produces some ideas, and thinks. So our understanding will be limited to those six consciousnesses. But you have one more, in actuality. The reason you make so many mistakes—the reason your understanding of life does not accord with the truth—is because you have one more faculty, the egoistic faculty.

According to Buddhism, you do not make mistakes without any reason. You know, there is a reason why you make mistakes--there is a big reason. You cannot see things as they are, although you have a mind and your five sense organs are perfect. Your eye is good, your taste and tongue are complete, but nevertheless you always make a big mistake. Why is this? There is a good reason. Do you know what it is? It is because of your ego-centered faculty, something which should not be mind. I don't know where this faculty is, whether it is in the faculty of your brain or not. I'm sure our brain does not make any mistakes, but something makes a mistake. What is it?

According to Buddhism, that is the ego-centered or seventh faculty, mana-shiki, in Japanese. This one always makes our judgement wrong. When your understanding is ego-centered, that is not right understanding. Your understanding is not universal. Your understanding is always ego-centered and partial. This is quite true with human beings. Without knowing that you are always making a mistake, you insist on yourself, your feeling, and you project your ego-centered ideas. That is why you make so many mistakes and we get into confusion.

But that is not all. According to Buddhism, there is an eighth consciousness that will correct the mistakes of the seventh consciousness. "You are mistaken," you may say. "You always make a mistake. Why is it?" it says. That is the eighth one.

So if we want to study Buddhism, we should not study it in the realm of the five sense organs or the mind. When you realize that we are always making a mistake, we say you have entered one step into the teaching of Buddhism. And when you understand what the eighth consciousness is, that is enlightenment—enlightened mind.

But usually almost all the teaching is limited to the realm of the first five or six faculties. This is what Dogen Zenji talks about in this fascicle. He says the mere stage of a little bit more than good and bad, right or wrong, agreeable or disagreeable to your six senses may be mysticism. A little bit more than the six senses is mysticism, but not much more than that. What he says is very brief, but I have to explain it in this way: I want to explain what holy mind or divine nature is.

Dogen Zenji referred to that heretical understanding, which I read to you in the last lecture. They understand that holy mind is always clear, independent of our surroundings, and eternal. The things the mind sees or understands are not eternal, but mind itself is eternal and has limitless faculties. It reaches as far as it thinks, and there is no limit to the faculty of mind. It will reach to the moon or to various stars in space, and it reaches them immediately. It doesn't take much time, or any time. So in this way the mind has a great faculty, and mind itself has a divine nature. The mind sometimes is called atman or "big mind" or "great mind," in comparison to our small mind. This mind is limitless; that is why it is called divine mind. This kind of understanding is called the understanding of immortality. We have a similar word, but we do not mean by immortality something that is immortal. Our understanding of immortality cannot be understood by your thinking.

You may ask, then, how should I understand what immortality is? That is wrong too. "How" also belongs to your mind faculty. You wonder how, your eyes wonder, your ears wonder. "Why is it?" you think. That is not the way to understand what it is. By the time we finish this series of lectures, you will understand what I mean, but I don't think I should strive to make you understand right now.

He also talks about Buddhist philosophy in this fascicle. According to Buddhism, the origin of suffering is very deep. Originally, we understand that there is some unconditioned being. But when unconditioned being is conditioned, something happens. I don't know what it is, but something happens. When this unconditioned being makes some movement, it is the beginning of ignorance. When an unconditioned being remains unconditioned, that is wisdom. But when that unconditioned being takes some form or color or movement, that is the beginning of ignorance. Accordingly, that movement will result in suffering or problems. This is quite understandable, I think.

This stage is called the stage of ignorance, or as we say in Japanese, mumyo. Anyway, this word is not appropriate, and "ignorance" is not appropriate, but conditionality is what we mean by "ignorance." By "movement," we mean that unconditioned being is conditioned in terms of color or form. As soon as it takes color or form, it will create some problem. This is the subtle beginning of the problem.

As soon as this conditionality takes place, we have subjectivity of mind, and, at the same time, we have objectivity. Subjective and objective: something that sees and something that is seen. Here we have three stages already. In the first stage, conditionality takes place. The second stage is subjectivity. And the third is objectivity. This kind of functioning of our mind is very subtle. You do not usually realize it.

But the faculties of your mind become more and more clear as they become rough instead of subtle. When the activity of your mind is more vivid, "This is desirable, and that is not desirable," or "I like this one, but I don't like that one." The faculty of your mind is more vivid. And as soon as this kind of dualistic functioning takes place, we will have the idea of the continuity of our mind. That is the first stage of attachment. Actually, your mind is not continuous, but you want what you see to be continuous if it is pretty, if it is good. But if it is bad, you don't want it to be continuous. If you think what you see is not continuous, that is right. But usually we think our mind is working very well when we have some attachment to something. Actually you are already making a big mistake because you misunderstand your mind as something which is continuous. Our mind is not continuous at all—or it is more than continuous or discontinuous.

As soon as you have the idea of continuity of your mind, you will have some attachment to what you observe, and then you will have terminology —terminological conception. You will start to think in terms of concepts. You put labels on the many conceptions you create, but those conceptions are involved in attachment.

When you study logic, you think you have no attachment. But it is like mathematics. When you actually apply the mathematics in your everyday life, attachment is always involved. Big or small, good or bad, heavy or light—this is not pure mathematics. Pure mathematics is very abstract and doesn't actually exist. But this is a shadow of your attachment, a shadow of your mistake. This is actually true. But you are quite sure about the logical conceptions you have, so your study will create a bigger and bigger ego. Now our ego is pretty big. And as soon as you have some terminological conception, you will put it into action. Now you have to fight with each other. We call this karmic action.

But see what has happened to me. This is awful," you may say. You are creating suffering in this process, according to Buddhism.

This is the third subject Dogen Zenji talks about in this fascicle. First of all, he talks about our eight consciousness, and next about the usual understanding of holy mind or our divine nature, and then he talks about how we make mistakes in our everyday life, starting from ignorance or the subtle movement of our mind.

We say there are three subtle functions and six rough faculties of our mind. The delicate movement of our mind (ignorance),subjectivity, and objectivity are the subtle functions. The rougher functions are dualistic feeling (desirable or undesirable), continuity of our mind, attachment, terminological conception, karmic action, and suffering.

When we suffer, our mind becomes very rough. All the subtle functions of our mind will be lost. This is the last suffering, you know. Next will be peace. We will not survive the next one, so we have no taste of this as the last suffering, the last one. You should not be lost in suffering. That is why we study Buddhism.

So anyway, we have to know that we are turning our face to our own call. You should understand it is all right to listen to me, but you should not turn your ear to your own talk.

Form and Emptiness

There are four ways of understanding the relationship of form and emptiness: form is emptiness, emptiness is form, form is form, and emptiness is emptiness. "Form is emptiness" may not be so difficult to understand, but it will be misunderstood by some advanced, hasty people. "Yes, form is emptiness. There is no need for us to attach to some particular thing. Form is emptiness." This looks very clear, and this view of life is better than attaching to some particular form or color, because in it there are actually many, many views of life. And this view of non-existence is deeper than the view of seeing many things which actually look permanent and which look like they have some self-nature. But as we explained already, and as you have already understood, there is no special self-nature for anything, and everything is changing. As long as everything is changing, nothing is permanent. So this form is emptiness may be a more advanced view of life.

But "emptiness is form" is rather difficult to understand. The emptiness which is the absolute goal we will attain, which is enlightenment itself, is form. So whatever you do is enlightenment itself. This is rather difficult to understand, or to accept, because you think emptiness is some unusual thing. Something unusual is something very common. This is rather difficult to understand, especially when you practice zazen. Even though your practice is not perfect, that is enlightenment. This statement is very difficult to accept. "No, my practice is not perfect." But when we understand form is emptiness, and emptiness is form, back and forth in this way, and form is form, and emptiness is emptiness, when emptiness comes, everything is emptiness, and when form comes, form is form, and we accept things as it is.

So when we come to the understanding of, "Form is form and emptiness is emptiness," there is no problem. This stage, or this understanding, is what Dogen Zenji means by, "When the moon is in the water, the water will not be broken, nor will the moon be wet." Moon is moon, and water is water. This is "form is form, emptiness is emptiness." But here there is the possibility of the misunderstanding that there is no need to practice Zen. "Form is form, and emptiness is emptiness. If this is true, why do we practice zazen?" You will have this kind of misunderstanding. But each of the four statements also includes the other three, so there are four ways of understanding each statement. If it is not so, it is not true understanding. So all four statements are actually the same. Whether you say form is form or emptiness is emptiness, or form is emptiness, or emptiness is form, one statement is enough for you. This is true understanding of Prajnaparamita.

Here Dogen Zenji referred to the koan of Zen Master Hotetsu [Pao-ch'e] of Mount Myoho (Mayu) [Mayoku] fanning himself. He was a disciple of the famous Hyakujo Zenji, and he was a very good Zen master. "Hotetsu Zenji of Mt. Myoho was fanning himself. A monk approached and said, 'Sir, the nature of wind is permanent, and there is no place it does not reach. Why then must you fan yourself?'" If the wind is everywhere, why do you fan yourself? Do you understand? If everyone has Buddha nature, and form is emptiness and emptiness is form, why then must you fan yourself?'" Although you understand that the nature of wind is permanent,' the master replied, 'you do not understand the meaning of its reaching everywhere.'" Even though you understand form is emptiness, you do not understand that emptiness is form, in other words. "'What is the meaning?' asked the monk. The master just fanned himself." He did not answer, but just fanned himself. There is a very great difference between a man who fans himself and one who does not fan himself. One will be very hot, one will be very cool, even though wind is everywhere. "The master just fanned himself. The monk bowed with great respect."

This is an experience of the correct transmission of Buddhism. Dogen Zenji said, "Those who say we should not use a fan because there is wind know neither permanency nor the nature of wind. The nature of wind is permanent. The wind of Buddhism actualizes the gold of the earth and ripens the cheese of the Long River."

"Ripens the cheese of the Long River"—this is a quotation from the Gandavyuha [Bandavyuha] Sutra. The water of the Long River is supposed to be pure milk. But even though the water of the Long River is pure milk, if it doesn't go through the right process, it cannot be cheese, you know. Milk is milk, and cheese is cheese. So if you want to ripen cheese, you should work on it. Even though there is wind, if you do not use your fan, it will not make you cool. Even though there is a lot of gold on the earth, if you do not pick it up, you cannot get gold. This is a very important point.

People may think Zen is a wonderful teaching. "If you study Zen, you will acquire complete freedom. Whatever you do, if you are in a Zen Buddhist robe, it is alright. If you wear a black robe like this, whatever you do is alright. We have that much freedom in our teaching." This kind of understanding looks like observing the teaching that form is emptiness, but what I mean by "form is emptiness" is quite different. Back and forth we practice, we train our mind and our emotions and our body. And after that process, you will acquire the perfect freedom.

And perfect freedom will only be acquired under some limitation. When you are in one position, realization of the truth will be there, will happen to you. But if you do not work on any position, wandering about from one place to another without knowing where you are, without knowing the place on which you work, then there will be no chance for you to realize your true nature. Even though you use something to make yourself cool, even though you have a Japanese round fan and a Chinese fan and a big electric fan, if you are always changing from one to the other as you wish, then you will spend your time just changing your equipment to make yourself cool. And you will have no time to appreciate the cool wind. That is what most people are doing. If you are not in some condition, you cannot experience reality. Reality will be experienced only when you are in some particular condition. That is why we say emptiness is form. Emptiness will be very good, but it can only be appreciated in some form or color or under some limitation.

But we cannot be attached to it. Even though it is very wonderful to use a big fan in Tassajara, if you use it in San Francisco, what will happen to you? You cannot use such a big electric fan in San Francisco. So you cannot be attached to anything.

But you should appreciate, moment after moment, what you are doing right now under some condition. First of all, you must know under which condition you actually are. This is very important. If you are a teacher, you should behave like a teacher; when you are a student, you should behave like a student. So first of all you should know what your position is, or else realization of the truth will not happen to you. This is how we should understand our way. To realize our position and find ourselves is the way.

In this koan, he says, "'Even though you know the nature of wind is permanent and reaches everywhere,'" but strictly speaking, this is a kind of rhetoric or a compliment. Actually, the monk doesn't even know the nature of wind nor what is meant by permanence. This is just complete ignorance. "'Although you understand that the nature of wind is permanent,' the master replied, 'you do not understand the meaning of its reaching everywhere.'" How the wind reaches everywhere, and what is everywhere, and what reaching is, he has no idea. He doesn't know at all, about anything! When the nature of wind is permanent, and how it is permanent, is that when the wind works in some certain direction, in some spirit, under some condition, then the nature of wind will appear. You see?

"Reaching everywhere" means that the activity of the cool wind, which is blowing in some certain direction, in some spirit, covers everything. At that moment, the movement of the wind is the whole world, and the independent activity of the wind. Nothing can be compared with the wind under this condition. Ash is ash, having its own past and future, and firewood is firewood, having its own past and future. Firewood and ash are thoroughly independent. So is the wind. This is how wind reaches everywhere, and this activity is beyond the idea of time.

When we attain enlightenment, all the patriarchs attain enlightenment at the same time. You cannot say Buddha is before and we are after. When you understand enlightenment, you are independent from everything; you have your own past and future, as Buddha had his own past and future. And his position is independent, as your position is independent. If so, this realization is beyond time and space. In this way, the wind reaches everywhere. Do you understand? You cannot say Buddha is before and we are after, like ashes are after and firewood is before. In this way, you should understand that the wind reaches everywhere. In this way, you should realize the nature of wind, which is permanent. The monk did not have any understanding of this kind. For Hotetsu Zenji, it was impossible to explain this direct experience of reality, so he just fanned himself, appreciating the cool wind.

This is a very famous statement: "The wind of Buddhism actualizes the gold of the earth and ripens the cheese of the Long River." Only by your practice, when you practice zazen in this way, aiming at this kind of goal, will you have a chance to attain true enlightenment.

How Not to Study

Buddhism is not any special teaching, and enlightenment is not any particular stage that you attain. When you understand your life completely, that is enlightenment. So though the approach to it is not the same, as long as you study sincerely, you will reach the same goal. You may think you have discovered a new teaching, but almost all the teachings we discover have already been discovered by Buddhist teachers. You may say Buddhism is the accumulation of our human experience. So whatever you make effort on, there is the way.

Some people are always trying to discover some particular way for themselves. That is not the true way to study; this kind of idea is utterly wrong. So we say, "Don't seek for any particular enlightenment." Enlightenment is not something particular. When you start to study Buddhism, thinking that it is good to expect that Buddhism will give you some particular teaching, if you cannot satisfy your expectations, you will give up. This is not how we study.

So here (in the Shobogenzo "Genjo-koan") Dogen Zenji says, "When a fish swims in the ocean, there is no end to the water, no matter how far it swims. When a bird flies, there is no end to the air, no matter how far it flies." When you think the sky or the water is something special and try to discover its end, you cannot. You have no chance to study, because you cannot reach the end of the water or the limit of the air. So he says no matter how far it flies, there is no end to the air.

"However, the fish and bird do not leave their elements." A fish or bird does not go out of the water or air. The water or air we want to study is for everyone, they are not particular things. You cannot live without water or without air.

"When the use is large, it is used largely. When the use is small, it is used in the small way." Anyway, whether you are aware of it or not, you are in the air and you are in the water, and according to the way you live, there may be more or less water. The water under this limitation is not the whole water you want to study. But even though it is a small amount of water, it is water, and it is the sky.

"Though it flies everywhere, if the bird leaves the air, it will die at once." Our way which we study is like air or water. So before you try to figure out what it is, you should practice it, you should live in the water or the sky. That is how you study Buddhism. Not by trying to figure out what it is intellectually, but with all of your mind and body, you should practice our way.

"The bird makes life and the fish makes life. Life makes the bird and life makes the fish. There are further analogies possible to illustrate [this]." The bird and life, which is water or sky, are the same thing. So the bird makes life and the fish makes life. Fish is fish made of water; bird made of water, and life made of bird, and life made of fish. Life and bird or fish, or water and sky and fish and bird, is not different. "There are further analogies possible to illustrate." There may be many ways of analyzing this truth.

"In this way, practice, enlightenment, mortality and eternity." So mortality and eternity are one, and enlightenment is one. Bird and sky is one. We should understand it in this way. So where you practice it, there is the way, there is enlightenment.

"However, if a bird or fish tries to reach the end of its element before moving in it, this bird, or this fish, will not find its way or its place. When we find our place at this moment, when we find our way at this moment, then practice follows, and this is realization of the truth. For the place and the way are neither large nor small." Our way cannot be compared with some other practice. Each practice is perfect, including everything, and independent.

So, neither subject nor object: "There is no subject who practices it and no object which is practiced. They have not existed from the beginning." When you practice it, reality appears. Reality did not exist before you practiced it. "They have not existed from the beginning, and they are not in the process of realization." Each moment is realization and is not in the process of realization. Do you understand? It is not process, you know. At the same time, it is in the process of changing into some other practice. But although your practice is a continuous one, at the same time it is discontinuous. Today you have done something, and what you have done will be continued tomorrow. But even though we do not know anything about tomorrow, tomorrow is included in the present. Your work has its own tomorrow and past. Tomorrow what you have done will have its own past and future. What you have done today will belong to the past tomorrow. So it is not the same. Do you understand? Not the same at all. Tomorrow is independent, and today is independent.

There must be some relationship, but although there is a relationship, you cannot compare what you have done today to the things you will do tomorrow. So you must be satisfied with what you did today. Tomorrow you should be satisfied with what you will do tomorrow. You cannot compare them. Oil is oil and water is water. You cannot say which is better. We cannot ignore the relationship between two things, or between many things, but each one is independent. So each one includes everything. You may say what you have done is small, but that's because you compare it. Actually, you should not compare.

"They have not existed from the beginning, and they are not in the process of realization." They are not in the process of realization. Do you understand? Your practice is not in the process of realization. So will you give up? "Your practice is not in the process of realization—it's better to give up if there is no hope." This kind of practice is not our practice. Even though you practice our way for a whole lifetime, some of you may attain enlightenment and some may not. You see? If so, do you give up your practice?

When I say some may and some may not, it means I am comparing someone's practice to someone else's practice. But your own practice itself is originally independent and perfect. So what is wrong is the comparison. You are limiting the actual value of your practice. Your small mind is a big limitation to your true practice, that is all. So it is not the practice that is good or bad, but your understanding makes practice seem good or bad. This is why we say do not seek for some particular enlightenment. You should be satisfied with your practice and practice hard moment after moment. Then there is enlightenment.

"Thus, in our practice of Buddhism, when we gain one truth, we must have mastered that one truth. And if we encounter one activity, we complete the activity. Here is the place, and here leads the way." When there is place, there is way. That is complete practice without calling it good or bad practice. When you encounter one activity, you should do it with your best effort. That is the way.

Therefore, he says, "Understanding is not always possible, because it is simultaneous with the complete attainment of the Buddha's teaching." The complete attainment is simultaneous with when you practice. So it is not possible to understand what it is. If they come one by one at different times, you will have a chance to see what Buddha's teachings and actual practices are. But when they come at the same time that you are practicing them, there is already attainment. So there is no way for us to know the other side, which is attainment.

When you are busy working on something, it is not possible to see what you have done. If you want to see, you have to stop doing it. Then you will know what you have done. Even though it is not possible to see what you have done, when you have done something, there is attainment. There is no doubt in it, but usually we are very curious about what we have done. That is all right; but when you see it, you have already put your practice in a limitation, and you are comparing it to some attainment. When your attainment is better than what you did before, or better than what someone else did, you will be pleased with it; if it is not, you will be discouraged. But that is not because your attainment is not good enough or is not perfect.

"Understanding is not possible because it is simultaneous with the complete attainment of the Buddha's teaching. Do not suppose that what we realize is knowledge in terms of concepts." So your knowledge about what you have done is not the same as what you realized. "Though we have already attained supreme enlightenment, we may not necessarily see." Some may, and some may not. This is a very important point and is the secret of the teaching. "Don't suppose that what we realize is knowledge in terms of concepts." Though we have already attained supreme enlightenment, that secret attainment, attainment which is more than you understand, cannot be seen by you. The way it appears to you is not necessarily the same.

As you know, we live in a world which is mostly perceptions. It is difficult for us to be satisfied with everything when our understanding accords with what we see or think. But we have to know that everything we see or think is under some limitation. You are not seeing or thinking about the thing itself. This point should be remembered. What you see, what you understand in terms of concepts is not always true. This is the secret of Buddhism. This point should be remembered completely.

So don't be disturbed by the ideas you have in your mind. This does not mean that you can ignore your thinking. Thinking should be systematic and should be right. But even though it is right, that is not complete. And what you think is right is not always actually right. Most people attach to the truth which they understand. The confusion arises from this hasty understanding. This is a very, very important point.

"As It Is"

Tonight I want to give you a correct idea of Buddhism or Zen. In a word, Zen is the teaching or practice of seeing "things as it is" or accepting "things as it is" and of raising things as they go. This is the fundamental purpose of our practice and the meaning of Zen. But it is, actually, rather difficult to see "things as it is." You may say you are seeing "things as it is," but actually, you do not see "things as it is." I don't mean that it is a distortion of sight, such as when something of one shape looks shorter than something of another shape. I mean that, as soon as you see something, you already start to intellectualize it. As soon as you intellectualize something, it is already it is not just what you saw.

When I was young, I wanted to practice true practice, and I wanted to know what the way-seeking mind is in its true sense. I thought that to do something good might be the way-seeking mind. So I got up very early, and washed the toilet and sink before the other students got up. I thought that would be a very good thing to do. But while I was doing this, I was afraid someone would see me. I wanted to do it just by myself without being noticed by anyone else. "If someone sees me, that will not be pure practice," I thought. But, before they saw me, I was already going wrong in my mind. I asked myself whether I liked doing it without being noticed by anyone, or whether I wanted it to be known by someone else. Why am I doing something like this? So, in a way, I couldn't accept my way-seeking mind. I was not so sure of the purity of my way-seeking mind.

When I saw a lamp lit in one room, of course, I hid myself. I thought that someone had gotten up already and might come down. It seemed as though I was at least trying to do something good with a pure mind, but that my mind was not so pure. My mind was wandering about. I couldn't make my mind sure, and I was at a loss for what to do. I suffered a little bit. And I thought, and thought, and thought about what I should do. One day, when I was listening to a psychology lecture, the teacher said, "It is impossible to catch our mind exactly. It is especially impossible to know what we have done. The mind which acted some time ago, the mind which belongs to the past, is impossible to catch. And even the mind which is acting right now is impossible to catch, actually." So I thought, "no wonder it is so difficult for me to understand my mind." And I gave up trying to be sure of my way-seeking mind. Since then I have done things, without thinking, just because they were good. And, at the same time, whether or not people saw me was not my problem anymore. So when you want to see, or be sure of, your mind, you cannot catch it. But when you just do something, and when your mind is just acting as it is, that is how you catch your mind in the true sense. Anyway, it is rather difficult to see "things as it is," because seeing "things as it is" is not just the activity of our sight or eyes. This is why we put emphasis on practice. To do something without thinking is the most important point in understanding ourselves. Since it is difficult to see "things as it is," we should practice our way.

People may say if the purpose of Zen is to see "things as it is," then there is no need to practice. That is the big problem. I think in your everyday life, the root practice may be to raise flowers or to grow your garden. That is, I think, the best practice. You know, when you sow a seed, you have to wait for the seed to come up. And if it comes up, you have take care of it. That is our practice. Just to sow a seed is not enough. To take care of it day after day is very important for the good gardener. When you build a house, your work is finished. If someone has written a book, that is enough. But for a gardener, it is necessary to take care of the garden every day. Even though you have finished making that garden, it is necessary to take care of it. So I think our way is nearly the same as making your own garden, or raising some vegetables or flowers.

Each seed, or each plant, has its own character and its own color. If it is a stone garden, each stone has its own character. A long stone has a solemn, profound feeling; a round one expresses perfection; a square one expresses some rigidness or feeling of austerity. If it has moss on it, it has some deep, profound, mystical spirit to it. Those are the characters of each material you use in your garden.

People may say, "Whatever we do, that is Zen," or, "I am seeing 'things as it is.'" They usually see things one by one, but that is not enough. You may say you see "things as it is," but you are just seeing each material and each material's character.

It is necessary for a gardener to make his garden beautiful. If possible, the gardener should express some meaning, or some particular beauty, according to what has been ordered. If someone wants him to build a calm garden, he must make the garden accordingly. If he wants a solemn or austere feeling, he makes the garden austere. He has to choose the material and make it more austere by contrast, or by association, or by harmony. There should be some rules. The way to create harmony is have a rule. We have many colors, and two colors may clash, or may be in harmony, or may be in contrast. If you arrange the six colors in order, starting from red, and going to orange, yellow, green, blue, and violet, that is the color order. But if you use red and yellow together, that is harmony. And if you use red and green, that is contrast. By using those rules, you will accomplish your purpose, and you will have a beautiful garden. So just living however you like is not the way to live. If you want to live, you should follow some rules. If there is a sharp, straight, narrow stone, it expresses some mystical feeling. If the stone is this way, it expresses calmness or peacefulness. And these two shapes are in contrast. But a round stone will be harmonious with every stone. It goes perfectly with any kind of form. A stone which has a wide base expresses a stable feeling. This stone is in contrast with a massive stone, and a long, upright stone and a massive stone are in order. You cannot make a beautiful garden if you just arrange the stones in order. So you should also use some stones which are in contrast with the other stones you're using. There must be some rules.

So, if you want to live, in the true sense of the word, in relationship with others, and in relationship with the "you" which has been living in the past, and which will live tomorrow, there must be some rules. Although it looks like there are no rules, actually there are strict rules. To live day by day, in the true sense, means to live by some perfect rules. This point is also emphasized in Zen. Zen is not just personal practice, and our enlightenment is not just personal attainment. When we attain enlightenment, everything should be enlightened. That is the rule of enlightenment.

When we find our position in this moment, we say we attain enlightenment. And when we live with other beings, we say we attain enlightenment.

So if you think enlightenment is just a personal experience, this idea of enlightenment is like collecting only square stones or only round stones. If someone likes beautiful stones, in which you can see something blue and something white, if that is his enlightenment, he will keep collecting the same stones. But with so many of the same stones, you cannot build an interesting garden. You should use various stones. Enlightenment is the same. If you attach to some particular enlightenment, that is not true enlightenment. You should have various enlightenments. And you should experience various experiences, and you should put more emphasis on relationships between one person and another. In this way, we should practice back and forth, according to the position in which we find ourselves.

This is the outline of our practice and how you attain it. If enlightenment is just collecting, or just being proud of a kind of experience, that kind of experience will not help you at all. And if that were enlightenment, there would have been no need for Buddha to strive hard to save people after he attained enlightenment. What is the purpose of wandering about the dusty road of illusion? If attaining enlightenment is the purpose of zazen, why did Bodhidharma come to China from India and sit for nine years on Shaolin Mountain? The point is to find our position moment after moment, and to live with people moment after moment according to the place. That is the purpose of our practice.

Zazen and Activity

In usual activity, as you know, our effort is directed to outside, and our activity is concentrated on some particular things. This activity of particularize something create many things. But this kind of creativity is— at the same time creates some fear. This creativity will result some feeling —whether it is good or bad—a good and bad feeling we have—we will have.

Before—before you do—if before the concentration happens to you, your mind is just big and something—your mind is something which you don't know. You do not have any feeling about yourself. But once you have involved in something or you are concentrated on something, there your mind will crystallize, and you will have some clear idea of yourself— subjectively and objectively. That subjective crystallized self reflect— project itself to the objective world, and you have some clear objects within your mind. There you have various feeling about the object. But as that object is the projected of mind of yourself, that—that you do—if that feeling is good or object is good, you will naturally cling to it. That—when you cling to some object, it means you are clinging to yourself at the same time because that object is the projected self. And if it—that attachment will result you some fear, if it is good. Because you attach to it, you try not [to] lose it. But nothing is permanent. Everything is changing. So even though you cling to it, that object will change even though you know that you have fear of losing it.

In this way the more your mind is particularized or crystallized, you will have at the same time uneasiness. That is what will result by your effort in its ordinary sense, while zazen practice will not result this kind of fear or attachment. Our effort will be directed the opposite direction. So the more you practice our way, the more you—your mind resume your fundamental state—big, where there is no feeling and where you do not think anything; no discrimination, no attachment and no fear. This kind of —this is the difference between zazen practice—the effort in your zazen practice and the effort in your ordinary activity.

I said sometime—I remember I says something, you know, very extraordinary , you know: Even though you die, nothing will happen . Even [though] the earth is, you know, broken piece by piece, nothing will happen, I said. If you—if your—if you practice zazen, your mind will resume where nothing—before nothing happens. In our mind, there is no star, no earth, no sun—nothing whatsoever. But everything will come out from that nothingness where there is nothing. So even though we pass away—we die, if we know that all of us came—arise from this nothingness, to die is to come back to the source of life. So for everything to appear means the possibility of resuming original state from where we appear.

We live in the realm of time and space. Even though the earth disappear, space exist, time exist. As long as the space exist, time exist. Something will happen in time and space. So as long as time and space is here—is there, there is nothing to be afraid of, even though there is no form appears in this time and space. No one can doubt that there is time and space. But according to Dogen Zenji, this kind of understanding is not deep enough, but tentatively we can acknowledge— we can't deny that the time and space is here.

So why do I—do we have fear of losing ourselves? Even though our form will disappear—disappear, as long as time and space exist, it is—it is all right. Nothing will happen. One after another something will appear. Actually some—that—which does not appear does not—which does not disappear does not exist . Because we disappear we, you know, we are quite sure about our existence. If we do not disappear, we don't know what we are . Maybe more than ghost . If we, you know, exist forever, we should be afraid of ourselves . You don't know where to go. But fortunately we disappears, we die. So as long as we die, it is obvious that we are—we exist in realm of time and space. So we are completely saved.

Even though you cannot deal with your fear, nothing happens to you, you know. Even though you go insane, that is all right . Because we are normal, we have that kind of fear. That we have the possibility of going insane is —should be lucky—we should be lucky, you know, to have possibility of going insane. But usually, you know, we are trying not to be insane . That is opposite effort to our zazen effort. We rather practice zazen to go to insane or enjoying possibility of going insane . It means, you know, we are alive—we are human being . There is no possibility for dog and cats to be insane . Because we are human being, we should dress up in some way. If we go insane, we will, you know, walk around without any dress, you know. If we do so you think—if we do so it may be terrible . We don't want to do so . That is, you know, human being. But for cats and dog there is no such fear.

Whatever happened to us, you know, after all—if we are—if we know what is our life completely and where we go completely, there is no fear whatsoever. But you—you will be—even—however, you will be very sorry for someone who lost his ordinary activity of their mind, because partly they are insane and partly they are not. They are still human being. And so he will make best effort to be human, but he cannot do that. Even though he want to be human, for him it is not possible because he lost his control. But even though you are in the same condition, for you there is nothing to be afraid of. As old Zen master said, "If fire come, you should be burned. If the water come, you should be drowned." That is our way.

So whatever happens to you, as long as you know the bottom of the suffering, bottom of the fear, you are—you feel quite safe. When you do not know the bottom of it, there you have real fear. You don't know what to do with yourself. Even before you go—before you die, you don't know how to live in this moment when you think of it. But as long as you know what will happen to you after your death, there is nothing to be afraid of.

Our practice is to resume our ordinal—original state of being which is universal. All the being in the world or in the cosmic scale in space—time and space.

Dogen Zenji said, "Think unthinkable." We think, but direction of our thinking is opposite. Instead of trying to attain something, we try to forget. Instead of keep thinking, we try to stop thinking. What you will acquire through this kind of—this practice will be tremendous, and every activity should be based on this kind of readiness of your mind.

So all the practice—Rinzai or Soto, or five schools of Zen, or seven schools of Zen, and many other practice should be based on this power. In old time—in ancient time, the people practiced or applied various way in our practice. Sometime they meditate on white skeleton;

sometime they meditate on water; or sometime they practiced zazen to obtain detachment—thinking filthy bag containing , you know, lung and stomach and many nasty things within it. Even the beautiful person contains many things in her.

There are many kinds of practice for us. You are just laughing at them, but if you are in the situation, you will do it. But in America, this kind of thing will never happen . All those practice, when it based on this true way of zazen, it works. But as long as those practice is directed to one way only, it doesn't work.

Because this—the attainment by this way of practice is—something is missing, and that is only delusion for us. It is not real. So true understanding of zazen is necessary, whatever practice you apply, if you do not understand our way as it is—our way of life as it is.

Evolution of living being is going on in the course of specializing the original nature. You know, something like our human life started from some—a kind of amoeba, you know, in the muddy pond in which something was lived, and they divide their body in two and four and eight. In that way our life started. The more and more our life specialized as a human being or animal or plant—the more our life is specialized, the more complicated our life activity become. So a human being has more complicated life. Human being has the more complicated life. So to be divided or to be specialized means to evolve ourselves—evolution of life going in this way.

Nowadays we have very complicated life. But in this direction, as long as we are making effort to reach the moon or the Venus, if that is only way we know, there is no hope for us to be—to attain liberation. The other day —the last year, or the—no—the year before last year, I went to Yosemite and saw a waterfall. I was watching it. It was one sheet of, you know, white pearls hanging on the rock. But a part of it, you know, separated from—by the rock. Part of the water separated from the rock and falling down. When I saw it, I felt very sorry for the separated water, you know. It is—it was almost going to be mist, you know, but still water. If it become completely mist, there will be no problem for it. But they are not mist yet and water. So it has to travel one thousand feet, you know, all the way down to the bottom. If, you know, when—if I didn't see that separated water, I have that kind of feeling for the water. But separation from the original source creates some feeling for us.

The evolution of life creates many problems for us. So I don't—I do not regret—I am not regretful about our civilization to be—to enjoy this civilization. I enjoy it very much. But at the same time, we should know that there is no complete freedom or complete renunciation in this kind of civilization. Only when we know that even though evolution of life brought our individual life to this point where we have many fears, we know how to resume our original life—source of life. Then, you know, we can enjoy this civilization at the top of evolution of life activity. So without this kind of understanding, we cannot enjoy anything. When you are involved in it you may be all right, but what will happen to next time? You will be very regretful.

In Chinese character—no, in zazen, we should get rid of, or we should be —in zazen, our mind should not be instead of contamination or in the state of sleepiness, you know. If [we] are sleeping, we cannot practice zazen. But on the other hand, if our—we are—our mind is state of agitation or state of extreme joy, we cannot practice our way. And describing this extreme joy,

Chinese people used two words—two characters. One is culminating joy, you know. One is culmination of joy. And one character is regretfulness , you know. This is very, you know—it describe to the point if the culmination of joy happens to us, next moment will be the regret .

So if we do not know how to resume the source of life, what we will have is the culminating joy and regretfulness. We cannot enjoy our life in its true sense without this practice. That is why Dogen Zenji put emphasis on this practice. It does not mean to slight the other practice, but if we forget this point, whatever practice it may be, it doesn't work. It doesn't help us in its true sense. On the other hand, if we understand this point, to apply whatever way you apply—way of practice you apply, it will work.

In this way, to open up your mind for everything and to be ready for accepting various difficulties is the purpose of zazen.

What is Zen Buddhism

First of all I am supposed to talk about our teaching. Zen is, Zen is, for you, some special teaching. But, for us Zen is, Buddhism is and not special teaching from the other schools of Buddhism. So, if you ask me to talk about our teaching I have have to, what I will talk is mostly teaching of Buddhism started by Buddha and developed by their teachers in India, China and Japan.

Buddha's teaching put the emphasis on selflessness because even Buddhism it's, is not special culture heritage. It is part of Indian thought. And so before Buddhism there must be some similar teaching or some opposite teaching which form a pair of opposites with Buddhism. As you see in Upanishad there are many similar teaching based on selflessness. Why, I think, why he put the emphasis on selflessness is because people at that time had very difficulty because of the strong idea of self, ah self.

So Buddha on the contrary put emphasis on selflessness so that there you have more balanced understanding of our life. And for the people who find, who were trying to find out something a pleasure of life in this actual modern world, he put the emphasis on suffering so that they can understand their life from both sides. So naturally even so his purpose of sitting or his teaching is through or form some harmonious teaching. So, sometime he put emphasis on self, you know, instead of put the emphasis on selflessness. He sometime rather emphasis on self.

We call this kind of nature of our teaching is double construction, or double construction or double nature of Buddhism. And actually without paradoxical or opposite, two opposite understanding, we cannot think things clearly. And what we think will be clear if we only, when we take at least two opposite viewpoint then you will have some reality without being caught by some one-sided idea. But, mostly, in general, Buddha's teaching is based on the teaching of selflessness. But later his teaching was more settled down in some static? teaching, like everything changes or teaching of interdependency or teaching of cause and effect.

And in Mahayana we have more advanced philosophical setting of that teaching, like, I don't know how to translate something it into English but ah some teaching you will study by Kegon Sutra or Lotus Sutra. Kegon put emphasis on jijimuie?. Jijimuie is harmony of each beings and jijimuie means harmony with the truth and the phenomenal world.

And Lotus Sutra puts the emphasis on the understanding which you will have after attaining the idea of emptiness or the experience of emptiness. This is something like Zen. Zen extended this kind of idea by practice and brought this philosophical teaching into our actual experience and how to bring this philosophical teaching to life by practicing Zen. In Zen school, in short to, you know, to wipe up everything, on the, every dust on the mirror. And to see everything, to see everything on the reflection of the mirror is our way, you know. Or to write to, to erase everything from the blackboard and to write something on it, is Zen.

And we continue this kind of activity, you know, wipe it up and write something on it and wipe it up. But, because I try to, from, try to explain it you know, more psychologically or more as a, our human experience, I put it in this way. But actually what we are doing is to continue this kind of effort you know. This is in other words detachment.

Detachment means, you know, to erase something but, actually we can not, you know, erase what we did . Actually that is not possible. But, you feel as if, you know, you, you, wipe up everything and you delude yourself. When you are absorbed completely absorbed in your activity or in your everyday life, you experience this kind of development of our life, our life force in this way.

So, but actually nothing happens even though you study Buddhism. And nothing happens even you practice zazen. But when you feel in that way, in your practice, that is enlightenment, you know. Because mostly it is difficult for us to wipe up everything, you know, from our mind. And actually there is no need to do so and it is foolish to eliminate all, everything what you have done or result of your previous activity. That is not possible. And it is foolish to try to do that. But there is way to, to develop our everyday life without being bothered by, you know, our previous activity or result of that previous activity. This is how I could explain, you know, how I can explain what I have in my mind about teaching of Zen.

Now, one by one, according to this little piece of paper? I want to explain this kind of double structure of our teaching. To me everything real could, should be understood in this way. For instance, you know, idea of time has, you know, double structure. One is cont - idea of continuity, it's of course time, you know, continuity, at the same time this continuity is the idea of time. If the continuity of time is the idea of time there is no need to have watch here. When I say it is half past ten, you know, it means that, at that time I have discontinuity of time, my idea of time, is discontinuity. You know it is, it is not actually half past ten, you know, maybe more, or while I'm watching it, it go more, continuously it's going. But I have to say, you know, as long as I have watch, it is, if someone asks me what time is it, I have to say half past ten. So that is the idea of discontinuity of time.

But, it is not actually so, it is continuous, time is, the idea of continuous. So discontinuity of time and continuity of time, in this way, real, you know, reality has double. Only by double structure of our reasoning we can figure out what is reality. And self is also, selflessness and self is same thing, you know, not different.

According to Buddhism, the basic teaching maybe for it's settled, more logically, it's everything changes. This is basic teaching of Buddhism and because of this teaching his descendents or his disciples treated Buddha as a teacher of heaven and earth, you know. He is not only a teacher of this world: he is a teacher of heaven. Because even though you go to heaven this teaching, that everything change, we must be different, you know, is also true in heaven. So he called a teacher of heaven and earth because of this teaching that everything changes. And this is the basic foundation of Buddhism - Buddhist teaching.

So, if everything is changing, you know, how about yourself? You know, self is also changing. If so, you know, even though he says self, there's not such substantial being as self. Self is as, I, we learned last night, we, have learned last night a self is not typically? temporarily? we call our function of mind and body - self. But there is no such thing as self. This is also true with

Buddhism. So we say, we put the emphasis, as long as everything changes self cannot be exception.

And the teaching of suffering comes from this point, from this teaching too. We, you know, although everything, including self, changes always we expect, you know, everything not to change, you know. This is also true. This is also marvelous fact (?), of our, you know, nature. In one hand everything change and on the other hand we try not think everything changes. And so there we have suffering, you know. When we expect things not to change, but actually everything is everything is, everything betray our hope. That is how, you know, we suffer.

But if we understand the reality that we hope everything not to change is true and that everything is changing is almost not true. So if we accept, you know, the two side of the one reality then there is no problem when we say everything is change; it's ok. When someone says everything does not change then that is true, but when you could accept in this way, even for a moment. That is enlightenment.

Enlightenment will happen to you, you know, when you are very, very, very truthful to the fact or truthful to, not to, truthful to, although you are not truthful toward reality or fact on both sides, but even, you know, if you very truthful to one sided view of life, you know, then you have chance to attain enlightenment, you know. And whether you attain enlightenment or not, you know, this is true. So other intellectual, intelligent people, you know, there might be no need to attain enlightenment.

You know, you would break into this pattern, this way of thinking and you will more get accustomed to this kind of, way of life or understanding of life and some day we will actually experience, you will enjoy this kind of paradoxical world. So enjoyment, you know, we mean is very much different from the enjoyment made by the people who just go along one-sided view. Onesided understanding of life. This is completely different, you know, we, so Buddhists are in one hand they are very, sometimes they are very, they look very joyous people. On the other hand they are very, you know, dismal and gloomy people. We are very gloomy. This is also double structure.

One person express, you know, their feeling in two different way. That is possible you know. He may be very strong and tough in one way but on the other hand, he may be very gentle and very soft. My teacher used to give us some, refer to, some, refer to famous, the most famous, the best sword maker Massamway.

One day Shihero, you know Shihero, not sword maker but spear, spearhead maker, visited him, but spear or blade, visited him. Fortunately or unfortuantely, you know, Massamai was not there, was not at home. Before Hiroshimai asked his wife to show him some of his sword. And she brought a small sword, as long as this sword, you know, and he was watching it, but he did not, his expression was not talking he's wondering, you know, if he if this is good or bad he is wondering about it. So wife asks him is there something wrong with his sword and if he has some criticism please tell her, she said. And Hiroshimai, you know, take out that spearhead from his pocket and putting his sword on the floor and when he you know, think like this, big hole, you know, was on the sword Massamai made. His wife was amazed at his, you know, strong power, strong quality of the spearhead. And Hiroshimai went back. But his wife promised him, as he was going, to come again to and to meet her husband. And one week after one week or so, he came back and Massamai was not moved a little, was not moved even a little. And he, you know, he asked him to show him, you know, his spearhead. And he was watching. And Massamai said give me that, I want to see your spearhead. And as soon as he receive it he draw, drew his sword and cut his, cut the spearhead in two. With that sword which had big hole in it. And he said, so your spear not able to ? ? because if you need to, is this spearhead, this spearhead is easily cut so this is rather dangerous, he said. Massamai, you know, saw it as double structure. It is soft, soft it is not easily be cut, but it is sharp enough to cut everything. So this is one of the example of double structure or double nature of the reality.

This is also, this, you know, is also selflessness. When you, when the meaning of selflessness is to annihilate all the evil desires or then to give up the idea of fame or profit - that is selflessness. That is one-sided idea. So, selflessness is also mean strong self. The toughness of the self and which is always free from personal attachment. Which is -able?, that is self- selflessness.

Dogen the founder of Soto School of Zen explained this point. You should not think firewood, you know, become ash. Firewood does not become ash. You should not think firewood become ash, firewood has it's own period (?) and ash also has it own period (?). And ash has its own person future, so does firewood. So firewood is independent and ash is independent. When we understand self in that way, you know, that self include everything: its own person future and everything which exist with firewood or ash. That is, that it does not mean to have some substantial idea of ash or fire. It is not some substance but it something ash, something named ash, include everything and related to everything. This is also the understanding of reality and understanding of self. When we -only when we understand in this way, we can understand Buddhism, not only Buddhism. I think, I hope, your understanding will be available to understand your life and to understand other's life and to understand science and everything.

When we just rely on one-sided understanding you lose the purpose of our study. For to study Buddhism to, according to him, to study Buddhism -Buddhism means here, not only, you know, Buddhist teachings everything, to study, everything is to study ourselves. And to study ourselves is to forget ourselves. And to forget ourselves is to be enlightened by things we study, you know. Some thing you study will teach me, teach us something, you know, it is real and true. So he say, he said, to study ourselves [is] to be enlightened by everything. And this enlightenment goes forever, in this way, wiping the enlightenment and having enlightenment again. In this way this enlightenment proceeds you where you go on and on and on and you will understand everything in its true sense.

So this is what is reality according to Buddhism and what is the teaching of selflessness of Buddhist. And this selflessness is one of the three important banner? or seals for Buddhism, that everything change, that everything has law? , when we say say so, it includes many things. There is nothing is also. Nothing is ? meant by this teaching of selflessness. We think, you know, it is possible to attain or to get contact with something, yeah, to understand or to grasp something perfect. But to attain some stage of perfection but according to Buddhism that is not possible, it is not possible. When you understand that is not possible, that understanding is perfect understanding and that is enlightenment.

We understand, that is second point and when we realize or when we have this enlightenment or as long as we have this enlightenment, then here we find nirvana. Right here in this moment that is the three seals, seals of Buddhism.

If some teaching or if some teaching have whatever on the teaching its, if that teaching has this three elements, that is Buddhism. For we call it the three important seals of Buddhism. And this basic teaching will be extended to the Four Noble Truths or the Eightfold Holy Path which was told by Buddha when he saved four of, five of his men who escaped from the castle with him. This world is world of suffering, that this world, that, that is the cause of suffering, and the way to get out of the suffering and what is Nirvana. Where do we attain Nirvana? Where is Nirvana? This is the Four Noble Truth. But those teaching are a different version of ,you know, truths. And then whatever the way of understanding about life may be, if we do not miss this point that is Buddhism.

Zazen as Organization

In zazen practice, what does it mean to put this leg here and this leg here. This is supposed to be our activity, this is. More or less this is openness, this is calmness of mind and this is activity. If this is wisdom this is practice. And when we put one leg, left one, on the right side, it means we don't know which is which. So here we have, you know, already oneness, symbolically. Here this side is, you know, already activity and wisdom and hand and our posture. Our posture is vertical without tipping right or left back or forward. This is also expression of the perfect understanding of teaching which is beyond duality of the teaching.

I want to explain this kind of idea into our rituals and/or precepts. When we extend this kind of practice into relationship between teacher and disciple naturally we have there precepts, idea of precepts, how to observe our precepts and what is the relationship between teacher and disciple. This is also extended idea of, extended practice of zazen practice. Zazen, this posture, is not only, not originally maybe a kind of training or something but it is not just training it is more the actual way of transmitting Buddha's way to us. Through practice we can actually transmit Buddha's teaching because words is not good enough to actualize its teaching. So, naturally how we transmit it through activity or through contact, through human relationships. Here we have relationship teacher, between teacher and disciple. Disciple, of course, can, will, must choose his teacher. Teacher should accept disciple when he wants job, when he's job should accept him as a disciple. This is sometimes teacher may recommended some other teacher for, you know, disciple. Or else, you know, human relationship will not be perfect. So if a teacher think, think his friend is maybe more perfect teacher for him, he may recommend him as a teacher. But, between teacher there's there should not be any conflict.

So, it is quite natural for some teacher to recommend some other teacher for some disciple. Once he become a disciple he should try hard to devote himself to study his way. At first, and because he maybe he, disciple like him, you know, just because, not just because he want to study Buddhism but for some other reason he may want to study under him, but it doesn't matter, you know, anyway if he devote himself completely to the teacher he will understand, he will be his dis.. teacher's disciple and he can transmit our way. And teachers should be, should know what, how a teacher should be. And teacher, relationship between teacher and disciple is very important and at the same time it is difficult for both teacher and disciple to be teacher or disciple in its true sense. On this point, both teacher and disciple should make their best effort. And this is relationship between teacher and disciple. If, when we have our teacher or our disciple there we have various rituals. Rituals is not just training, it is more than that.

Through rituals we communicate in its true sense and we transmit the teaching in its true sense. That is the meaning of ritual. And we have many precepts. Precepts of the relation is also based on this idea of relationship between teacher and disciple or between disciple and disciple. Rituals, true of all ritual or precepts its to understand our teaching in it's true sense. We put the emphasis on selflessness so teacher and disciple, as long as they have their observation of rituals or precepts it's, is not selfless then that is not true ritual. For instance, when we observe one thing together, we should forget, you know, our own practice, we should practice when we, when we practice something with people it is partly each individuals practice and it is partly it is also, it is also others practice. So, we say, for instance, when we recite sutra, we say, recite sutra with you ear, really?, you know, to listen, you know, to some other chanting. So with my mouth we practice our practice and with my ear we practice, we listen to other's practice. So, this kind, here we have the complete egolessness in it's true sense.

Egolessness does not mean to annihilate or to give up our own practice, you know, individual practice. Egolessness, you know, true egolessness should forget egolessness too. So as long as you understand my practice is egolessness, then it means you stick to, you know, ego too, ego practice too, you know, practice of giving up ego center practice. So, When you practice your own practice with others true egolessness happen. That egolessness is not just, you know, egolessness, it is also maybe ego practice. And at the same time it is practice of egolessness. So this egolessness is beyond ego or egolessness . Do you understand?

This is also true in observation of precepts. If you observe precepts you know, that is not true observation of precepts. When you, when you observe your precepts without trying to observe precepts, then, you know, that is true observation of precepts. So, we say, in observation of true precepts there is positive way of observation and negative way of observation. And two of that and not two of that, there must be, you know, for our ways. But those four ways, should be, should not be different. To observe precepts should be, not to observe precepts at the same time. Not to observe precepts means not just observing precepts but when you do not try to observe it then there you have both observation of truth and not observation, not observing precepts. So, one is positive and one is negative. Looks like so, you know, but in its true sense, anyway we have to observe it and out inmost nature, you know, help us to observe precepts.

So, when we understand our precepts from our, from some point of inmost nature that is not observation of truth precepts it is, you know, the way as we want, or way as it is and there, there is not precepts, you know. Precepts is not necessary. So, we are not observing any precepts. But, on the other hand, inmost nature is so, but we have on the other hand, the opposite nature, we are double nature, so on the other hand we want to observe precepts or we, we fear we have to observe it, you know, and we fear the necessity of precepts which will help us, you know.

So when we are helped by precepts that is the coming of the, the blossoming of the, blossom of the true nature. And when we understand precepts in a negative sense, spiritually, as a, spiritually sense that is also expression of true nature but that is negative way of expression of our inmost nature. So precepts observation has two sides, one is negative and the other side positive. And we have choice, you know, to observe it and not to observe it. This is some of the different way of analysising the way of observing precepts.

When we cannot observe, ten or more precepts, then we have to chose some precepts which is possible to observe. And we have this choice, it doesn't mean precepts observation is not some set up, is not ruled, set up by someone, you know, it is the expression of our true nature. And so if something wrong with our expression of the true nature, you know, Buddha will say that is not the way. That is wrong way. Then you have precepts.

So, rules is not path, but the actual event or ? so this the nature of precepts, so we have chance to choose, you know, our precepts. If you go this way, you know, you will have some precepts and if you take the other way you will have some other precepts. So weather you go this way or that way is up to you. So if you go this way you have some if you go the other way you have some other precepts, because precepts is not something set up is not set up rule by Buddha. So, this is actually the extended practice of our zazen practice.

Not rules, in its true sense. When we say rules, rules is for everyone. But our precepts is not for everyone. It is the precepts is his own way of obervation of practice. This is a characteristic of Buddhist precepts.

We have chance to choose, you know, choose precepts. And precepts observation is both negative and positive. Both expression of our true nature. And it has prohibitory meaning too. To prohibit, you know, some conduct is up to your teacher. Teacher, you know, knows whether his way is good or bad, which way is more appropriate to him (you?). Before you are not familiar with our way you should depend upon your teacher, that is the best way. So, in this case we have prohibitory precepts. But when you become familiar with your way you have more positive, you have more positive observation of precepts.

If we start to talk about precepts I think we have to explain our, you know, sin or guilty conscious too. This guilty conscious or idea of sin is, I don't know, Christian way of how you think about things, but Buddhist thinks our by nature as we say Buddha Nature, Buddha Nature is birth? a nature to everyone, that is more good nature, not sinful nature. That is our understanding of our nature. And, in its true sense it is not either good or bad, that is complete understanding. But, in its usual sense it is more good nature rather than bad nature.

And, how sinful or guilty conscious appears in our mind because of karma, you know, because of our accumulation of personal or social karma, activity. Accumulation of inappropriate way of observing our way, will result some power, you know, which drive us to wrong way. That it is our idea sin or karma. And karma is not just, you know, what you did, but also it is more personal. One way it is social and on the other hand it is more accumulated. It is not just created by our body, this body, but our ancestors or our before like, you know, created by our former life.

If when we understand sin or karma in that way it is rather difficult to surmount to ? it just by our confidence or decisions. It is more than that. So in this point I think there is some similarity of Christian sin and our idea of sin. Both for us and Christian this idea of sin is something inevitable and something impossible to get out of it. This is, you know, the idea of karma or sin for us.

And how to get out of it is to best answer is by our practice. But before we go to the best answer, where we have no idea of good or bad, I think or... not simple. There we have to go pretty long way in our practice, which is little by little we should improve ourself. Even though you attain enlightenment in something but you cannot change your karma as long as you live here. So, we have long way to go.

So, this impossibility of solving our problem or sin we have vows as a bodhisattva. Even though our desires are innumerable we vow to cut it, you know, put and end to it. Some thing like this, you know. Even though our way is not attainable, we want to attain it. This is the vow we should have forever. In this way, Buddhist way, will have its own life. If Buddhism is some teaching which is attainable, you know, if you attain it that's all, there's no Buddhism, there's no need to study Buddhism. But fortunately, I didn't attain anything, so we have to strive, to attain it. And here we have double structure, one is, it should be, you know, we should attain it, but on the other hand it is something not attainable. And, how to solve this problem is to practice our way, day by day, moment after moment, to live on each moment is the best answer.

When we satisfy with our attainment moment after moment, with some improvement, we have there composure of life. We have satisfaction. So in our way, there is no idea of complete success, you know, complete enlightenment. And yet we are aiming at, you know, we have some ideal, but we should note that, we, ideal is something which you can't reach, you know, because you cannot reach that ideal. So, ideal is ideal and reality is reality. Now, we should have both reality and ideal, or else we cannot do anything. So ideal and reality, both ideal and reality will help our practice.

And we should not treat ideal or reality something desirable or something not satisfactory. We should, you know, accept ideal as ideal and reality as reality. So even though our practice is not perfect, you know, we should accept it, without forgetting, without rejecting ideal. How to do that is to live on each moment. On each moment we include reality and ideal. So everything is included on each moment. So, there's no other way to be satisfied with what we have on each moment. That is only approach to the ideal.

And we have, we understand Buddha as the ideal, as a perfect, you know, one. At the same time we understand him as one of the human beings, you know, although we have ideal there is no need for us to be bound by ideal. The same thing is true with rituals and precepts. There is no need to be bound by precepts and there is no need to be bound by, to observe, you know, our rituals as some formality.

And in Soto practice, you know, we do not put too much emphasis on enlightenment, you know. When we say enlightenment I. we mean something perfect, perfect stage, you will have, you will attain. But actually that is not possible, you know.

Everyday Mind is Dao

Koan is not something to—something to explain. Why we talk about is to give some suggestion, you know, about how you practice zazen. It is suggestion. We don't talk about what koan means directly. We give you just suggestion, and you, according to the introduction or suggestion, you work on koan. That is how we explain koan and how you listen to koan.

So you don't—you must not think—if I, you know—if you remember what I said or if I—if you understand what I said, you—that is—there is no need for you to solve the koan, you know. So I am not trying to explain what is everyday mind or what is dao, but through this koan—by this koan, I want you to—I want to give you some suggestion how you practice shikantaza.

Actually, shikantaza and koan practice [are] not exactly the same, but there is not much difference. Shikantaza is more condensed practice, more essential practice, or fundamental practice than koan practice. The purpose of koan is same as shikantaza. Anyway, I want to—I want you to understand how you practice our way by explaining this koan of "Everyday Mind Is Dao. Everyday Mind Is Dao."

You may think, you know, that if you practice good enough then you have power which could be extended in your everyday life. It—it is so—actually it is so, but how—then how you, you know, acquire this kind of power is different matter. When you have power, you know, then you can extend that power to everyday life. But the next question will be how you can obtain that power will be the next question. But—and you may wonder what kind of experience you have when you have acquired the power . That kind of—this kind of question will continue endlessly. How —how you will acquire that kind of power, or how to extend the power to everyday life.

So anyway I will explain, first of all, this koan:

Joshu, you know, asked his teacher Nansen, "What is dao?" What is dao?

And his teacher Nansen answered, "Everyday mind is dao."

And Nansen asked his teacher again, "How—how to accord with the dao?" or "How to follow the dao? Tell me how to accord with the dao." That was, you know, Joshu's question.

And Nansen said, "If you try to follow the dao," you know, or "The more you try to follow the dao, the more you will lose the dao." That was his [answer]. And he continued, "The true power does not belong to the matter of attaining it," or "matter—matter [of] aware of it or not aware of it, or attaining it or not attaining it. If you," you know, "if your practice goes beyond the matter of attaining it or not to attaining it, your mind will be boundless blue sky—like a boundless blue sky. And you will have no problem in your everyday life." That was his answer.

Now I want to come back to the discussion between one of you student and me. He said he want to—to have vacation or to go to see someone, and he want to leave Tassajara for one week, he said. And, you know, I— I wanted to know why, you know, why he was—he feels in that way. And at—at last I found how is that. He wanted to—before he rigid—rigidly, you know, strictly attached to or strictly observed Tassajara way. But now he feels to—to observe his way, you know, strictly with the idea to observe Tassajara way is right and not to observe—not to practice even for one day is not good.

So he—he was—his practice, in other word, involved in right or wrong— right practice or wrong practice. And found out that our practice should beyond, you know, go beyond right or wrong. "If so," you know, "what is wrong in my idea of going—leaving Tassajara for one week? Before I saw in that way, but right now I don't understand our way in that way—in that way. So I don't understand our way so rigidly. So sometime we can take—we can leave Tassajara. What is wrong with you to leave Tassajara when I want to leave?" That was his—that is why he now want to leave Tassajara.

Before, you know, as you see in the question and answer between Nansen and Joshu, Joshu said—Joshu asked him, you know, "If I do not try to observe the way, how—how will—can I follow the way— don't—if we—if I don't try to observe it?" It—or in other words, "Is it possible for me," you know, "to observe our way without trying to observe our way?" But Nansen said, "If you try to observe our way, that way is not true way." How you will understand this point? It means that, you know, until you have some power or some experience of real practice, you will not understand what is true way.

Even though I explain what is true way, and even though you understand what I say, that is not true way. Only when you have actually you have that power to extend your experience to everyday life. Then, and without trying to observe our way, naturally, intuitively, when you are able to observe our way, that is true. You understand?

So to—to follow our way rigidly, you know, to—to attain some power or some enlightenment or experience is not, you know—may not be true way. But while you are doing so, unexpectedly your enlightenment will come to you. And that enlightenment is not the enlightenment you expected . That will [be] how, you know, you will experience our true way.

So Dogen Zenji says—always says, "Don't try—try not to attain enlightenment. Just practice it, even though," you know, "you—you have some idea of enlightenment—like a picture," you know, "like a beautiful picture." To attain, to realize, to actualize that idea, you practice zazen. What you get is quite different thing. It will not be the paintings, you know, [of] rice cake. What you will get is something quite different. That is true.

So in koan practice, you know, you try hard to attain enlightenment. In shikantaza, you know, we do not try to attain enlightenment. Or in shikantaza we have no time, you know , to expect something. We have—we have, you know, pain in our—on—in our legs, and sometime it may be very cold . So to remain in right posture is difficult, you know. And if you [are] involved in our practice with right posture, with good breathing, you—you have no time even to, you know, try to—even to have beautiful picture of enlightenment, . It is already hard enough to sit, and you have no other idea of—to have some imagination.

So actually, what will—we do in the same, and what we will attain is same. But, you know, what you attain is something completely different [than] you expected.

So he says, you know, if you try to—if you try to follow the way, you will be far away from it. That is what Nansen said. But what, you know—after what you will attain is something quite different. It is not something to describe, so we call it emptiness. Or sometime toilet paper. Sometime cats. Sometime fox. Whatever it is, you know, it is another name of something which cannot be described. That is true enlightenment. When—only when you have it, you know, then you may say, "everyday life is true way." Even toilet paper is true way . Whatever you do, that is another name of the true way you attain—you have.

This morning I didn't, you know, explain so—so far, but even though I say it may be—I agreed with his idea not to—to go—to leave, you know, for one week or two, it does not mean that is the true way . True way is not something like that. You know, to—sometime to observe our way, sometime we don't. That is not true way. But even so, I don't mean that you should, you know, stay here. Some day he will realize the true way, then he may understand why I said you should—why I—I agreed with his idea of leaving Tassajara for a while. Or sometime don't wear so—so much clothing. Or you should practice rigidly and strictly enough.

To be completely involved in our practice, some day he may understand but I meant. But at least, you know, right now I don't think he understood what I said. I didn't agree with his idea. Or I didn't agree with his rigid practice—what is the true practice. True practice is not in the realm of, you know, "This is true practice and this is not true practice." True practice is beyond right—the idea right and wrong, and beyond experience, beyond human suggestion.

I think old all student may have very difficult time with me because I do not say anything definitely . "Yeah, that is all right. That may be all right. Do whatever you like." And, you know, sometime I don't feel so good, you know, so—so old—old student will wonder, you know, why he is not—he doesn't feel so good when he said, "Oh, whatever you like. Do whatever you like." Or without saying, "Do this. Do that."

So, you know, he may understand, you know, his —he doesn't feel so good. Why is—the true way, you know, is not something you can achieve in term of good or—right or wrong, or successful or not successful. But the important point [is] to have always composure within ourselves whether we are successful or not. To have deep mind, to include everything within ourselves—that is, you know, true way or dao.

So everyday—when you have—when you accept even toilet-paper buddha, you know, you have to true way. So anyway, the point is to—that you can accept things as it is, as you accept Buddha as your teacher. That is true way. And as our patriarch and buddhas did it, it is possible for us to attain that kind of true way.

So there is no difference in everyday problem and true—and koan. There is no difference between bird's or fish's way and Buddha's way. And to attain that there is many ways and various ways to attain that kind of true way—true way experience which is your own, which could be your own, and which will be different from each other's way, and which is quite independent way from other's way—at the same time which is universal way to everyone. That is true way. If so, you know, how can I explain what is true way?

But—only way to, you know—although Nansen and his—great teacher Nansen and his disciple Joshu have this kind of discussion, it does not mean anything to those who do not understand the true way. But it will give us some suggestion, and it will give you some encouragement to practice our way even though here is—he—here may be some Rinzai student or Soto student.

You may think that—for—it is nonsense for Rinzai student to come to Tassajara and practice shikantaza, but it isn't so. Koan practice could be shikantaza. Shikantaza could be, you know, koan practice. Actually if you really practice koan practice with right understanding—with right—under right instruction, that is shikantaza. If you practice shikantaza under the right teacher it will be koan practice. There could not be—if you understand our practice—what is our practice, there is no two practice. Your practice is pointing one way. It looks like various way because you understand it in term of "Rinzai or Soto," "shikantaza or koan practice." That is your fault , not, you know, teacher's fault. Or he is—you may say I am Soto priest, Soto teacher, but actually, you know, you may be—my lineage is Soto lineage, but actually our—or way directly came from Buddha.

Actually, you know, what I meant is—anyway, you should practice zazen . That is what I wanted to say. But you should practice it. You should—should be completely involved in your practice. That is what I meant in short. Then everyone will attain enlightenment. That is what I said in short. You cannot waste your time. It is not possible to waste your time. But you think I am wasting time, that's all . But you are not wasting your time.

So anyway, if you trust in words, you know, it's better to practice zazen without any doubt. And it's better to be completely involved in your practice, forgetting—putting everything aside. That is what I mean.

And we shouldn't be fooled by Nansen and Joshu, even though he said, "Everyday life is true way." So if you are fooled by them, you will say, "Whatever you—we do, that is true way." "There will not be no need to practice zazen. What is wrong not to practice zazen? Even though we do not sit in cross-legged position, that is true way." It means that when you understand in this way, you are trying to understand koan literally without knowing what they really meant by those discussion.

I am so glad to see that you have experienced here in last time period. So after you did it, you understand what you have done . Before you do it or when you—is coming back to Tassajara, or it doesn't mean anything to sit with a teacher, but after you did it, you—you must have experienced what you have done.

Nothing Definite

There's, as I always say, there is no need for you to remember what I said as something definite, you know. I'm just trying to help you, so it is just support of your practice. So if you stick to it, it means that you stick to the support—not, you know, tree itself. You know, a tree, when it is strong enough, it may want some support. But the most important one is the tree itself, not support.

I have, you know, I am one tree, and each one of you are a tree of itself. And by itself, you should, you know, stand up. And when one tree stand up by itself, we call that tree a buddha. In other word, when you, you know, practice zazen in its true sense, you are really buddha. So buddha and tree is one, in that sense. It may be sometime we call it a tree; sometime we call it a buddha. "Buddha" or "tree" or "you" is many names of one buddha.

When you sit, you know, you are independent from various being, and you are related to various being. And when you have perfect composure in your practice, it means that you include everything. You are not just you. You are whole world or whole cosmos, and you are a buddha. So when you sit, you are ordinary man, and you are buddha. So in this sense, you are both ordinary man, ordinary man, and buddha. So you are not just ordinary man—ordinary man. Before you sit, you know, stick to the idea of "you" or idea of self. But when you sit, you are both, you know, ordinary man and buddha. So you are not the same being. When you sit you are not same being before you sit. Do you understand? Because, when you sit, you are ordinary man and buddha.

You may say it is not possible to be ordinary and holy . You may think so. When you think so, your understanding is, we say, heretic understanding or one-sided understanding. We should understand everything, not just from one standpoint. We call someone who understand things from just one side, we call him "tamban-kan." Tamban-kan in Chinese or Japanese means "a man who carry a board on his shoulder." Because he carry a big, you know, board on his shoulder this way, he cannot see the other side . He is always, you know, carrying big board on his shoulder. Almost all the people are carrying big board, so he cannot see the other side. He thinks he is just ordinary man, but, you know, if he take off the board, he will understand, "Oh, I am buddha, too . How come to be a buddha and ordinary man? It is amazing," he may say. That is enlightenment.

So when you experience enlightenment, or when you are enlightened, you will understand things more freely. You don't mind whatever people call you. "Ordinary man." "Okay, I am ordinary man ." "You are buddha?" "Yes, I am buddha," you know. How come to be a buddha and ordinary man?" "Oh, I don't know why, but actually I am buddha and ordinary man." Doesn't matter. Whatever they say , that is all right.

The buddha, in its true sense, is not just different, special one from ordinary man. So ordinary man, in its true sense, is not someone who is not holy or who is not buddha. This is complete understanding of ourselves. With this understanding, if we practice zazen , if we practice zazen, that is true zazen. You will not be bothered by anything. Whatever you hear, whatever you see, that is okay. Actually, but before you have this kind of actual feeling, of course it is necessary to be accustomed to our practice. Although intellectually we understand ourselves, but if we haven't actual feeling with it, then it is not so, you know, powerful. And so that is why you must keep on our practice. If you keep practicing our way, naturally, you know, you will have this understanding and this feeling—actual feeling, too.

Even though we use—we can explain what is Buddhism, if you do not have the actual feeling with it, we, you know, cannot call him real Buddhist. Only when you, you know, your personality is characterized [by this] kind of feeling we call him a Buddhist. How we, you know, characterize ourselves by this kind of understanding or practice is always, you know—it is necessary, you know, for us to be always concentrated on this point.

It is rather difficult to explain how to be concentrated on this point. There are many koans and saying on this point. And those saying looks like very different, but actually they are all the same. Ordinary mind is tao, you know. Ordinary mind is tao, you know. Even though we are doing quite usual things, whenever we do something, that is actually Buddha's activity—Buddha's activity, but our activity , you know. Ordinary mind is tao. Buddha's mind, Buddha's activity, and our activity are not different.

Someone may say our activity is originated or based on Buddha's mind. And Buddha's mind is "such and such" is Buddha's mind, and the "so and so" is ordinary mind. You may, you know, say various explanation , but there is no need, you know, to explain in that way. Whatever we do, you know, if we, you know, do something we cannot say, "I am doing something," you know, because there is no one independent from, separated from, the others. When we do something, you know, it makes sound . What is the sound? When I say something, you are hearing it. So I cannot do, you know, anything by myself, just for myself. That is actually what we are doing, so I cannot say I am doing something. Everyone—if someone do something, everyone is cooperated. And everyone will do something. So there is no explanation , actually, you know. So just minute—moment after moment, we should continue this kind of activity, which is Buddha's activity.

But you cannot say this is just Buddha's activity, because you are doing actually . You may say then, I don't know what I—who is doing what. But why you say, "Who is doing what?" you know. You wanted to limit your activity, you want to intellectualize your activity, that's all, you know. So before you say something, the actual activity is here. That is, you know, actually who we are. We are Buddha, and we are each one of us .

Our activity is cosmic activity and personal activity. So there is no need to explain what we are doing. When you want to explain it, that is all right, but we should not think if we cannot understand it, you know, because of we—because it is impossible to understand it you should not feel uneasy. You know, actual you are here, right here. So before you don't understand yourself, you are you, you know. After you understand it, you are not you anymore .

But usually you stick to who is not you, which is not you, and you ignore, you know , the reality. And you feel uneasy with the reality, and you feel something, some satisfaction, you know, which is not real. As Dogen Zenji said, you know, we human being attach to something which is not real and forget all about which is real . That is actually what we are doing. If you realize this point, you will have perfect composure in yourself, and you can trust, you know, yourself. Whatever happen to you, it doesn't matter. You can trust yourself.

That belief or that trust is not usual trust or usual belief in [that] which is not true, [that] which is not real. So when, you know, you are able to sit without, you know, being attached to any image or any sound, with open mind, that is true practice. And that you can do that means you are [have] already absolute freedom from everything.

Right now I am put emphasis on, you know, one side of the truth. But it is all right with you to have, you know, to enjoy your life moment after moment because you are not enjoy your life as something which is concrete and eternal. Our life is momentary, and, at the same time, each moment, you know, include its own past and future. Next moment will include its own past and future. In this way, our momentary and eternal life will continue. This is, you know, how we lead our everyday life, how we enjoy our everyday life, and how we get freedom from various difficulties. How we not suffer from difficulties and how we enjoy our life, moment after moment, is our practice, based on true understanding.

I was in bed for a long time, and I was thinking about those things, you know. I am just practicing zazen in bed . I should enjoy my bed . Sometime it was difficult, but if it is difficult, I laughed at myself. "Why is it so difficult?" "Why don't you enjoy," you know, "your difficulty?" That is, I think, our practice.

The Only Desire that is Complete is Buddha's Desire

I was talking about denial of, you know, desires. This is very confusing, you know—may be confusing. Our way is not asceticism, but actually, what we—if you read, you know, our precepts literally, there is no difference . But what it means is completely different. What is the difference is what I want to talk about tonight. Or what is the difference between "to study" and "to listen to." "Go to the master and listen to what he says" and "to study." Or why you started to study Zen. There must be some reason why so many people come and—come to Zen Center and practice Zen and study Zen.

I think this is because of the—because our culture—our civilization—came already [to a] dead end, and if you realize that you cannot go any more—any further more. So someone who notice—people who notice that this is the dead end may come to Zen Center to find out some way to go further. That is, you know, your feeling, you know, whether or not you understand what is dead end or why we came to the dead end.

The foundation of our culture is based on individualism. And individualism is based on, you know, idea of self, you know. And from the time of Renaissance, we awoke in our human nature, and we started to put emphasis on our human nature rather than, you know, something which is called "divine nature" or "holy nature." We put more emphasis [on] how— what we are and what is human nature. And we wanted to express our human nature as much as possible. But—and, you know, the human nature—holy nature, you know, or buddha-nature, were replaced by human nature. And that human nature is not what we mean by buddha-nature. This is, you know, starting point of mistake. So whatever the— whatever sort may be—communism, or capitalism, or individualism—all those sorts are based on individual right, or individual power, or individual —supremacy of individual.

So, for an instance, you know, individualism or capitalism seek for the freedom of our desire, our freedom, you know. But capitalism—or—but communism rather put emphasis on equality of the profits or right. But equality of—equality and freedom is not, you know, compatible, you know. If you want to be free, you know, from everything, if you want to extend your desire freely, limitlessly, you know, you—you cannot divide things equally, you know, because you want to extend your desire as much as you can. If each one of you extend, you know, their desire, it is not possible to—or have—to possess things equally.

But our conscience—our conscience always tell us, you know, "You should be free from— you should be free in extending your desire. It is all right. It should be all right to act freely, to possess things as much as you can, if you don't disturb people." But if you have too much, you know, when others do not have so many—so much, you don't feel so good. So that is not compatible thought—those are not compatible.

Why, you know, this kind of—this individualism and to—and—or desire— freedom of desire and equality of our right is compatible is because our thought is based on, you know, self-centered idea. We, you know—when we say "equality," equality means, you know, equality of our human power. When we say "desire," "limitless desire," "freedom of desire," it means "our" freedom, "my" freedom, or "someone's" freedom.

So there is no idea of holy being, or Buddha, or God. There's no idea of it which will make some rule to—some background to give appropriate position to equality and desires or freedom. So those idea—those thought —if it is necessary for—for us to accommodate those thought without difficulty, it is necessary to postulate some big fundamental idea of non-selfish desire or limitless boundary of—boundary of material or place, which is not just material or spiritual. Something beyond spiritual and material is necessary. That is so-called-it "non-selfishness."

As long as our life is controlled or based on a selfish idea, you know, it is not possible for every thought to find its own place without fighting with each other. So there's no wonder why we have difficulty in our life when we—when our life is based on just, you know, superficial idea of self or individual.

Asceticism before Buddhism—asceticism before Buddhism put emphasis —they practiced asceticism for their future, you know, good life: to be born in some place where they have lot of enjoyment or more, you know, perfect world. That is, you know, a kind of selfish extension— extended selfish practice. But our mortification is not based on selfish desire. The purpose of our practice is to control our desires so that our desires find its own place and act properly. We control our desire. And so that every one of us, you know, without any difficulty, to extend our desire, we practice mortification.

So difference is our mortification is based on non-selflessness. And before Buddha's mortification is practice of mortification based on selfish desire or extended practice of selfish practice. When you practice—when you study Buddhism, you know, you have a lot of selfish idea: "I study. I must know what it is," you know. When you want to listen to your teacher, there is not much self, you know—selfish idea. That is the difference. This is very important point.

Why you should have a teacher is, without extending selfish practice or understanding, to learn the truth in its pure form, excluding selfish practice. Study is also, you know, practice. It is not just intellectual. It is intellectual practice. So it is nothing—it is not different from zazen because it is based on non-selfish idea. It is not selfish—extended selfish practice.

Why we say you should practice zazen without "gaining idea," you know: Gaining idea [is] based on selfish idea. And when you just sit because you are told to sit, because that is Buddha's way—only because that is Buddha's way—then you have not much selfish idea in your practice. When you have—you eliminate selfish idea from your practice, that is actually non-selfish practice—the true way of practicing true—true—truth.

Why We Practice

Before I try to explain our practice, I think I should explain why we practice, you know—why we should practice Zen when we have buddha-nature. And this is the great problem Dogen Zenji had. And he worked for this question before he went to China and met with Nyojo Zenji.

And this is not, of course, so easy problem, but if you understand what do we mean when we say everyone has buddha-nature, and everything has buddha-nature. What does it mean? And he explained very carefully in Shobogenzo, on the—in the first chapter.

When we say "buddha-nature," you know, you may think buddha-nature is some innate nature, you know, because we say nature. In Japanese we use same words—nature—buddha-nature. But actually it is not nature like nature of human being or nature of plant—or nature of cats or dogs, you know. It is not, strictly speaking, it is not that kind of nature.

"Nature" means something which is there whatever you do. Whatever you do, there is nature. Nature is not something which is there, you know, before you do something. When you do something, you know, at the same time, nature appears. That is nature, you know. What he meant.

You know, you—you think, you know, we have buddha-nature within ourselves or innate—as a innate nature. And because of this nature, you do something, you know. That is usual understanding of nature . But that is not his understanding. Or it is not like some seed, you know, which is there before plant come out you know. "That is not the nature which I mean," Dogen Zenji said. That kind of understanding of nature is, you know, heretic understanding of nature . It is not correct understanding of nature.

That kind of nature is some idea, you know, you have in your mind. "Here is plant," you know. "So there must be—before this plant appear—there must be something—seed or within the plant, there must be some nature which promote the—its activity. Because of that nature, some flower is red and some flower is yellow." Most people understand in that way. So why we practice—when we think why we practice zazen is, you know, because we have nature—buddha-nature.

"So after," you know, "after practice—after training—after eliminate various selfish desires, that buddha-nature will," you know, "appear." That kind of understanding is based on unclear—unclearness of your understanding of observing—observing things. According to Dogen Zenji —he, you know, worked on this problem for a long time, so his understanding is very clear.

Only when you, you know—when something appears, there there is nature, you know. So nature or outlook of things is two names of one thing, one reality. Sometime we say buddha-nature. Sometime we say enlightenment or bodhi or buddha or attainment. But those are just—those are the two side of one reality. So not only we call it from those two side, but also we call it, sometime, "evil desire."

"Evil desires," we say , but it is another name of buddha-nature . You say, you know, "evil desires," but for Buddha, that is buddha-nature, you know. There is of course, layman and priest , but usually you understand in that way, but actually there is no particular person to be a priest, you know. You may be—each one of you can be a priest and I could be a layman, you know. Because—just because I wear a robe I am priest. Because I behave like a priest maybe—like way, I am a priest. That's all, you know. There is no special person for priest or for layman.

So whatever you call it, that is another name of one reality. Even though you call it mountain or river, that is another name of one reality. So we should not be fooled by words of "nature" or "result" or "buddhahood." We should see thing itself with clear mind. In this way, we understand buddha-nature.

Then why we have evil desires at the same time is, as I explained, that is another name of buddha-nature. Then why we practice zazen—where— from where that evil desire , you know, come up, there is actually no place for evil desires. But actually, you know, we have so-called-it buddha-nature—evil desires which should be annihilated. Why is that? And where should I, you know, should we—after you eliminate, you know, buddha-nature—evil desires from us, you know, like this—here is evil desire. Where do you throw this away ?

You know, when we start to think in this way, we are already started to understand things in heretic way . That is just name, you know. Just name of one thing. There is no such thing to pull out, like this, and to throw away.

You may feel as if you are fooled by me, you know, but it is not so. It is not a laughing matter. You know, we are seriously confronting with our selfish desires, and we are always observing things in wrong way. When we come to this point, it is necessary for us to understand our practice—our practice of shikantaza.

I said, where should I throw evil desire? There is very famous koan, you know. A man who climb up to the top of a pole. If he stays here, he is not enlightened one. When he jump off from the top of the pole, he may be a enlightened one. This is koan.

How we understand this koan is how we understand our practice. Why, you know, we have something which should be take out from us is because we, you know, stay here, you know. Because you stay at top of a pole, you have problem, you know. But actually there is no pole for a—no top for a pole—for actual pole is continued, you know, endlessly forever. So you cannot stop here, actually.

But you think when you have some experience of enlightenment or something, you think we can rest here, you know, observing various sight at the top of a pole, forgetting all about to climb up—to continue climbing up a pole. We say, you know, this is—because this is koan, if— we say "usually," but "usually"—people think, you know, on the top—on the top for the pole. Usually we think in that way. But there is—actually there is no top for anything. Things are continuously growing or changing to something else. Nothing exist in its own form or color. So actually there is no top. But when we think, "Here is a top," that is already misunderstanding.

So accordingly, you have problem whether we should jump off from here , you know. Actually you cannot jump off where we—it is not possible. And even though you try to, you know, stop on the top of the pole, you cannot stay here because it is growing continuously . So you will be continuously, you know, higher and higher. You cannot stop here. But you think it is possible.

That is the problem, you know. That is why you should practice and you should forget all about the top of the pole. If so, you know, where should I forget or throw our misunderstanding is right here, you know. Not this way or that way or past or future. Right here. You should, you know, forget all about the misunderstanding when the place where you are right now. Do you understand? You should, you know, forget this moment, and you should grow to the next— you should extend yourself to the next one. That is the only way. I think you must have understood our practice.

For an instance, you know, my wife —every morning, when breakfast is ready, he hit, you clappers—like this. If I don't answer for it , you know, I—he—she may continue to hit it until I feel rather angry . Why we have that kind of problem is quite simple. Because I don't answer, you know. If I say "Hai!"—that's all . Because I don't say "Hai!" she, you know, continue to—she has to continue because she doesn't know whether I heard it or not .

Sometime she may think: "He knows but he doesn't answer." Eei! That is what will happen. When I don't answer, you know, I am, you know, on the top of the pole . I don't jump off from here. When I say "Hai!" you know, I jump off from here. Because I stay at the top of the pole, I am—I have something to do—something important to do — something important at the top of the pole: "You shouldn't call me! You should wait!" So before I say something I determined to shut up—not to say anything. "This is very important! Don't you know that?! I am here, on the top of the pole! Don't you know that?" That is how we create problem.

So the secret is just to say "Hai!" you know, and jump up from here. Then there is no problem. It means that, to be yourself—always yourself, without sticking to old self. When you say "Hai!" you know, you forget all about yourself and [are] refreshed into some new self. And before new self become old self, you should say another "Hai!" or you should work to the kitchen. So the point is on each moment, and to forget the point and to extend our practice, forgetting ourselves.

So, as Dogen Zenji says, "To study Buddhism is to study ourselves. And to study ourselves is to forget ourselves on each moment." To forget ourselves is—means to be yourself on each moment. Then everything will come and help you, and everything will assure your enlightenment. That is enlightenment, you know. When I say "Hai!" you know, my wife will assure my enlightenment. "Oh, you are a good boy! But I stick to the "good boy"—you know—"I am good boy." I will create another, you know, problem. "Oh, you are good boy. Then you have to help yourself," she may say. So I shall not be good boy any more. I shall not be enlightened one.

So on each moment you should be concentrated yourself, and you should be really yourself. At that moment, where is buddha-nature, you know? Buddha-nature is actually when I said "Hai!" That "Hai!" is buddha-nature itself, in its true sense. Buddha-nature which you have proudly within yourself is not buddha-nature. Actual buddha-nature is when you say "Hai!" or when you become you yourself, or when you forget all about yourself. There is another name— you will have another name of Buddha or buddha-nature.

So "nature" is not something which appear—which will appear in future. Buddha—true, real buddha-nature should be something which is actually here—there. If you cannot see actually what is buddha-nature, it doesn't mean anything . It is rice cake or painted rice cake. It is not actual one. If you want to see the actual rice cake, you should see it when it is there. So purpose of our practice is just to be yourself. When you become yourself in that way, you have really— real enlightenment is there. The enlightenment you have in your mind, you have attained—you attained long—you attained long time ago is not actual enlightenment.

Back and forth when we—you understand our practice, you will enjoy your practice, thinking about what kind of practice you had had before you attained actual enlightenment. Sometime you will have pity on someone who has—who is involved in wrong practice. And sometime you will laugh at yourself, you know, when you fall in—when you are involved in wrong practice. "Oh, what are you doing?" You will, you know, laughed at you—you will tease yourself: "What are you doing?" You will have various feeling. All the real compassion or real love or true encouragement or true courage will arise from here. You will be not only courageous person but also you are very kind person when you reach— when you understand yourself in that way.

So one practice include various virtue, and one feeling of practice will result [in] various feeling like a wave on the sea. So we say, "One practice covers everything"—various virtue. And when you practice your practice in that way, you may be a piece of stone, you may be a tree, you may be a star, you may be a ocean. So you cover everything.

That is how we practice zazen when—before you attain enlightenment. Actually, enlightenment is, you know—will be there only before you attain enlightenment, or just before . You will say—if you say, "I attained enlightenment," you know, it is too late to say . You should say, you know, you should say before smallest particle of time imaginable, if you want to say . But if you cannot say, maybe better to be silent. Better not to say anything.

So to talk about enlightenment is rather, you know , foolish— rather foolish. But sometime we have to talk about it in this way until we lose our, you know, "eyebrow" . You know, to talk about it is to lose our eyebrow, you know—to lose ourselves. Instead of being ourselves. In this sense, we say "be yourself" to be natural. If you say, "This is the way to be natural," you know, that is not natural. Only when you are you in its true sense, on this moment, at this place, that is "naturalness." So there will not be any particular way to be "natural."

For me, you know, to be here right now is naturalness. And to wear robe is naturalness. And to shave my head is naturalness, as a priest . In this way, we should—our practice—we should practice our way and we should remember this. It is not so easy to be natural. Not so easy.

If we have, you know—in our practice if we have a smallest gap, you know, we will, you know, fall into hell. So our practice should be, you know, continued. Continuous practice is necessary. And we should not, you know, rest. We should continue it, if possible, without trying to, you know, continue it. Just, you know, to have generous mind and big mind and soft mind is how to continue our way. And we should be always flexible, you know. We should—we should not be—stick to anything.

I will not repeat same thing over and over again . I think this is enough.

Bodhisattva's Vow

We say "bodhisattva's vow," but actually this is not only Mahayana Buddhist vow but also all the Buddhist vow. When we say Mahayana, we also—it means that something—usually it means that the something superior teaching in contrast with Hinayana. But this is—may not be real understanding. According to Dogen Zenji, this is not right understanding, to say "Hinayana" or "Mahayana."

From the beginning of—the Agama Sutra is supposed to be the oldest sutra—Buddhist sutra, but even in Agama Sutra this kind of thought is there. It says, Shujo muhen—"Sentient beings are numberless. I vow to save them." Why Buddha, you know, come to this—came to this world is to save sentient beings. Usually those who do not believe in Buddhism comes to come to this world because of karma. But for Buddhist—for Buddha, he did not come to this world because of the karma.

In Agama Sutra, they say Buddha passed away by his own choice. And because he finished his task, he—because he has nothing to do more in this world, he took nirvana, it says. When he finished, you know, his task he took nirvana. It means that already [the] purpose of his coming to this world is to save sentient beings or to help others. So if that is, you know, the reason why he come to this world if he finish his task—when he finished his task, there is no reason why he should stay in this world. So he took nirvana.

So underlying thought [is] already to help others, to save sentient beings. Usually, you know, Mahayana Buddhist denounced Hinayana Buddhism. Only Mahayana—Hinayana Buddhist just practice our way to help themselves, not to help others. That is what they say, but actually when they say in Agama Sutra that he took nirvana because he finished his task in this world, it means that already he came to this world to save others. And [in] various Hinayana—so-called-it Hinayana sutra, we find this kind of thought everywhere. Anyway, those vows are supposed to be Mahayana—Bodhisattva's vow or Mahayana vow, but it is actually—those four vows actually [are a] vow for all Buddhists. All Buddhists should have this vow.

To take vow is very important. To believe in Buddhism means to take vow. If you don't take vow, life will be life of karma. Only when we take vow, we—our life is life of Buddhist. And how to take vow may be the most important point. How to take vow.

Another reason Mahayana Buddhist denounce Hinayana—so-called-it Hinayana Buddhist is they are rigidly caught by precepts or teaching or what was told in scriptures. And they have no freedom from precepts or teaching. That is another reason why we denounce—why Mahayana—so-called-it Mahayana, Buddhist denounce Hinayana Buddhist.

But when Buddhism [was] started by Buddha, Buddhism was Mahayana. So if I dare to say, that was Mahayana. Mahayana Buddhist arising was mainly Buddhist teaching of Buddhism or teaching of Buddhism became more and more concrete or caught by concrete idea of some particular teaching or some precepts. And they rigidly try to stick to the teaching. At first it was they respected the teaching too much and preserved—tried to preserve teaching, and that was the purpose of the priest especially. And this kind of effort result [in] very rigid understanding of precepts or teaching. So when, for an instance, they had—they—at first, Buddha did not have no idea of setting up precepts. And some—when someone do something wrong, Buddha just said, "That is not right. Why don't you do it this way?" That was the precept—the original precept. So there was no precepts in term of "Don't do—this is a precepts all the Buddhist should keep."

But when we count precepts in—like Ten Precepts—Ten Prohibitory Precepts, it is, you know—we feel as if we—if we fail to observe those Ten Precepts, you know—if you miss—if you cannot [if you violate] even one of the ten, you will not be the good Buddhist. So the purpose of precepts, receiving—taking vow or taking precepts is just to, you know, observe those things literally. That is maybe the usual way of understanding of precepts. But a true purpose of precepts is not just to observe precepts so that you can attain enlightenment.

Why we observe precepts or why we take vow is to actualize Buddha's spirit—Buddha spirit. So to take vow I, you know, this is the way: "Sentient beings are numberless. I vow to save them." The sentient being are numberless, you know—if it is numberless, you know, how is it possible to save them? Same thing will be true with keeping precepts, you know. We should not kill: We should not take life without reason. "Without reason" is, you know, extra, you know. Without reason —we shouldn't say "without reason." We should just say, "You should not kill." That is enough, you know.

When you fell into the idea of more usual, you know, secular understanding of precepts, you should say, "without reason" , if it means that if there is some reason, we can kill. By saying so we are making some excuse to kill. But why we have to make this kind of excuse is because you think the purpose of keeping precepts or taking vow is to attain enlightenment. And if you do not kill, or do not observe precepts, or do not take vow, you will not be a Buddhist or you will not attain enlightenment.

But purpose of—if you understand the purpose of observing the precepts is—precepts is to arise buddha-mind, then when you say "I will not kill," at that moment you have buddha-mind. There is no need to think, "I have to keep or observe precepts or vow forever." Even though—actually we don't know what we will do in next moment . It is very difficult to know, to be sure about our future. But even it is so right now "I will not kill!" That is enough to arise buddha-mind. Even though it is not possible to save all sentient beings, but moment after moment if you say, "I must save all sentient being"—then you have buddha-mind.

So to arise—to be a Buddhist, moment after moment, we take vow. So it is not necessary to think about whether this is possible or not. When you take vow or when you keep precepts in this way, your way is already is not Buddhist way. You are fell into the superficial practice of "you should do" or "you should not," or "you should take vow" or "you shouldn't take vow." To take vow is to observe our way. So this is one of the way—many ways to practice our way, like zazen practice.

So "Sentient beings are numberless": Maybe, you know, it means that sentient beings are numberless. I vow to save them moment after moment, continuously. But "moment after moment, continuously" is not necessary. "I vow to save them" is strong enough and good enough. "I vow to save them." If the sentient beings are numberless, we will take this vow numberless times, that's all . In this way, we feel another, you know, quite—feeling of quite different quality. We feel the eternal practice of our way, of our Buddhist way. So that it is—"Sentient beings are numberless" means that our practice is—will continue forever.

"Desires are inexhaustible. I vow to put an end to them." If our—the purpose of keeping precepts is to annihilate our desires. This vow is a contradiction. But if the purpose of vow is to arise our buddha-mind, then it makes sense. The "inexhaustible" is some —gives us some encouragement, and we can continue our practice forever. And we—we will have firm confidence in our practice which continue forever. So we will be encouraged by this vow forever.

"The dharma is boundless. I vow to master them." Here it says also "boundless," the boundless dharma. I vow to master it. So our vow will continue forever, and we—we can believe in our boundless dhamma.

"The Buddha's way is unsurpassable. I vow to attain it." The same thing will be true with this vow.

In this way, we should take vow and we should keep our precepts. When you receive precepts, you know, you say, "I will," you know, "keep it," you say. When I give you precepts, you say, "I will keep it."   It is not even promise. When you say, " I will do it," by words that is how you keep precepts. "I will do it." That's enough.

But you —you may think, you know, when you don't know, you can keep the precepts. To say "I will keep it" is, you know, not so conscientious, you may say. When you take the precepts in that way, or when you receive precepts in that way, you are not receiving precepts in its true sense as Buddha expected. Why don't you say, "Yes, I will do it." That is what Buddha wanted you to say. That's all. And whether you can keep it, you know, in next moment or next day is not the point. Do you understand? So it not so—it is not difficult at all to receive precepts. We say so—so we say, to receive precepts is to arise buddha-mind. To receive or to give precepts is to arise buddha-mind at that moment. It is not matter of keeping precepts literally or not. To arise buddha-nature, buddha-mind [we say], "I will do it!"—you know. That's enough.

You know, when you say "I will not say so because I don't know whether I can do it or not," that is maybe a kind of arrogance, which is the enemy of Buddhist. People may say, you know, people who is not so conscientious may say, "I will do it." But a person like me who is very conscientious will not say , "I will keep it." You see? Big arrogance is there . Anyway, you know, you say—when you say, "I will keep it!"—you know, there is no arrogance. There is soft mind, which we Buddhist expect is there when you say, "I will do it. At least I try to do it." And "try to do it" will not be so good, you know. "I will DO it!" , you should say. "I will try to do it" is you are hesitating. "I will do it" is like to jump into the ocean. "I will do it!" Then there is no trouble.

The other day I told you about to climb up the top of the pole and to jump off the top of the pole. We say—usually we say to climb up the top of the pole is easy but it is difficult to jump off from it. I don't think this is true . To climb up, you know, to the top of the, you know, pole is difficult, but to jump off from it is not difficult. The way is just so say, "I will do it!" When you think which is easier, you know, to climb up to the top of the pole or to jump off from the top of the pole, which is easier? When you—because you are thinking that way, it is difficult. When you don't think, when you trust Buddha, and when you say, "I will do it!" that is way—easy way.

We are liable to be caught by something we see or something we experience, and we liable to compare one experience to the other and say which is difficult. So you say to climb up, you know, to the top of the pole is difficult—too easy in comparison to jump off from the pole [which is] not so difficult, but to jump off is very difficult. But you shouldn't say so —or because you say so, because you think so, because you compare the experience of jumping off from the pole to the experience to climb up, you hesitate to do so. So how you keep this—those—how you keep precepts or how you take vow, four vow, is to—to do it, you know, without being involved in some idea of vow or practice or precepts.

In Japan, Buddhist receive precepts—we say jukai—and everyone says, "I will keep it." And when I was young, you know, I thought this is nonsense. How they keep precepts, you know? When they go home have to eat eggs, meat, even they eat rice, that is living being. They are killing everything as long as they live. How is it possible to say, you know, "I will keep it. I will not kill"? But later, you know, I was strucked by them when they say, "I will keep it." [I thought], "Oh, that is the way," you know, "to keep precepts."

In this way, we should take vow—Mahayana vow. This is the way the Buddha's disciples—direct Buddha's disciples took vow. Later, you know, Buddhism became more and more idealistic or more rigid, and we lost the important point. Those things is not something which we should be told. Actually we are doing—we are leading our life in this way. If you observe carefully our everyday life, we are actually doing so—doing in this way. When we understand our life in some sophisticated way , you get into trouble.

So if you want to study our way, we must not forget this point. It is necessary to study, of course, but in your study if you lose this point, your knowledge or your study will not work. You cannot own your knowledge in its true sense.

The Need for Strong Conviction

Dogen Zenji says: "Everything is encourages us to attain enlightenment. Mountains and rivers, earth and sky: everything is encouraging us to attain enlightenment." So, of course, a purpose of lecture is to encourage —to encourage you attaining enlightenment. So we call our lecture, you know, teisho. Teisho means "with teaching—with koan," to help people to attain enlightenment.

And usual lecture—sometime to explain the context of teaching—like to explain philosophy—to understand our teaching in philosophical way is more a "lecture"—a kowa. Kowa is more philosophical. And purpose of to listen to kowa is to have intellectual understanding of the teaching. While teisho is to encourage students to attain enlightenment, or to have perfect understanding of—to have real experience of—to have real Buddhist experience.

And same thing will be koan to encourage—to encourage us to attain, to have direct experience of our life. Even though you think you are studying Buddhism, actually, you are, when you are just reading, you know —it is—it may be—it may not be true or it will not help to have direct experience of Buddhism but just intellectual understanding of it.

That is why we, when we study Buddhism, it is necessary to have strong conviction and to study it with mind and body, not just, you know, not only just mind but also body. So if you attend lecture, you know, even though you are sleepy, you know, and unable to listen to it, just to attend the lecture in spite of the drowsiness will be, you know—will bring you some experience of enlightenment. And it will be the enlightenment itself.

So intellectual understanding is necessary, but it will not—it will not complete your study. Through—by actual practice you can study it in its full meaning. So intellectual study, we say, doesn't make much sense , but it does not mean to ignore intellectual understanding or— enlightenment experience is quite different thing from intellectual understanding. And the true, direct experience of things could be intellectualized. And to try some intellectual explanation to our direct experience is necessary to help your —to help your direct experience. So, for us, both intellectual understanding and direct experience of it is necessary.

Sometime even though you think that is—you think this is enlightenment experience, it may be just, you know, intellectual, extended explanation of —or extended experience of intellectual things, and not true experience— direct experience. That is why you must have true teacher who knows the difference between extended experience of common experience in its dualistic sense. Direct experience will come when you are completely involved in your practice, or when you are completely one with your activity, and when you have no idea of self—not only when you are sitting, but also when you are—your way-seeking mind is strong enough to forget your selfish desires. Or to forget selfish desire when you do something, study something with your whole mind and body, you will have direct experience.

That you haven't—that you have some problem means your practice is not good enough. When your practice is good enough, whatever you see, whatever you do—that is direct experience of the reality. This point should be remembered. And if you know that, it is not so easy to say "this is right" or "this is wrong"; "this is prefect" and "this is not perfect."

Anyway, [for] most of us, it is not possible to say "good and bad" or "right or wrong." Usually we, you know, without knowing this point, you say, "this is right, this is wrong." That is, you know, ridiculous when we know what is real practice. Because you are just involved in usual judgement of good or bad, right or wrong, you can easily say, "this is right, this is wrong."

We Buddhists—you may say, for Buddhists there is nothing wrong. Whatever you do, you know, "Buddha is doing it, not me." And so, "Buddha is responsible for it, not me." But that is, you know, also a kind of misunderstanding.

When we say we have buddha-nature, that is, you know, the statement to encourage you to have actual experience of it. To encourage your true practice we say, "we have buddha-nature." It works only to attain enlightenment, you know, to encourage your true practice. Purpose of the statement is just to encourage true practice, not to give you some excuse, you know, [for] your lazy practice or your formal—just formal practice.

People misunderstand the true meaning of, or true purpose of our words, and you abuse and—or you make excuse for your lazy practice, referring to Buddha's words, understanding the statement in relative sense. This kind of mistake is everywhere. "It works," you know, "only this way and not that—the other way." Do you understand?

Everyone has buddha-nature. Period. No more. You shouldn't say, "so" or "but". You should put "period," you know. "Everyone has buddha-nature." No more statement. If you say something, you know, you will be—you will get big slap. Whap! You have to put "period" here. If you don't, you know, your teacher will put big "period".

So we say, you know, in China, people carry something on their head. Honey or water in big jar. Sometime he may, you know, dropped, you know, of course, by mistake. But if you do not, you know, look back, like this —it is all right. You should go on and on , even though there is no more honey or water on your head. If you go on and on, that is, you know, that is not mistake. But if you [say]: "Oh! I lost it!

Oh, my!" If you say so, that is mistake. That is not our true practice.

When skillful martial artist use their, you know, sword, he could be able to —he should be able to cut fly on your friend's nose, ffft!— without cutting off your [his], you know, nose. It means that, you know, if you have some fear of cutting his nose, that is not true practice. When you do it, you know , you should have strong determination to do it! Whei! without any idea of skillful or not, or dangerous or not. You should just do it when you have to do it.

When you do it with this kind of conviction, that is true practice. So when you do—do it with this conviction, it is true enlightenment at the same time. Not just because of the skillful—skill. It is necessary to have strong conviction to do it, conviction beyond "successful or not successful." Beyond any feeling of fear. You should do it. That is real practice, and that is the way-seeking mind, which is—which goes beyond the idea of— dualistic idea of good and bad, right or wrong.

Now—can you hear me?

So if you should do it, you should just do it. We shouldn't mind whether it is—whether you will be successful or not. That is our vow, you know, four vow. We—we must do it. We must help people just because we must, you know. Sentient being are numberless, so we don't know whether we can help completely all of our sentient being. That is out of question. Our practice should go beyond it—the idea of numerous sentient being or some limited number of sentient being. A part of it or all of it—it doesn't matter as long. As we are here, we should continue our practice. That is true, you know, practice.

Of course, there is no limit in our understanding of the—our teaching. The meaning of Buddha's teaching is limitless, but we should do it. Whether you understand it or not, we should try to understand it. This kind of conviction is necessary when you—once you started to study Buddhism.

"Incomparable teaching" or "supreme teaching" does not mean this is the best of all or something like that, in its comparative sense. When you have right attitude in your study, the teaching you study is the absolute teaching. So, as Dogen Zenji says, "We do not discuss the meaning of teaching in its comparative sense, but we should practice it in its—our practice should be right." With right practice we should study. As a right practice we should study the teaching. We should try to accept teaching with right attitude. Whether teaching is profound or lofty is not the point. But the point is our practice, our attitude to study it. So whatever the teaching is, we do not, you know, we do not discriminate teaching in Zen. Kegon Sutra or Lotus Sutra or Agama Sutra, we don't mind. Whatever the sutra is, the sutra is—all the sutra is our fundamental teaching. We do not discriminate: "This is scripture for Soto." Or "This is the koan for Rinzai." Or "This is scripture for Nichiren Sect." Or "This is the scripture just for Pure Land School." And all the sutra is our sutra.

Whatever the teaching is, if we have right attitude towards the—in our study, that is our teaching. This is characteristic of Zen and characteristic of true Buddhism. We do not set up any system of Buddhism, but we put emphasis on true practice.

In this sense, we say "Zen school." Zen means "right practice." It means to extend Buddha's practice, you know, day by day. That is, you know, how to be Buddha's disciple. That is why we started Zen Center here, or Tassajara Mountain Center: to practice our way in its true sense. It may be rather difficult to study our way in the city, but if you understand, you know, this point, you have no excuse for not practicing zazen. All the rules we have—but all the rules we have here is just to make your practice easier. Not to make our door narrow, but to open up our door for everyone.

Maybe Tassajara door is narrower, you may think, but wider. To have rules is to help your study. Because we know, you know, how difficult it is, so we set up some rules to help your practice. That is the purpose of having rules in Zen Center. If there is no—no pole, you know, to climb up, it is rather difficult for you to experience what kind of feeling you will have when you jump off from the pole. If a baby has no toy, you know, it is rather difficult to—to have actual experience of human being, as a human being. We have—we must experience many things, but if there is nothing, you know, even though whatever things may be—things in our room could be, you know, devices to experience human experience. But if we have, you know, special toy for babies, it is easier to experience our human— develop our human experience.

The, you know, rules we have is just a kind of toy to help your experience as a Buddhist. But toy—it does not mean toy is always necessary, you know. When you are young it is necessary, but after you know how to handle a cup or how to work, it is not necessary for you to have some wheel to, you know, push, or to have some cup or toy made of, you know —miniature, you know, cup made of plastic. If you want to have taste food better, plastic, you know, cup is not so good, you know . It is better to use some ceramic, you know, or cups made of—mud? How do you say it? Clay. You taste better.

So you don't—it is not necessary for you to stick to toy always. And you should extend your way of life deeper and wider. But it is—even so, you know, beautiful, you know, ceramic is not necessary. If you have, you know, if you are ready to appreciate things, and if your practice [is] always encouraged by things you see, things you eat, you know, any special things is not necessary. Whatever it is, things will encourage your true practice.

If you can enjoy your life in its true sense, even though you lose your body, you know, it is all right. If you are not conscious of your mind, it is all right, you know. Even you die, it is all right. If—when you can—when you are encouraged by everything, you know, and when you realize everything is always helping you, then there is no difference whether you are dead or alive. It doesn't make, you know, any sense. It is all right, quite all right . That is complete renunciation.

And your practice will be vigorous—enough to continue this kind of practice forever, regardless of life or death. In this way, our enlightenment should be—could be explained. And how to, you know, have this kind of practice is up to you. I cannot, you know, explain your understanding of Buddhism. You should explain your way of life as a Buddhist in your own way.

So, you know, my talk is just to encourage your practice, but even though you memorize what you say—what I said, it will not help you in its true sense. Maybe it will give you some suggestion.

Zazen is Not Personal Practice

It is rather difficult for us to figure out why we started to practice zazen. It is rather difficult, and I think it may be same for you. But the more you think why you started zazen practice, the more you will find out how deep it is—the meaning you started zazen practice. And once you start our practice, even though your determination is not so strong, or you don't feel your determination is not so strong, but you will find out how strong the determination has been.

It is rather difficult, you know. You think—when you are here, you think sometimes or, you know, once in a while it may be better to give up . But actually to give up our study or practice is not so easy. But you have some, you know—when you—your determination—you think your determination is not so strong—when you think in that way, your— you will not make much—much progress. So anyway once you study— start to study zazen, it's better for you to have strong, you know, determination not to give up our study or our practice. That is why we Soto students put emphasis on way-seeking mind or determination to practice our way forever. And trust in our true nature, who—which is always seeking for our true nature. You know, we say, "True nature is seeking for true nature." You know, true—because we have true nature, so naturally we seek for [it]. It is quite natural for us to seek for true nature. So, "Buddha seek for buddha," we say.

Anyway, you know, even though—once you study—start to practice zazen, even though you stop it, or you leave Tassajara, or Zen Center, I am sure you will come back . I am quite sure about that. But it is rather, you know, waste of time. So once you stop, you are caught by buddha-nature which you have, you know. So it is better to continue it until you have complete freedom even from sitting zazen. That is much better.

So to get through, you know, our practice until you have freedom from it. Then, whenever you do, that is extended practice of zazen. If you—if you stop practicing it until you have freedom from even zazen practice, your life will be always shaky, you know. So you feel as if you waste your whole life.

For a man who realized what is practice, even though we haven't attained enlightenment—so-called-it "enlightenment," we don't feel we waste—we have been—our practice have been waste of time. We don't feel in that way. If you—you are—even though your practice is not perfect, you think someday or in next life you will, you know, sure to—you will have—sure to have that kind of feeling. And we are quite—we know what kind of life we should have.

So even though you don't feel your life was perfect, you will leave for your descendent some problem which they should solve. So your descendent or some of you will find out the meaning of our practice, and find out it is necessary for human being to solve this problem and to continue our practice. So if no one start this kind of practice, your descendant will not find out what is our true life and what is the way to solve personal problem as well as social problem.

Especially, I think, in America not much people knows the meaning of practice. And even in Japan, too, you know, it is—in Japan, I think there are—they have wrong understanding of layman and priest. The priest is, you know—priests are quite different Buddhist from layman. But that is not right. So although priests practice zazen, layman doesn't. Layman don't practice zazen. Of course, some of them do. But quite few people practice zazen. They understand—they think zazen practice is too difficult, you know, for layman, so the priest only should practice zazen.

But that is—they have this kind of idea. So I think most of Japanese people doesn't understand why we practice zazen. It is not matter of layman or priest. For all of us, it is necessary to practice zazen: not only Buddhist but also for all followers of various religion.

But zazen practice is not just personal practice. Buddhist practice is for each one of ourselves and for the others too. And to help themselves and to help others is the purpose of practice and reason why we practice zazen.

I think it is—now it is the time to practice zazen for—with every one of us. So if you realize this point, our practice is not just, you know, for ourselves. And we should know this point. I know the American people are very individualistic, you know, and so their practice is very sincere. I know that. But their practice is just—tend to be just for himself. And so if he think, you know, he has—he thinks he has freedom of choice whether you should practice—whether he should do it or not. But we—actually we don't practice our zazen just for ourselves. And here I feel some difficulty, some, you know—in spreading our true way in America. Maybe, you know, personally I think you may have very good teachers. But—and good teacher will give up personal things, you know, and sacrificing their—his own life, and he may devote himself to the practice in its true sense. But people may think, you know: "That is just," you know, "his choice. It doesn't," you know—"just his choice. So for him that may be," you know, "very good thing, but I don't—I don't," you know, "agree with him." Or, "His practice is nothing to do with —with me-with our life." So even though you have—you may have good teacher, I think you will appreciate his value, or his practice, his being so much—you may not appreciate him so much.

But that is, you know—that kind of understanding of individualism is not so good. Individualism, in its true sense, is very good. And our religion should be for each one of us, you know, first of all. He should do it for his own sake. He should not [be] concerned about other's criticism, you know. He should have strong determination to do it. In this point, individualism is very good. But if you think individualism is absolute, you know, teaching, like bible or scripture , it is, you know—we don't take that kind of understanding.

For Buddhist there is no absolute teaching. Even though it is good, we should know good side and bad side. We should know our tendency. We should know that it is human beings who believe in some kind of teaching. And human being originally has some difficulty to accept teaching as it is. Usually we accept teaching just to make some excuse for himself—for ourselves. You know, "In scripture," you know, "it is said so-and-so. So it is good to do so," without thinking about it so much. "Scripture says this is American way. That is the Japanese way." You know, we don't accept teaching in that way. When you want to study—accept teaching, you should know what it is. American way is not always good. Japanese way is not always good. If there is good side, there must be bad side. So we should be very careful to accept the teaching. We should know the both sides of the one teaching.

You may say this is difference of the cultural background. So Buddhist— Buddhism should be extended or should be developed according to the cultural background. And, "In America there must be American Buddhism —in Japan as Japanese," you know, "Buddhism, is based on or extended on the base of the Japanese cultural—culture."

But this is, you know—one of the important characteristic of Buddhism is whatever the, you know, cultural background is, Buddhism has some power to penetrate into the cultural background. We do not ignore the cultural background, but Buddhism is the deeper foundation of various cultural background. That is why, even though Chinese—Indian Buddhism, Chinese Buddhism, and Japanese Buddhism are different, quite different, are very different, I may say, but there is some traditional, you know, understanding of Buddhism which is always the same.

So I think until you understand your culture, good side and bad side, and accept Buddhism as a deeper, you know, foundation of your culture, I think you—your effort will—you will make a vain effort. So we should know that all of us are just human being. You know, I am Japanese and you are American. But I think even though you say you are American, you know, I don't know who is true American and who is not .

Dick [Baker]—the other day Dick wrote me [from Japan] saying: "I thought," you know, "you are—you are not—I didn't know you are not so Japanese." But when I came to America I thought many people like me, you know, in Japan. The more he understand Japanese people, the more he understand how, you know, difficult Japanese was. If I am, you know, among you, even though I—if I don't wear this robe, I don't know, you know. You may—you don't think I am Japanese. But if you go to Japan, seeing people like me , you will immediately realize, "Oh, he is Japanese"—maybe especially you saw me from, you know, back. You know, "Oh, same figure is—same figure as you see in Japan. You will find same figure, you know, you saw in Japan in me, you know. But even, you know—I think that is the idea of Japanese, you know. If there is many people like me, you know—if you see many people like me, you will have idea of Japanese. But if I talk personally with you, there is no idea of Japanese or American. And if we are just here, even though I am Japanese, when I am talking with you like this, I have no idea of Japanese. And I don't think you have any idea of Japanese.

So "Japanese" or "American" is just idea. "American way" or "Japanese way," you say, but actually there is no such thing. There may be same, you know, people doing same thing, but it does not mean he is Japanese. People may say, you know, people may have some idea of Japanese, that's all. As Dogen Zenji said: "No one say," you know, "he is—he is Zen Buddhist or Soto Zen student. No one calls himself Soto Zen student— teacher. But people may say he is Soto. But that does not mean we should call ourselves Soto students."

So we—when you make some excuse, you say: "This is—we are American people who is raised in American cultural background." I don't think that is proper—that is right. Actually, for each individual there is no American way or Japanese way. That is his own way. So he should—he is responsible for his own way of life and understanding.

And—and I think we should not try to propagate Zen in America, you know. That is not Dogen Zenji's way. One by one is enough. If we have, you know, good understanding between your friend, that is enough. If you love someone, you know, you should try to make—make him understand you. That's all. That is quite natural for us. But we should not try to propagate Soto Zen or Rinzai Zen in America. It is same thing, you know, [to] try to force Japanese way—way of life to American people, or American way of life to Japanese people, which is not really exist.

That which exist in its true sense is, you know, mutual understanding between one and the other. I think that is true Buddhism in its true sense. We have—all human being or living being has fundamental tendency to try to find out some composure in identifying himself to others, you know. If some worm or frog—frog stay in green, you know, leaves, they change their color to the green—into green.

But we have to realize a deeper, you know, nature than—than we feel or than we feel or see. We have deeper nature which is called buddha-nature, which is not various nature—or which is not one of the various nature, but which is the basic nature for various nature. Deeper nature than we see. That is human tendency, you know, to identify ourselves to —to the majority. But, that is—for us, that is the nature to be aware of, or to be careful about, rather than to follow it with our eyes, our thinking mind, our five senses stopped, and our reason stopped. That is the nature we should be careful about.

But most people, you know, make some excuse, numbering various nature we have. One by one, when we face to the problem, we should know our nature. And we should be careful our nature, not to stop our— not to limit our basic nature, so that we can extend our fundamental basic nature without any trouble.

So it is important to know American way or Japanese way. But more important thing is to know our own cultural background, and to have eyes to see our—each one's own cultural background, and what kind of tendency you have. If so, it—it may be very helpful for you to have Japanese friend and for Japanese to come to America and study Japanese way, or to have—to listen to criticism by American people. Then we will be aware of our tendency, which is difficult to—to notice. Not to, you know, not just to stick to American way or Japanese way, but to know our weak points. This kind of effort should be continued.

You think you have, you know—as you are in America, you know, I think you—you may say: "We have no cultural background." But you have. You, you know—I noticed, you know, many, you know, characteristic of American people. That is, you know, your cultural background. Here at Tassajara what are you doing is not just American way or Japanese way. And we are studying what should be our human way, day after day. There may be many reasons why I came to American without knowing this kind of thing. When I came to America, you know, what I thought was: "Anyway, we are all human beings , so I think I can survive" . That was what I knew—only thing what I knew. I, you know, I didn't know where is San Francisco, even. Anyway I came to—I bought a ticket , and I came to America. That's all. And, you know, I was rather angry if people say, you know: "He is Japanese" , you know. Why I am Japanese? You know, those who come to America is American people, you know. Whatever nationality he is, they are all American people.

Some of them must have come a long time ago, but all of them, anyway, except Indian— American Indian—they are people who came from other country. Why they call me Japanese?

And, you know, sometime: "That is Japanese way." Why? I didn't know myself. But now Dick wrote me, "I find—I found—at last I found you typical Japanese," you know. And I realize, "Oh, maybe so." Because there are many people like me. It may take pretty long time to study the true relationship between various, you know, people—various—various kinds of people. But I think we should start to study our basic human nature.

And we should start to study our weak point. If you want to be really strong, you should know your weak point. Without knowing your strong— weak point, you cannot be really, in its true sense, cannot be strong person. And if you don't know your weak point, you will have various worry, and you will have various problem, and you don't have real courage to do something. If you know your weak point, you know—because you know, "My weak point is here," you know, so you—you know how to protect yourself from it. But if you don't know where is your weak point, you will—you must have protect yourself covering all parts of your body. Maybe best thing is to enter a big bag . That will—may be the best way, but you cannot survive in that way. So you should know the weak point only, and protect weak point and extend strong arm, you know. If one—left arm is, you know, not so strong you should fight with right arm. If you don't know which is—which is stronger, you don't know what to do.

A scroll given to me by my teacher says: "Piece of stone in the air. Piece of—piece of stone in the air." "Piece of stone in the air." It means that the created problem, not real problem. There is no stone in the air. There may be bubbles, you know, but there is no stone in the air. But we create—we hit against stone in the air, always. "Oh!" That is what we are doing. If you know, you know, real, you know, problem, you will not hit against so many stones which doesn't exist, you know. Maybe— sometime there may be stone in the air—even in the air. But there—there is—I don't think there is so many stones in the air . So if you know that there is stone, you know, but you know the way to go through the room even though several stones [are] in the air. But most people has many stones in the air, not only one piece of stone. That is, you know, the problems we have because we don't know ourselves.

Most—most of the problem are the problem we create because we don't know ourselves. If you know yourself, you will have, you know, problem. But that is actual problem which will help you—help your way of life. It is much better to have some problem than no problem. If you want to help others, the best way may be not to involve others in the problem you created . Not only you have, you know, various problem created by yourself. You may involve many people in your problem, in your created problem. If you stop doing it, that may be great help, I think.

I may, you know, point out something, you know, always, but it does not mean to criticize you. Because it may be difficult for you to—to know your weak point, I may point out, you know, sometime. So don't be angry with me too much, okay?

Form and Emptiness II

We previously have studied the relationship between— relationship between real and seeming, or emptiness and forms. [By] "real" we mean something beyond our thinking. This is, you know,—there is no way to—whatever, you know, we say about it, it is the express, just suggestion, you know, not real or emptiness itself. It is something beyond our thinking mind, so we call it "emptiness."

It is not actually something which we can understand in term of good or bad, real or not real. And seeming and all—whatever it is—all what we say, you know, everything what we say or what we see is forms. And we actually live in the world of forms and color, you know. And we don't know, actually, what is emptiness itself. Even—we call it "emptiness," you know, there is some rules, you know, how emptiness takes various form. So according to some rules, emptiness take its form and color. And we are explaining about the relationship between emptiness and form which we can see.

Right now we have been mostly discussing rather philosophical way, but tonight may be better to explain it more psychological way or physical way. According to Buddhist psychology, you know, of course, we have five senses, and thinking mind, and to—some faculty to lead our thinking mind in false, you know—to make our thinking mind mistake, you know. That kind of faculty we have. And there is also some faculty to point out the mistake of the seventh mind, you know. Five senses and thinking mind, that is six. Seventh one is, you know, to make our mind made— make mistake. That is the seventh one. That is the mind which let our thinking mind stick to something, you know. There is no need to stick to something, you know, actually. But seventh mind, you know, make sixth mind to stick to something.

The truth we think—idea we have is not always—should not be always same. It should change. But we [are] liable to stick to some—some idea. Why we do so is because of the sixth mind we explain. And that sixth mind is, of course, mistake, you know. We should not stick to some idea always, because everything is changing. If things in reality [are] changing, our mind should change also. But we [are] liable to think, you know, something always exist, something which we see—which we saw always exist and some conclusion we reached is always true. But it is not so. Today's, you know, conclusion will not be true anymore tomorrow, maybe. But we [are] liable to stick to some conclusion or idea. That is the seventh mind.

And eighth—eight one—eighth one told us—tell us, you know, that is also mistake. And eighth one—eighth sense is at the same time the storehouse of various, you know, ideas and knowledge. And eighth— eighth sense is just the purpose of—motto of the eighth sense is just to keep things as it is, old and new. Everything is mountain and river, whatever it is, you know. What we see is always kept in our mind. That is eight—eighth one. And it include also not only knowledge or ideas but also outward object—so-called-it outward object: objective world, including mountain and stones and river and water. Everything, you know, which we call "objective world" is included in our eighth mind. So eighth mind or sense is both subjective and objective, and material and spiritual.

But most of us—most of us are very much involved in thinking mind, and we do—we ignore the more fundamental minds—mind. Because we put more emphasis on thinking mind, so we ignore, you know, our tummy [hara], you know, which is the center of more vegetable-like nervous system. We call it—I think you call it "autonomic nervous system," you know. This is the center of the autonomous system. And, you know, our brain is the center of thinking mind, you know. And it—our nervous system connect both center, you know, like this

We know many things about our brain system, but we don't know whether have mind here or not. But from ancient time, Oriental people studied a lot about this mind. And we—Chinese people call mind here is yang; and this mind here is yin. Some people understand yang is better that yin or powerful—more powerful than yin, but that is not right. Both yin and yang is important.

So yin means, you know, some—something which produce many things. That is yin, like earth, you know. Earth is yin, and the sun is, you know, yang. And yang, you know, help producing us many things. And woman is yin, and man is—a man is yang . I—we don't know which is more important Anyway, both is necessary, yin and yang.

And Chinese people thinks this mind we have here is—or this mind or nervous center—center of vegetable-like nerves is here, right here. And this is actually, you know, a branch of, you know, this nervous system, according to Chinese understanding of mind. So even though you cut off our mind from this mind, you know—cutting off the connection between this mind and this mind, still, you know, you can survive. And you—still you can—you will have children, you know. Still you can eat. If you cut off this mind from yin mind, this center, you know, exist, but this center stop, you know, working. So that is why, you know, we put emphasis on practice of here [hara], you know. If you practice—if you practice zazen, you will have more active autonomous nervous system. On the other hand—on the contrary, if you use too much thinking mind, it will affect the activity of your nervous center here and will create some indigestion or some—will create some trouble to your tummy or lung which is in—in your tummy [hara].

We, you know—by the way it [niku] means "flesh," you know, and this [do] means earth, which is in. And this character means hara. This is hara.

The flesh—earth—or in nature's flesh, you know, here [in the hara]. And it is—so this is very important part . It is not just to—tummy is not to just to keep your various things, you know—bag to keep it—various thing in it. It is very important, you know. Hara.

So in our practice we rather stop our thinking and encourage our activity of more vegetable-like nervous system. And this is nearer to the understanding of reality. We—we analyze things for some purpose, you know. But more important thing is to support ourself, you know, in healthy condition. And you can analyze things, and think about something, and try to make our life easy—easier. But first of all, we have to keep ourselves healthy.

So even though—so maybe, you know, that is why we are now more interested in medicine or medical science rather than philosophy nowadays, I think. And when you become more interested in medical science, eventually we will [become] more interested in study of our own hara. And Chinese people say—according to Chinese people, we have five, you know, five organ in our body. And each one of us—each one of them has some special—not thinking, but nervous activity. My friend is very—now in Japan, authority of Chinese medical—medicine, and he has been—he was a good student when we were studying together. But he started to—he became interested in herbs and Chinese medicine. And he is still continuing reading many books, and [studying] relationship between Zen and Chinese medicine. It is so voluminous that I have no time to follow his books, you know.

But what he describe in those magazine or books is very interesting. And he has big confidence in our future medicine, which is almost, you know, vanished from China and from Japan after Meiji period, when we are more interested in Western medical science. So, according to our law, we cannot be a doctor unless we study Western medicine. That is only way to be a—to have license, you know, as a doctor. And we have still therapy, for an instance—what you call it?—to burn our skin, you know, on some point, you know, or to put a needle, you know—by needle here we help some people. But they are just popular therapists. They have no—they have license, but they have no license to diagnose— diagnose a patient. If they come, they will see him, and, of course, you know, unless he knows what is wrong with him, he cannot use his therapy. But by law it is prohibited to make some prescription or [to] diagnose a patient. But if you study more—nowadays it is very difficult to have—to read books—to collect books because we haven't not much books even. In China, also, those valuable classics is no more. So he has very difficult time to study Chinese medicine.

This is not what I wanted to talk [about] tonight , but anyway what I want to say is, you know: Thinking mind—in our practice, you know, we stop—rather stop our thinking mind to make our more fundamental activity active. Sometime we say "direct experience." What does it mean physically or psychologically? More to stop our thinking mind and to open our basic mind—our practice, physically speaking or psychologically speaking. Anyway Eastern people or Oriental people—our base of—for Oriental people, base of our thinking is oneness, you know, oneness. And that one will be divided yin and yo— yin and yang. There is no yin and yang, or seeming or reality, quite separate element, you know. One—originally it is one element, and yin or yang is two side of one element.

So we catch, you know, our things in the picture of yin and yang, or seeming or reality, you know. That is just picture of one reality, you know. It is not—we don't think, "Here is seeming, and here is reality," or, "Here is yin, and here is yang," you know, and, "Yang is better than yin," or "Yin is better than—more powerful than yang." We don't think in that way.

And—our world will be divided [into] yin and yang, will be divided, you know. Our world will be divided in two. But temporary we can divide it in two, but it does not mean our world is consist of yin and yang. Yin plus yang is not our world. But we, you know, tentatively divide or analyze our world in two: yin and yang. Do you understand the difference? So it is difference of— base of the thinking mind. Your thinking mind is based on duality and our Oriental thinking is based on more oneness.

So even though we use those—this kind of formula, this is a picture of reality, you see? Just picture of reality. We understand reality in this way, that's all. It does not mean there is, you know, form and emptiness, something which is called emptiness and which is something called form. Form and emptiness is originally one. But because of our rigid, limited thinking mind, or to destroy our thinking mind, we use this kind of tools. This is a tools to destroy our thinking mind, or destroy—by "destroy" I mean to be free from thinking mind.

And tonight I think I have to explain this one: "Form is emptiness." Oh— excuse me. "Form is form." When we call "form," there is nothing but form—form—world of form only. After we understand or accept the formula of "form of emptiness, emptiness is form," and "emptiness is emptiness," we will reach the understanding of world of form only—form only.

I think you will understand the world of form only. Actually, you know, whether you understand Buddhism or not, maybe we are actually living in the world of form only. But this form include thinking mind too— everything: physical and spiritual. Whatever it is, what we think is world of form only. So actually we live in world of form only, but there is difference between Buddhist and non-Buddhist. Buddhist also live in world of form only, you know. But there is difference. The difference is, you know, Buddhist understand "form is emptiness, and emptiness is form, and emptiness is emptiness, and form is form," you know. But usual people understand—do not understand "emptiness is form, and form is emptiness, and form is form, emptiness is emptiness." That is the difference. Usual people, you know, in short, do not, you know, have any experience of zazen practice, any experience of stopping thinking mind to reach the world "emptiness is emptiness."

So for usual people, you know, to lose something is very discouraging, you know. Like the old Indian—Indian old woman, you know, who happened to see in her mirror no head .She couldn't—she couldn't see, one morning, her own head in his [her] mirror, so she was very much discouraged, you know. We Buddhist will not be discouraged, even though, you know, we die because we know form is emptiness. Originally we are empty. Originally we are not here, you know, because we are changing moment after moment. I am here, but tomorrow I shall be quite different person because I am changing always into someone— something else. I cough a lot tonight, but I may not cough tomorrow morning , so I'm not same person. So [if] I die in two days, you know, Suzuki and new Suzuki will be born in tomorrow morning. That is, you know, our understanding of ourselves. That is the difference.

But I am right here, you know, and I am doing something. I am talking to you and you are listening to me, so we are involved in same activity. So we are doing same thing, but our understanding of life is different. Actually difference is, you know, whether you understand our life in this way, you know, with five ways or with one way is the difference.

Usually we understand things—as I said, "Form is form." "I am I," you know. "Table is table." "Fire is fire." That is our usual understanding. And that understanding is called "dualistic understanding." So in one way, Western culture is enemy of Oriental culture, or good husband of Oriental culture, maybe. Enemy and, you know, good husband is same thing not different at all. Good, you know, good couple are always fighting —quarrel—get into quarrel. So we say, "You should not try to," you know, "[get] involved in the quarrel of husband and wife." He may be very good friend, you know. He is so good to continue their quarrel. But, you know—so whatever the relationship may be, it is all right, you know. For Buddhist it is all right. For non-Buddhist it is, maybe, big problem . So we must be able to, you know, have various picture of same reality.

Selflessness

We practice zazen so that we attain selflessness. This is very, you know, important and very subtle thing, the matter of self. We don't know where is ourself, but it is very tenacious one, as you know . Even though you think you are pretty well, but it is not so. Why selflessness means, you know—why we say "selflessness" [is] because each one of us is not substantial being. You think you are here, but there is no such thing as "you" exist here. You are not ghost, but at this moment, at this place, you exist here, but you don't exist here so many times. It is just, you know, just tentative being which is always changing. We know that by here, you know, but it is almost impossible to get rid of this idea of self or feeling of self.

To change, you know, to have good understanding is easy, we say, but to have right—I don't know what to say—to have right feeling or to accept it completely emotionally is very hard. Even though you know it, you know, but actually you have no feeling of it. Emotionally you don't accept it.

So it is easy to get rid of idea of self intellectually, like break small lock, you know. It is not so difficult to break some small lock if you hit it [with a] big hammer, you know, it is quite easy. But it is difficult to get rid of habitual thinking, or habitual way of thinking, or habitual way of understanding, or emotional, you know, feeling of it. [It] is as difficult as to break lotus root, you know . To break lotus root is quite easy if you right. You think I have diamond. I break—broke it in two like this. But string is, you know, still here in between, even though you pull as much as you can, string is always follows. It is so hard, like to break a lotus root in two. I think that is very true.

Dogen Zenji was so kind to explain this point in the—one of the fascicle of Shobogenzo, "Sansuikyo"—the sutra of Mountain and Water Sutra."Mountain—what is mountain? What is water? We know—we think we know what is mountain and what is the water. Of course you know. But water for human being, [is] of course water. But for the people in hell it is blood, you know, water is blood. For fish or for dragon, who live in water, [water] is a beautiful palace . And for human being, that is water.

He says a dragon or a fish knows—understand water is blood or palace— their own home, but they don't understand the palace for them is the water —is water for the human being. But you know—you think you know what is water. You are not like a fish, or like a dragon, or like a hungry ghost. "I know water," you know. But Dogen Zenji says you don't know water. You are almost same as—almost ignorant as the dragon or hungry ghosts in heaven. Even though you say you know what is water, Dogen Zenji said you don't know actually what is water.

I think that is why you don't understand why he took the water—leftover water, to take it to the river and return it to the river. Maybe—maybe he knows what is water, but we don't know what is water, maybe, according to him. Do you think what is water then? He says, "You don't know what is water. You are almost as ignorant as the fish." So he says mountain is mountain and water is water. This is point we should study or understand even in intellectual way.

I said last night—I explained last night how everything exist in this world. The teaching how things exist in this way is teaching of interdependency. Teaching of interdependence. Actually I explained last night, but may be better to repeat it.

That something exists means that some other thing exist before—in time-span before. Because something exist before, something else exist later here. Because this exist or because that exist, this exist here. And that something exists here means, at the same time, some other thing in space-span exist, you know. That you exist—that I exist here means you exist here at the same time. And that I exist here means my father existed. Because my father existed, I exist here. In this way, we are closely related to something else. So we do not—we cannot exist just as a independent being from others. It means that, that something exist here, the rest of things exist here. And many things exist—existed in past time.

So, you know, if water, if, you know, if water is here, you know, it means that mountain exist, and fish exist, and the stone exist, tree exist, frog exist, stars exist, moon, and milky river, and everything exist. So we said that water exist, you know, you—you—you may say that. When water exist, everything is water, you know. The water is representative of the whole world. So whole world is water. Nothing can compare to the water because the water is closely related to other things. So actually water may not be water. But if we say, "This is water," the rest of things can be the same thing. May be the water too. Just for convenience sake, we name it "water," that's all. When we reach this kind of understanding, even intellectually, we said—we may be said to have understood what Dogen meant by "water."

You exist here, you know, helping you. But actually there is no borderline between you and I. For me, you are everything. you know. When I—as long as I am here, you are everything. You know, like water, for—like for water everything is just water, just for water. A husband is—for your husband, you are everything . There is nothing but you for your husband right now. When you reach this kind of understanding, you know, you will live in this moment in its true sense. As long as you understand things in term of duality" "I am here and he is there," as if there is no relationship between you and others.

So water is not just water. The water I drink, if I drink a cup of water, the water is everything for us right now when—as long as I am drinking it. With this kind of feeling and spirit, you have to drink water, and you have to treat others. There is no separation between us.

So you say "star," star is only one being which include everything. If you say "mountain," mountain include everything. For mountain, you know, everything is just for himself. Do you understand? And if you reach this kind of experience by practice, you are said to have been practicing zazen. Do you understand?

So there is no wonder why Dogen Zenji says, "Water for you is just like water for the fish," because actually a fish doesn't know what is water. Even though you said you know what is water, but you don't know actually what it is. And you have no feeling of real water. That is something which is very little to do with you. You do not appreciate water. So there is no wonder why he had to—he couldn't help to return the leftover water to the river. Okay? There's big, big difference—

even—in Kegon Sutra. So how we exist in this world is very miraculous way. Even though you can reach to the moon, you cannot explain this point.

According to Kegon Sutra, you know, how we exist is—he—sutra—the sutra says, "I am Vairochana Buddha,who is sitting on a big lotus in— in a big miraculous shape of lotus named Lotus Seed. And in the Lotus Seed there is a lotus—big lotus. And sitting on it. And the lotus has thousands—a thousand petals. And I incarnated into thousand buddha and sit in each petals of the," you know, "lotus. And in each—in each petal—and then in each petals there is"—how many there ? "There is hundred millions of Sumeru Mountain—one millions of Sumeru Mountain, and—no, no, hundred millions of Sumeru Mountain— Mountains, and hundred millions of Four Seas, and hundred million of the world called Naiyenbudai."

So it makes—how—how much, you know, world there is. And in each world there is Bodhi tree. And under the Bodhi tree there are Bodhisattva Shakyamuni practicing zazen to attain enlightenment. And after he attain enlightenment, he will tell you the true story, true law. And that is very true, you know. In this world—I don't know how many beings is in this world. Even we don't know how many stars there are in this cosmic world. I think much more than one hundred million of world or earth, and that is very true.

And in each world there is Shakyamuni Buddha, who know the truth, who know what is water, what is this Bodhi tree, what is petals of lotus. So this is just, you know, a way of expressing the truth, but actually we cannot figure out how things exist in its true sense. That is actually the teaching of selflessness or teaching of interdependency.

Only when you understand our world or—in this way we will be free from suffering. So every existence is just for you, you know. If you ignore this fact, that is, you know, ignorance . Ignore the truth. You ignore the fact—this fact. Even though you cannot describe it, it is true.

And now I think I have to explain the Four Noble Truths: how to—how we should get out of the suffering. The Four Noble Truths are: All existence is suffering. The second, the cause of suffering—what is cause of suffering? Cause of suffering is because of our ignorance we don't, we do not know how we exist here. So cause of suffering is illusion or ignorance and desires based on ignorance. Desires—there is nothing wrong to have desires, but if the desire is based on, you know—based on ignorance, it is like a—like to, you know, drive a car when you are drunk . You don't know where to go with the desire. It is good to have a brand new car. That is okay. But, you know, you must drive the car pretty well, you know. You shouldn't be drunk. The cause of suffering is delusion and desire based on ignorance.

The third one is nirvana. Nirvana—what is nirvana? Nirvana is realm of free from suffering, you know. When we understand the "things as it is," like I explained—when we understand the teaching of interdependency then we are in nirvana—in realm of nirvana.

The fourth one is the means for attainment of nirvana—how to attain nirvana. And how to attain nirvana is the practice of hasshodo, or Eightfold Noble Path. How we suffer, why we suffer, and cause of suffering. He points out the cause of suffering. The cause of suffering is ignorance, illusion. And he pointed out if the cause of suffering is the illusion or ignorance, to be free from ignorance, or to get rid of ignorance, or to have wisdom is the way to attain enlightenment. The cause of suffering is directly related to the result of suffering—suffering which is resulted by the cause which is ignorance. So, you know, cause of suffering is here, and the end of the suffering, the result of ignorance is suffering.

So to—there is, you know, immutable truth between the cause of suffering and suffering. And this is the teaching of cause and effect. And you cannot, you know, get out of the cause—course of cause and effect.

So to—only way to be free from suffering is to transmute the ignorance to —into wisdom. That is the only way. Or to replace ignorance for the wisdom. And the relationship [between] wisdom and ignorance is the same, you know. The—it is two side of the one coin. And suffering and the relationship between suffering and nirvana is also two side of the one paper. It is actually one, but because of our ignorance we cannot see, you know, the other side of the wood like we can see the water but we do not actually understand what is water, like Dogen Zenji point out—pointed out.

Now how to—the practice how to attain nirvana. The one is to have—this is, you know—what I am talking about for—in three lectures are—four lectures are not Zen—teaching of Zen, but in its wider sense it is teaching of Zen, but in its narrow sense this—those lectures are lectures about Buddhism in its wide sense. And those teaching are called teachings for shravakas, or Hinayana Buddhist, or Theravada Buddhist. But it is true for every Buddhist—Buddhist.

And the Eightfold Noble Paths are: One is correct view. The second is correct thinking. The third is correct speech. Correct action. Correct livelihood. Correct endeavor. And correct memory. And correct meditation. Those are Eightfold Noble Truth— Noble Path. Here it says "correct," but there is no other word for this. So in Chinese or in Japanese we use "right": right thinking, or right speech, or right thinking, right view, right thinking, right speech, right activity, right livelihood. In this way, we say—we use "right." But this "right" is not the "right" in term of good and—right and wrong. This is more than that.

Anyway, we cannot say—we cannot explain it in one word. So "right," here, it means to have good understanding or, if possible, perfect understanding of the four teaching of: everything changes—everything— teaching of everything changes; teaching of selflessness; teaching of suffering—teaching of everything in state of suffering; and how—teaching of nirvana.

To have correct understanding of it is right understanding. As you have understood what is water, actual, you know. When you reach this kind of understanding, that is right thinking, right view, right viewpoint. Not partial, you know, onesided view, but correct view or right view. And right way of thinking. Just —it is not just thinking, but it is wisdom itself. And if you think accordingly, that is right thinking and right speech. Right speech does not mean to, you know, to speak—to give a speech in term of right or wrong, good or bad. Right action. The right action should not be one-sided action. We should speak impartially always. And the fourth one is right livelihood— livelihood. It want some explanation. And this is—it gives us very good suggestion what is right livelihood. Of course, this is for monks.

What is, then, wrong livelihood? To cultivate the land or to cultivate land for a monk is not right livelihood. But in China, you know—this is like a kind of precepts for Indian monks. There are the people who enter religious life after finishing their family life. And they are supposed to be supported by people—not only his family but also people in the town—in his the town.

So after they entered religious life, they are not supposed to cultivate land or cut the wood for fire. Or they should not [practice] compounding. They should not compound medicine, even. And they should not study astrology. They should not speaking by proxy for another. You should not be attorney . You should—you should not practice charms, you know, some magic. And you should not be fortune-teller.

What will be a monk—what kind of person, you know—what kind of personality is for monk, or ideal image of monks. They should not tell something, you know—they should not pray some magical power, you know. They should not fascinate people by some, you know, by some extraordinary way . Only his own personality, only his own everyday life, he should be a monk. Do you understand? They should not take some particular—they should not take some different activity. They should be plain, common, ordinary people, and they should be a good friend of others. And sometime they should be even a teacher of others, without having this kind of charm. This is how the monk should be—how Buddhist should be.

If you understand the teaching of interdependency, or if you understand what is water, actually, you will easily understand what will be the right livelihood for Buddhist. Okay? You should remember this. I don't prohibit, you know, those things, but you should know the image of the Buddhist. What will be the Buddhist? In this way, Buddha had many disciples.

Do you know Manjushri? He was a very alert fellow. How he joined Buddha's order is when he saw his—Buddha's disciple early in the morning on the street, walking, you know, straight, calmly, and gently. And he was strucked by his appearance. Just—when just he saw him, he was fascinated in its trueness, not because of some magic—magical power. And he decided to join Buddha's order.

In this way, you know, Buddha obtained many disciples. He did not play any magic. He did not say anything strange, special. The teaching he told for us is very usual teaching. It is very wide and big, but if you try to understand it, you know, it is bottomlessly big. But he did not tell us anything strange. This is right livelihood. I think this is very important, especially for you who want to be a pioneer of American Buddhism in its true sense. You should not depend on some, you know, power, or some wisdom, or some particular knowledge or study.

And right endeavor. This is also important, you know. It is rather difficult to—to have right endeavor. In short, when people get up you should get up. When people eat, you should eat. That is right endeavor. You should not get up too early or too late.

And right memory. Memory—something—to remember something which is important for our practice. And the last one is right meditation. Before Buddha, people practice zazen, you know, in various way, with various aim. But Buddha's meditation is completely different from those meditations. I think there is no need to explain about this. Okay? I think you will dust everything.

You cannot use, you know, what you have now. Even though you know many things, you should not tell—you should not use it, and just to sit is what you should do. Just to know what is meditation, what is water , why did you came here—that's all what you should know. And, in this way, if you continue your practice, you will be a good Buddhist in its true sense.

Teacher and Disciple

Emptiness does not mean annihilation; it means selfless original enlightenment which gives rise to everything. Once selfless original enlightenment takes place, very subjective and objective existence resumes its own nature (buddha-nature) and becomes valuable jewels to us all.

In Mahayana Buddhism every teaching is based on the idea of emptiness, but most schools emphasize its expression in some particular sutra—the Lotus Sutra, the Avatamsaka Sutra, the Mahavairochana Sutra, and others. In Zen we do not emphasize the teaching until after we practice, and between practice and enlightenment there must not be any gap in our effort. Only in this way it is possible to attain the perfect enlightenment from which every teaching comes out. For us it is not teaching, practice, enlightenment; but enlightenment, practice, and the study of the teachings. At this time every sutra has its value according to the temperament and circumstances of the disciples.

So it is the character or personality, the cross-current of teacher and disciple, that makes transmission and real patriarchal Zen possible— practicing from the point of view of the enlightenment of the Buddhas and patriarchs. So the relationship between the teacher or Zen master and disciples is quite important for us. By believing in one's master, one can attain his character and the disciple or student will have his own spiritual enfoldment.

Once when Yakusan Zenji was asked to talk about Buddhism he said: "There is the teacher of scriptures, there is the scholar or philosopher of Buddhism, and then there is the Zen master. Do not acknowledge me." Day after day, from morning until night, he behaved like a Zen master. "Why don't you acknowledge me" is what he meant. To practice Zen with disciples, to eat with them and sleep with them is the most important thing for a Zen master. So he said, "Why don't you acknowledge me? I am a Zen master, not a teacher of the scriptures or a philosopher."

So we say, "Only to sit on a cushion is not Zen." The Zen master's everyday life, character and spirit is Zen. My own master said, "I will not acknowledge any monastery where there is lazy training, where it is full of dust." He was very strict. To sleep when we sleep, to scrub the floor and keep it clean, that is our Zen. So practice is first. And as a result of practice, there is teaching. The teaching must not be stock words or stale stories. But must be always kept fresh. That is real teaching.

But we do not neglect the teaching or sutras of Buddha. Because we want to find out the actual value of the teaching, we practice Zen and train ourselves to have the actual living meaning of the scriptures. But this practice must be quite serious. If we are not serious enough, the practice will not work and the teaching will not satisfy you. If you have a serious friend or teacher, you will believe in Buddhism. Without an actual living example it is very difficult to believe or practice. So to believe in your master and be sincere—that is enlightenment. So we say, "Oneness of enlightenment and sincere practice."

I didn't know it at the time, but the first problem given me by my master was this story about Yakusan Zenji, which I have just told you. I could not acknowledge my master for a pretty long time. It is quite difficult to believe in your teacher, but we must know our fundamental attitude toward Buddhism. That is why Dogen went to China. For a long time he had studied in the Tendai school, the very profound, philosophical school of Buddhism, but still he was not satisfied. Dogen's problem was, "If we already have buddha-nature, why do we have to practice? There should be no need to practice." He was quite sincere about this problem.

Buddha-nature, you know, is neither good nor bad, spiritual nor material. By buddha-nature, we mean human nature. To be faithful to our nature will be the only way to live in this world as a human being. So we call our nature buddha-nature and accept it, good or bad. To accept it is a way to be free from it; because we do not accept it, we cannot be free. If the idea of human nature exists in your mind, you will be caught by it. When you accept it, you are not caught by it. So to accept does not mean to understand it psychologically or biologically. It means actual practice. No time to be caught, no time to doubt. Dogen tried to be satisfied with some teaching or answer which was written, but as long as he was concerned only with the teaching, it was impossible to be satisfied. He didn't know what he wanted, but as soon as he met Zen Master Nyojo in China, he knew. Dogen was quite satisfied with Nyojo's character and Nyojo said to Dogen, "That I have you as a disciple is exactly the same as Shakyamuni Buddha having Mahakashyapa." So that was the relationship.

In this way, Zen teaching and understanding is transmitted. Nyojo said, "You must transmit this teaching to someone." This looks as if he were trying to bind the disciple, but once you understand what he actually said, everyone you meet and everything you have becomes valuable to you. So Dogen said, "Everyone is your master, don't pay any attention to whether they are a layman or priest, a woman or man, young or old. Everyone is your teacher and your friend, but as long as you discriminate this from that, you will not meet a Zen master."

If we are real Zen students, we sleep where we are, eat what is given to us, and listen to the teacher, good or bad. The teacher may say, "How are you? If you answer, I will give you a hit, if you don't answer I will give you a hit." He doesn't care what you think about it. If you get hit with the stick, you will get something. Whether the answer is right or wrong, whether you get hit or not, is not the point. So Dogen said, "If you want to listen to a Zen master for absolute truth, you must not think about his rank, his accomplishments, deeds, or shortcomings. Accept him just as he is because he is a bodhisattva." That is the right attitude toward life—just accept it. If your attitude is right, everything you hear will be Buddha speaking. Then the master is not teacher or student, but Buddha himself.

Religious Activity

The more we attempt to manage religious activity, the more we lose our fundamental way. The more we study the teaching of Buddhism as if it were philosophy, the more we lose the original teaching.

The founder of Eiheiji Monastery, Dogen Zenji, respected students who sincerely practiced zazen rather than intelligent or learned students. Dogen emphasized organizing everyday life as the practice of Zen. He felt that this was the proper activity for Buddhist. When he spoke of the basic teaching of Buddhism, the transiency of life, he stressed it as an actual fact and not as a teaching of the sutras.

Dogen Zenji lost his father when he was three and his mother when he was eight. His mother was a Fujiwara, the most eminent family of the time. She had full experience of the teaching of transiency, and she wanted Dogen to be a priest of great sincerity. He decided to follow her will. After his mother died and he sat by her cold body; he reached a profound understanding of impermanence, watching a few lines of incense smoke drift. Dogen said, "I can walk on the edge of a white blade. I can do without food and drink, but it is not possible for me to forget my mother's last words."

In Zuimonki it is stated that Dogen said, "In order to have a strong introgressive way-seeking mind, it is necessary to see the transiency of life. This actual fact of life is not something conceivable in our brain or something to be dwelled on as an object of meditation. It is an actual fact. You should not wait even for Buddha's teaching."

In Denki it is stated that Dogen said, "When we are not sincere enough to be Buddhists, there is a difference between the intelligent and the dull .... If you lose your human life (Buddhahood can only be attained, when you have human life) you cannot have your life again." This way is Buddha's true teaching. We should encourage ourselves with great holy desire and devote ourselves to Buddhism under the guidance of a true master."

And again in Zuimonki he says in regard to right activity, "Some people think building a temple or pagoda means that Buddhism is prospering. This attitude is a great mistake. Even a building of gold and precious stone is not the prosperity of Buddhism. The only prosperity of Buddhism is the practice of Buddhism, without wasting a single moment."

The Traditional Way

To understand what the "Traditional Way" of Buddhism is and to actualize it in one's own life are the most important points in being a sincere Buddhist. The Traditional Way of Buddhism, although it is dependent upon no particular form for its expression, the sutras and rituals handed down to us from the Patriarchs are a great help to us. A part of the ritual which may be particularly difficult for Americans to understand and accept is the bowing. After zazen (sitting meditation) we bow to the floor nine times in front of Buddha's altar, each time touching the forehead to the floor three times and lifting the palms of the hands. (The story of the origin of his practice is that during Buddha's lifetime, there was a woman who wished to show her respect for Buddha, but who was so poor that she had no gift to give. So she knelt down and touching her forehead to the floor spread out her hair for him to pass over. The deep sincerity of the woman's devotion inspired the practice of bowing to this day). In our American culture there are no traditional forms through which we are accustomed to show respect towards a Buddha--a human being, who was not a god and who nevertheless attained perfection. Lacking such forms, there is a danger of neglecting or forgetting to respect Buddha, the Perfect One. This kind of respect is an essential part of the Traditional way. If we practice zazen just for the sake of our own self-improvement or to attain Enlightenment, our practice will be one-sided, and the true spirit of Buddhism will be lost. Because in America there is particular danger of this one-sidedness, we bow nine times to Buddha after each zazen practice, when in Japan it is customary to bow just three times.

Bowing to Buddha is actually to bow to oneself—to one's true nature. You, yourself, are Buddha. In a later lecture, Master Suzuki said that a common misunderstanding of the practice of bowing arises from our dualistic analyzing of the experience of bowing. We always think, "I bow to Buddha." But actually, when you bow, as Buddha himself did, there is no you and there is no Buddha; there is only the independent act of bowing which covers unlimited time and space.

But to say that you and Buddha are one can lead to another misunderstanding for someone who does not have the experience of zazen practice. It is true that you yourself are Buddha, and yet at the same time you are also Buddha's disciple. In the sutras, this is expressed by the words: "Not one; nor two." You and Buddha are one and at the same time two. If your tendency in practice is to there is no good or bad, right or wrong, then the sutras say to you: "Not one?" (i.e., you are not just Buddha, but also Buddha's disciple; you are taking the lazy way out of practice and not trying hard enough; your understanding of Buddha nature and the deep truth of "no good, no bad" is very superficial). On the other hand, if you are unduly discouraged and self-critical, and dismiss your practice as not very good, then the sutras say to you: "Not two." (i.e., you and Buddha are one; on each moment of your practice, Buddha nature is there, whether you are aware of it or not. It is Buddha himself who is practicing zazen; how can you say that it is not good?) These two aspects of reality--the duality of oneness and the oneness of duality-are essential to a true understanding of our bow based on the experience of zazen.

After bowing, the Prajna Paramita Sutra is recited three times: once to Buddha and his first disciples (Arhat); once to the Patriarchs, and once to our ancestors. The Prajna Paramita Sutra is the teaching which Buddha, after his Enlightenment, gave to his disciple, Sariputra, saying: "Form is emptiness; emptiness is form." One meaning of this sutra is that our ordinary perception and understanding of things is illusory. Usually we do not perceive things as they really are. We mistake for real and permanent what is actually constantly changing. This is true of human beings too when they are caught by the idea of self. This theory of the transiency of all things is one of the basic tenets of Buddhism, and an understanding of it is essential to follow the Traditional Way.

Before breakfast at the weekly Saturday morning meditation practice, and before each meal during sesshin, sutras and gathas are chanted. One of the most important phrases in these chants is: "May I, along with all sentient beings, achieve renunciation of the three attachments." "Renunciation" can also here be translated "emptiness" or "detachment."

The three attachments refer to the three aspects of giving and receiving: the giver, the receiver, and the gift which is given. Giving should be a free act, unhindered by calculation of amount or reward. The receiver likewise should not be greedy; he should be grateful for what is given to him, but on the other hand he should not be overly humble. And we should not discriminate the gift itself. The attitude of renunciation or detachment consists in not evaluating the thing as good or bad. (Thus it is helpful in our practice to recite these words before each meal).

After going over the sutras and rituals, Master Suzuki devoted the remaining lectures to general discussions of the Traditional Way to help us understand how we can actualize it in our daily lives. The following is the gist of his talk on Wednesday evening of sesshin.

In the morning we say the Prajna Paramita Sutra the first time to Buddha and the Arhats (the first disciples). Part of the prayer that the priest or leader of zazen says at this time is that we may attain sah-myo roku-tsu. San-myo means the three powers of mind; roku-tsu means the six powers of mind; the former contained in the latter. Power of mind means the power to fully understand sentient beings and our own human nature. The first power of mind is the capacity of sight and the second power is that of hearing. To understand someone we must first see with our own eyes and then hear what they say with our ears. The third power is the cognitive capacity to understand the words that we hear. The fourth power is to understand what is really meant by what was said. (Not just to understand the word, but to understand what the person means to say by them.) The fifth power is to comprehend the mind of the person speaking and to understand why he suffers. Finally, the sixth power is to perceive nature as it really is—as pure Buddha nature itself.

In order to obtain to the sixth power of mind, it is necessary to annihilate all evil desires and all thought of self. The way to its attainment is understood in different ways by the Hinayana and Mahayana Buddhists. For Hinayana Buddhists, the lower powers of mind are hindrances to the attainment of the sixth power of mind. But to the Mahayana Buddhist, when you see or hear or think, it may be done in the sixth way. For the Hinayana the lower faculties are obstacles and the seat of evil desires; they tend to take an annihilistic attitude with regard to them. The Mahayana attitude is more positive and not so strict in the physical sense. But with regard to the idea of self,

Mahayana is more strict than Hinayana. The sixth power is emancipation from all ideas of self; to perceive in the sixth way is to see or hear or think, but not from an egoistic or self-centered point of view. To have any idea of self involved in your perception is to be prey to evil desires; what you then perceive is not reality and you can have no true understanding of human nature or sentient beings.

There is an old Chinese story which illustrates the power of mind or understanding when one is truly free from any idea of self. A famous old Zen master, Esan was taking a nap, his face to the wall. His disciple, seeing that he was asleep, passed by very quietly to avoid awakening him. But Esan turned over and soon awoke. His disciple said: "Oh, did I disturb you? Why not sleep some more." But Esan only answered: "I had a wonderful sleep and dream; do you know what it was?" His disciple at these words, left the room without replying and came back with a basin of fresh water and a towel. Esan washed his face saying: "That's wonderful!" The a second disciple came into the room. Esan asked him the same question: "I had a good sleep and a wonderful dream; can you tell me what my dream was?" The second disciple left the room and came back with a cup of fresh tea! Esan was delighted with his two disciples. He said: "Why, my two disciples are even better than Sariputra!" (Sariputra was one of Buddha's first disciples, a disciple of great Mahayana spirit, the one whom Buddha addresses the Prajna Paramita Sutra.)

This story has deep meaning. Most people want to help others and try very hard. But it may be quite difficult to know how to help people. In order to help another it may be necessary truly to understand him. For this, the sixth power of mind, or absence of any idea of self is necessary. Our Traditional Way transmitted from the Patriarchs is the way of the sixth power of mind. When you are one with what you are doing, there is no idea of self. The transmitted way of practice is to become one with what you are doing, and to practice without cessation to express this oneness. To do something is to help others, and at the same time to help yourself. When you sleep you help yourself, and you help others too. When you take a cup of tea, you help others and you help yourself. Even if you sit alone in the zendo (meditation hall, you are helping others. And even if you do something quite different, you are sitting in the meditation hall. Practice is one. It is continuous and uninterrupted; there should be no discrimination of activities. Your attitude when helping yourself should be the same as when you help others. You are all quite sincere when you are helping yourselves; how about when you are helping others? We find it easy to want to help those we like.

So practice is not just to come to the zendo and sit in meditation posture; it is everything you do in your everyday life. It is, for example, to anticipate the wish of someone and bring a bowl of water, if such an activity be done with true zazen spirit (without thought of self). If your attitude is right, when you help another, you help yourself and vice versa. Sitting in zazen is the easiest, safest way to help yourself and others. It may be pretty hard to help others by kind words, by giving some good gift, or in some special way. Trying to help often creates more problems than it solves. But if you sit in zazen you will come to respect yourself and others will then respect you. Then you can help them quite freely and naturally, without imposing any burden or obligation or gratitude. Ungan asked Dogo: "That great Bodhisattva of Mercy (i.e., Avalokishevara, Kwan Yin or Kwannon, often represented with one thousand arms and one thousand eyes, symbolizing the all pervading-mercy) how does he manage to use those many hands and eyes (in helping sentient beings)? Dogo said: "It is like when, in the dark night, we straighten out our pillow with our hand (though not being able to see with our eyes).

If you think zazen is some particular thing you are doing right here, you are quite mistaken. Practice is each moment every day all year long; over and over we repeat our activity. Our practice is like 10,000 miles of iron road. We run on iron tracks in a straight line, never stopping. The tracks are iron, not gold or silver. There is no special way for sages and another for fools; both are the same train. There is no special person for Buddhism, Buddhism is for everyone; there is no special activity of sitting for Buddhists--everything you do should be practice.

You remember the famous Zen master Joshu, the one who always sat in a broken chair. Once a young monk came to visit him, and Joshu asked: "Have you had breakfast?" Joshu was not talking about rice-gruel (but rather enlightenment)! But this monk was very brave and confident, and he answered: "Yes, I have!" (i.e., I have attained enlightenment and know everything and am quite ready to converse with you on any subject!) Joshu replied: "Well then, wash you bowl!"

That is our way—step by step. After eating, wash your bowl. It is always the same on the same iron road. Sometimes you want to take an airplane, but that is not the right way! You should always stay on the train.

There is an old story about three animals crossing a river: a hare, a fox, and an elephant. The hare skipped across the surface (using stones?); the fox swam across, but the elephant walked slowly steadily across, touching bottom with each step. The Traditional Way of Buddhism is the last, and in our practice we should all be elephants.

Bodhidarma's Understanding

In our practice the important thing is our physical posture we take, and breathing...way of taking breathing. Those are very important because we have...we are not so much concerned about our deep understanding of Buddhism. As a philosophy Buddhism has very deep and wide and firm system in our thought, but Zen does not concerned about those philosophical understanding but we emphasize our practice. But why it is so important...we must understand why our physical posture and breathing exercise is important is...there is some reason and instead of discussing or having deep understanding of the teaching we want strong confidence, or you may say faith, a kind of faith in our teaching that we have originally Buddha Nature. And our practice is based on this faith. Originally we have Buddha Nature. If so we have to behave like Buddha is why we practice zazen.

You may feel rather funny in our reason why we practice zazen but if you compare the various practice or training with our...to our practice you will understand our practice better. Before Bodhidharma came to China, there were, of course, there were many people who were interested in Zen practice and there were many literature which looked like Zen. You may.. .almost all the famous stock words were originated even before Bodhidharma came to China. Sudden Enlightenment...Sudden Enlightenment is not the right translation but tentatively I say sudden enlightenment. Enlightenment comes all of a sudden to us. That is true enlightenment. But before Bodhidharma, people thought that after long preparation, sudden enlightenment will come. So, this is actually.this Zen practice is a kind of training to gain enlightenment. Actually many people are practicing zazen in this idea. But that is not our traditional Zen. Our traditional understanding of Zen, from Buddha to our time now is without any preparation, when you start zazen there is enlightenment. That is traditional understanding of Zen. Whether you practice zazen or not you have Buddha nature. Because you have Buddha nature in your practice there is enlightenment. That is our practice. The point we put emphasis on is not the stage we attain, but our strong confidence in our original nature which is nothing different from Buddha nature, and to practice Zen the same sincerity with Buddha's. The transmission...to transmit our way is to transmit our spirit from Buddha. That is the most important point we have. So we have to harmonize our spirit with the traditional way, or we have to harmonize our physical posture or activity with the traditional way. That is the main point in our practice. Not.you may attain some stage, of course, but the spirit should not be based in egoistic idea. Buddhism.. .traditional understanding of our human nature is (egolessness) in Buddhism. Egoistic idea is delusion. When we have no idea of ego we have Buddha's view of life. Because of ego-centered idea our Buddha nature will be covered by the delusion of egoistic idea. So our spirit should not be based on egoistic idea. So we should be very faithful to the Truth only.. .not without having any egoistic idea.. .at least we should try to give up your egoistic idea. You may have...we always are creating some egoistic idea and are following the egoistic idea, and we will repeat this process over and over again, and our life will be occupied by egoistic idea completely. This is so-called karmic life.karma.

The Lotus Sutra

The Nirmanakaya Buddha comes into this world with the vow that he will save all sentient beings. Not by karma, but by vow, he appears in this world, practices the Bodhisattva's way, attains enlightenment as Buddha did, and saves all human beings. So he is called an incarnated body. He changes his form in various ways, sometimes to a bodhisattva, sometimes to a buddha. He takes on various forms to help people, so in the widest sense of the word, everything is Nirmanakaya Buddha. But in the narrow sense, those who appear in this world by vow instead of by karma are called Nirmanakaya Buddhas. The Sambhogakaya Buddha is the original source of the Nirmanakaya Buddha: it gives birth to the Nirmanakaya Buddha. In order to explain the Dharmakaya Buddha, it is necessary to explain the Sambhogakaya Buddha more. Then you will understand what the Dharmakaya Buddha is naturally.

The Dharmakaya Buddha is called the fundamental, undeveloped Buddhakaya. In Buddhism, when we say the undeveloped, or fundamental, body, it means that it is the original source itself. But there are two interpretations for one reality. When we understand it as something which is very calm, which is not in activity, we call it the Dharma Body. But the Dharma Body does not actually remain calm and inactive—it is always active. When we understand it as activity, we call it Dharma Nature. "Dharma Nature" means something in action, and "Dharma Body" means something which is not in activity, or which is not developed. But the whole Nature exists in the Dharma Body as a potentiality. So we have two understandings of one reality: Dharmakaya [kaya = body] and dharma nature.

The Sambhogakaya Buddha is the Buddha who realized this dharma nature in activity, or as something which has a nature. And when we understand the reality which has various potentialities to act or to develop, that is called Dharmakaya Buddha.

Figuratively speaking, the Sambhogakaya Buddha may be like the sun. Instead of observing things objectively, he understands his Buddha Nature, which is always in activity within himself, figuratively speaking of course. So, like the sun, although he is not trying to illuminate everything objectively, he is actually illuminating everything. He is actually helping others without trying to help. He can illuminate everything because originally he has that kind of power or potentiality. But the most important thing for the Sambhogakaya Buddha is to attain enlightenment inwardly, or to illuminate himself, instead of illuminating the objective world. Instead of observing each thing respectively, one by one, he observes his nature within himself. When he observes his inside world, as the sun does, he finds himself as earth. That earth nature is universal. This earth is also earth, and the sun is also earth. Everything is earth, so there is no difference between the objective world and the subjective world. To be enlightened in his inward nature is to be enlightened outside in the objective world. So for him the whole world is his inside or subjective world. When he reaches this kind of world, we call him Sambhogakaya Buddha.

His world is limitless. It includes the sun and stars and everything. So his virtue and wisdom are also limitless. He is the Omniscient One, who knows everything as being within himself. For him there is nothing outside his being. That is the Sambhogakaya Buddha. When we understand reality in this way, our understanding includes everything. And the reality which includes everything as an undeveloped reality is the Dharmakaya Buddha itself, Dharma itself, Being itself.

Our way of understanding things is exactly the same as our zazen. We say, "Just sit!" What does this mean? When we say, "Just sit," it includes all the potential activity which we have. We remain in an inactive state, but we have potentiality. So in this sense, our practice includes everything. When we sit, we are just sitting. Each one of us is sitting, and each one of us is Dharmakaya Buddha. But within ourselves, even though we are sitting, we take breaths and our heart is beating, so we are also Sambhogakaya Buddha. We understand reality in this way.

So the Sambhogakaya Buddha or the Dharmakaya Buddha is the source of all buddhas, which exists before Buddha. In this sense, Buddha is eternal, perpetual being. So we call it tathata in Sanskrit, or shinnyo in Japanese. And the Lotus Sutra is the sutra which describes this kind of reality, the world of tathata. That is why it is told on a big, cosmic scale. We say in Japanese jisso, the way everything exists in the realm of reality or the realm of tathata. In this sutra, everything presumes this world of tathata. Of course, it is described in a very dramatic way, but what it means to show is how things exist in this world, in this dharma world or world of tathata. The purpose of this sutra is to give a dramatic version of tathata This is an important point.

This sutra was told by the Sambhogakaya Buddha, with his wisdom, to save all sentient beings. It verbally tells us what dharma nature is, not with a substantial idea, but rather in a dramatic, figurative way. And this sutra especially puts emphasis on dharma nature instead of on the dharma body, because the dharma body is inexplicable. You cannot talk about the dharma body because it is something beyond our world, beyond our wisdom, beyond our understanding. That is why we say the dharma body does not talk. My mouth talks, but my body doesn't talk. When we say "body," it is a source of activity, but not activity itself. But without the source, there is no activity. So when there is activity, there should be a source. But the source does not always have any activity. You can have the idea of source or body without activity.

There is something which is not in activity. That is the Body. But actually, there is no such thing. Whatever it is, it has some activity. Even a stone has some activity. So there is no such thing. We cannot talk about the Body itself, so what shall I do? If I talk about something, that is already the dharma nature, how dharma goes, what it is like. When I say what it is like, that is the Nirmanakaya Buddha. Objectively speaking, that is form. More subjectively speaking, it is its nature. But what the source of that Nature is, no one knows. We know it, but we cannot say anything about it. If you say something, it is not the Body, it is the Nature, or it is an attribute of the Body. So we do not talk about what the Dharma Body is, but we understand that there must be some source.

That is the dharma body, the dharma nature, and the dharma attribute, or form and color. That is the outlook of dharma, nature of dharma, and dharma itself. And the Nirmanakaya Buddha, the Sambhogakaya Buddha, and the Dharmakaya Buddha. Did you understand? The Nirmanakaya Buddha is the form of dharma, the Sambhogakaya Buddha is the nature of dharma, and the

Dharmakaya Buddha is the dharma body, which is beyond words, which we cannot describe. So this sutra tells what the Dharma Nature is, and when we listen to it, we will understand what the Dharmakaya Buddha is and who the Nirmanakaya Buddha Shakyamuni was.

I say there is no way to talk about the Dharma Body, but if you will allow me to say something about it, we can call it "Truth Itself." Truth is something which you cannot see. You can see the apple, but you cannot see the theory of gravity. But there is some theory, some truth. So nothing happens just by accident. When something happens, there should be some reason. It is caused by Dharma. In this sense, truth is close to the Dharma Nature. But we can understand it in some way, we can figure out some rules. In Buddhism, those rules, or that truth, is sometimes called the Dharma itself. That is the way in which we call it the Dharma Body. It is the source of all truth.

When we say "nature" it is, of course, truth. But nature is something which includes what we see. In its strict sense, truth is not something which we can see. Buddhists figure it out in this way: because many people ask us, "What is Dharma Body?" we must say something about it, so we try to figure out what we should say. In this case, we give a very difficult explanation. If I don't say anything, you may say, "He doesn't know anything about the Dharma Body. He is not such a good teacher." So I must make a narrow escape. The way to do it is to talk about some truth. Nature and truth are not exactly the same. Truth is nearer to the Dharma Body. The idea is also pretty close to the Dharma Nature, but it exists just in between the Dharma Nature and the Dharma Body.

So sometimes "Dharma" means "teaching," sometimes "reality," and sometimes "being," just "something," just "there." Ri means "truth," and ji means "event" or "being," something which exists, like a stone or like water. Ri means, not "water nature," but how it becomes water from air. So another side of water is truth, and that truth is not something which we can see. You can see the nature of water: it flows from a higher place to a lower place.

The Japanese term for truth is ri, and the Japanese term for various beings is ji. Ji and ri are very important, key technical words in Buddhism. When we realize ri in its true sense, we are Sambhogakaya Buddha. When we observe things as we observe the objective world, and when we want to help people involved in the objective or materialistic world, we are Nirmanakaya Buddha. The way to help others as Nirmanakaya Buddha is to take various forms and give them some handy [appropriate] help. But as the Sambhogakaya Buddha we should realize that there is no "I" or "you"—it is all one being. When we realize this nature, which is universal, we can help others without trying to help them, because whatever we do, that is our activity.

You are a part of me, you know. When we reach this kind of understanding, when we become Sambhogakaya Buddha, then when you practice zazen you have no "you" and no "others"; your practice includes everything. So everything will take place within yourself. There is no objective world anymore. Without trying to help others, you will help them anyway. That is the Sambhogakaya Buddha.

But when we realize that our practice includes everything, why don't we include the Nirmanakaya Buddha? Shakyamuni Buddha is included in our practice. So all the Shakyamuni buddhas, and all the Nirmanakaya buddhas which were spoken of by Shakyamuni Buddha will attain enlightenment all at once when we practice zazen. Do you understand? The Nirmanakaya Buddha is within ourselves.

Before we reach this kind of understanding, the Nirmanakaya Buddha is just a hero. He has no eternal life. He is one of the great heroes of our history. But when we understand Shakyamuni Buddha as the Sambhogakaya Buddha or the Dharmakaya Buddha, for the first time, he has perpetual life. This is a more traditional understanding of Buddha. And actually, this kind of understanding was supported by Buddha when he was alive, although it took several hundred years before we understood who Shakyamuni Buddha was in reality. This kind of understanding, which was accomplished by his disciples, gave Buddha new life, made him a perpetual buddha. In this sense, he is called the Tathagata.

This is a history of the development of the understanding of Buddha, and at the same time, the true understanding of his teaching. He did not stick to the words he said. He was like a doctor who gives his patients prescriptions. According to the people, he gave various prescriptions. He didn't have any idea of giving the same prescription to various patients. What he said was for him like a paper.That is actually what he did and how he understood that he should help people. But the reason he was Buddha is that he was the Enlightened One. He was illuminated in his own nature, Dharma Nature, and everyone's nature, so he knew who he was. For him there was no disciple and no objective world. So he said all sentient beings are his sons, are part of him. That was Buddha.

Since we have arrived at this kind of understanding, there is no need to talk about what Theravada or Mahayana Buddhism is. All Buddhism, whether it is Theravada or Mahayana is one whole Buddhism. This is how we have transmitted his teaching from Buddha to us. And the purpose of this sutra is to describe our Dharma Nature.

Since it may be difficult for you to understand the Lotus Sutra, I wanted to clarify who is supposed to have told it. The sutras usually look like they were spoken by the historical Buddha himself. But our Buddhist sutras were not actually spoken by him. So when you read a sutra, if you think it was spoken by Buddha himself, you will be confused, because there are actually many elements in it which did not exist in Buddha's time. Afterwards, when the sutra was compiled, it was interspersed with various thoughts that existed then. Buddhist thought itself developed from the understanding of the direct disciples of Buddha to that of Buddhists several generations afterward. So you will be very confused when you read the sutra as if it was spoken by the historical Buddha.

Actually, the sutra was told by so-called Mahayana Buddhists several hundred years after Buddha passed away. Buddhism had developed from the sravaka to the Mahayana understanding. If I say Buddhism developed in this way, then you may think it developed or changed. But in reality, it did not change or develop, but tried to resume the original understanding of Buddhism. In this way, for many thousands of years, Buddhists have been trying to restore Buddha's teaching. It looks as if this effort changed Buddhism from the original way to some different teaching, but that is not so. Do you understand what I am saying? It is rather difficult, with my language problem, to explain this part. This sutra was told by someone who was a Mahayana Buddhist. It looks like the historical Buddha, over here, spoke this sutra, but actually someone who was over here told it. And Buddhism itself developed from here to here. So you may say what is taught in this sutra is not Buddha's teaching, but a teaching which developed from Buddha's teaching. So if you are attached to Buddha's original teaching, you may be disappointed, you see?

But what I want to say is that there is no need for you to be disappointed, because what Buddhists have been trying to do was to find out what was fundamental Buddhism. So they thought, this is not fundamental Buddhism, and this is not, until finally they thought this is Buddha's original purpose in teaching. When they reached this kind of understanding, someone invented this story with such conviction and on such a great scale. That is why this sutra is called the king of all sutras. Do you understand?

Nowadays we have various sects in China or Japan, but the reason so many founders of various schools continue to make that kind of effort today is only in order to understand who Buddha was. When someone found that Buddha was such and such a person, he became the founder of some school. All the effort we have been making has been to know who Buddha is and what his purpose for teaching was. Do you understand this point? For a Buddhist, Buddha is not just a historical person—he is truth itself. We think he should be truth itself, and the historical Buddha cannot be perfect. But the background of the historical Buddha should be truth. If so, truth itself should be the real Buddha for us.

Then what is truth? How should we understand the truth, or how should we accept truth in the situation of this age? Because of questions like that is why we have various schools. Do you understand? In this way, with that kind of attitude, this sutra was told. So it is necessary for me to tell you about the history of Buddhism from the original, fundamental, form to the Mahayana form. If I say "Mahayana", there is also the "Hinayana" school, its opposite. When the Mahayana Buddhists reached Buddha's original teaching, they called all the teaching from before Mahayana Buddhism arose "Hinayana". But while the Mahayana school was being established, there was no Hinayana school.

According to the Tendai school, which was founded by Tendai Chih-i in China, there are two kinds of Mahayana. One is the last stage of the development of Buddhism, which is very different from the so-called Hinayana, or teaching of the sravakas. The Pratyekas have no teaching, because they are the ones who have no teacher, who studied by themselves. So there is no school for the Pratyeka Buddhist. They have no way that they are teaching; they have no written material for their disciples. The trees we see, the flowers we see, the stars and moon, or the mountains and rivers, are the teaching. So there is no Pratyekayana. But the Sravakas have a teaching, and the Mahayana teachers who reached this point, criticized the sravakas by calling their way the Hinayana. Of course, according to the Tendai, this is not the real Mahayana, or real teaching. The real teaching is the one which can include Sravakas, Pratyekas, and the so-called "one vehicle" or "great vehicle" teaching. That is the true teaching. So the Buddhists who discriminate between Mahayana and Hinayana are not true Mahayanists.

For the true Mahayana Buddhist, there are no Sravakas, Pratyekas, "Great One Vehicle," or "Mahayana." This is called the truth vehicle, while the other is called the special teaching. The special teaching is not good enough. It should be perfect teaching. So according to the Tendai analogy, there is the perfect teaching, the special teaching, and the teachings of the Pratyekas and Sravakas. This is a more proper understanding of Buddha's teaching.

In this way, our understanding of Buddha's teaching improved more and more. Finding out how we should improve and accept Buddha's teaching as a perfect teaching is the effort we have been making. So Buddhism should change, it should not be completed. One after another, we must have new teachers, and we must improve our understanding of the teaching from an immature one to a mature one. We should study this sutra with this in mind. Did you understand what I'm trying to say?

We exist moment after moment, as taking form and color of great Sambhogakaya Buddha. That is true. (chuckle) Don't you think so? If I say Sambhogakaya Buddha, you know, by technical term—because of technical—because you don't know, what does it mean, definition of Sambhogakaya Buddha, it makes you, more difficult maybe. But we exist here; and we are not permanent being. Only in this moment we exist as like this. But next moment I will change to— tomorrow I will not be the same person. This is rue. Next moment I shall be future Buddha. Yesterday I was past Buddha. In this way there is many and many Buddhas. And you will be another Buddha. In this way, there are many Buddhas, but Source of—or—we are incarnated body, with some certain color and form and character.

So there must be source of Shakyamuni Buddha, who is called, Nirmanakaya Buddha. But when he realize this point, he accept himself as Nirmanakaya Buddha, as Sambhogakaya Buddha, as Dharmakaya Buddha. When we understand ourselves in this way, you know, what will be the way—why we live in this world is to try to continuously try to express Buddha Nature, moment after moment. And that is the effort we should make, instead of being caught by some certain color or form. But even so (laughing), we should not ignore—we should make our best effort in each moment. So that is a kind of attachment. But this attachment is, at the same time, detachment, because next moment you should make best effort (chuckling). So, it means detachment to the last being. In this way, moment after moment, we exist. So this kind of understanding will be expressed by our technical term of Nirmanakaya Buddha, Sambhogakaya Buddha, and Dharmakaya Buddha.

What is told in this sutra is the view of the Dharmakaya world, Sambhogakaya world and Nirmanakaya world. We say shoho jisso [the real state of all elements or dharmas]. Shoho means various dharmas or various beings. Jisso is reality. So this is the right view of life and the world, in which various famous disciples of Buddha and arhats and various Sambhogakaya Buddhas and Dharmakaya Buddhas and Nirmanakaya Buddhas would appear. I think it's better to start little by little.

The first chapter is an introduction to the whole sutra, and it describes the scale of the sutra. "Thus have I heard." All sutras are started with these words. Nyoze gamon, "Thus have I heard." At the meeting of the compilation [of the sutras] after Buddha passed away, the leading disciples decided on [the correct form of] Buddha's words. So they started with, "Thus I heard." All the sutras are supposed to have been spoken by Buddha, but it is not actually so. It is a kind of formal way of starting sutras.

Thus I have heard:"Once upon a time." It doesn't say when.

Once upon a time the Lord was staying at Ragagriha, on the Gridhrakuta mountain, with a numerous assemblage of monks, twelve hundred monks, all of them Arhats, stainless, free from depravity, self-controlled, thoroughly emancipated in thought and knowledge, of noble breed, (like unto) great elephants, having done their task, done their duty, acquitted their charge, reached the goal; in whom the ties which bound them to existence were wholly destroyed, whose minds were thoroughly emancipated by perfect knowledge, who had reached the utmost perfection in subduing all their thoughts; who were possessed of the transcendent faculties; eminent disciples, such as the venerable Ajnata-Kaundinya, the venerable Asvajit, the venerable Vashpa, the venerable Mahanaman, the venerable Bhadrika, the venerable Maha-Kasyapa, the venerable Kasyapa of Uruvilva, the venerable Kasyapa of Nadi, the venerable Kasyapa of Gaya, the venerable Shariputra, the venerable Maha-Maudgalyayana, the venerable Maha-Katyayana, the venerable Aniruddha, the venerable Revata, the venerable Kapphina, the venerable Gavampati, the venerable Pilindavatsa, the venerable Vakula, the venerable Bharadvaga, the venerable Maha-Kaushthila, the venerable Nanda (alias Mahananda), the venerable Upananda, the venerable Sundara-Nanda, the venerable Purna Maitrayaniputra, the venerable Subhuti, the venerable Rahula; with them yet other great disciples, as venerable Ananda, still under training, and two thousand other monks, some of whom still under training, the others masters; with six thousand nuns having at their head Mahaprajapati and the nun Yasodhara, the mother of Rahula, along with her train; (further) with eight thousand Bodhisattvas, all unable to slide back, endowed with the spells of supreme perfect enlightenment, firmly standing in wisdom; who moved onward the never deviating wheel of the law; who had propitiated many hundred thousands of Buddhas; who under many hundred thousands of Buddhas had planted the roots of goodness, had been intimate with many hundred thousands of Buddhas, were in body and mind fully penetrated with the feeling of charity, able in communicating the wisdom of the Tathagatas; very wise, having reached the perfection of wisdom; renowned in many hundred thousands of worlds; having saved many hundred thousand myriads of kotis of beings; such as the Bodhisattva Mahasattva Manjusri, as prince royal; the Bodhisattvas Mahasattvas Avalokitesvara, Mahasthamaprapta, Sarvarthanaman, Nityodyukta—

This is very difficult. I may bite my tongue.

There are many names, but I will only explain some of the important ones among them.

Thus have I heard. Once upon a time the Lord was staying at Ragagriha, on the Gridhrakuta mountain, with a numerous assemblage of monks, twelve hundred monks, all of them Arhats.

Sravakas practice their way in order to attain arhatship. Arhatship is called, "no learn." It means there is nothing more to learn or study after reaching arhatship. An arhat was a perfect being—not Buddha himself, but next to Buddha. As you know, after Mahayana Buddhism arrived, there were the bodhisattvas and buddhas above the arhats.

Those who attained arhatship were free from depravity, stainless. Stainless means that they annihilated all the stains, or all the evil desires.

Free from depravity, self controlled.

You know the difference between controlling self, or desires, and annihilating desires? There is a slight difference. Do you remember? Sally asked that question. Controlling desires is a more autonomous or voluntary way. You do it by yourself. Annihilating is a more negative way. You annihilate some desires because they are evil and we have to get rid of them. Self control is a more positive way. If you switch your practice over from negation to self control, it becomes more religious in its true sense.

Actually, this difference between the attitudes of annihilating or controlling divides Buddhism right in two. You may not like either of them. You don't like to control your desires, but that is not Zen. We have limitless desires, so if you let all your desires go as they want, what will happen to you? You must do something with them, that is true. Do you agree with that? You may say, "Desires as they are," but that does not mean to let them go as they want.

Usually when we say "desires," they are not just desires, they are desires plus something. That something may be various powers or faculties you have, and even reason will act with those limitless desires. With the aid of all the faculties we have, those limitless desires will extend themselves until we get lost. So something should be done with them. The first stage is to know what they are and how they work. When you know what they are and how they work, you will know how to develop them. That is actually our practice. I tentatively call this kind of effort "self-control" or "controlling desires". Control is not such a good word; you may find some better, beautiful, fancy word for that. But what I mean is to know the nature of desires and how they work, what kinds of friends they have, and what kind of things they do. We should know this and develop desires appropriately; that is self control. So instead of annihilating them, we should know what they are. Instead of trying to attain arhatship by annihilating desires, one by one, you will develop them.

These are opposite ways—one is negative and the other is positive, and Buddhism is divided in two. One way goes from top to bottom, the other from bottom to top. Hongaku homon [the dharma gate of innate buddha-nature] means to start from Buddhahood and work on our world and our desires. Shikaku homon [the dharma gate of realizing one's buddha-nature by undergoing religious exercises] means to begin with annihilating greed, and annihilate more and more subtle desires until you attain enlightenment. But the other way is to start from Dharmakaya Buddhahood, or Sambhogakaya Buddhahood, and come down to our world to help others.

Hon means origin, gaku means enlightenment, shi means beginning. It looks like the two ways are quite different, but what we actually do is not different. To annihilate or to control is the same thing, because desires are coexistent with our being. That I am here means desire is here. If you annihilate all the desires, you don't survive. So to annihilate actually means to control, because you cannot annihilate them. If you say to cut out all desires, that looks like there is a strong feeling of controlling them. "Cut out!" If you cut them out, you will die, but that much confidence is necessary. If you extend the practice of annihilating seriously, it will end in asceticism. But if you know the real nature of desires and how they work, those two practices are the same.

If you think that they are evil desires which we should get rid of, and you are worried about them, then that is not our way. So it may be better to say to control them. Here, in the sutra, it says "self controlled," but for sravakas, it is a more annihilistic way.

With a numerous assemblage of monks, twelve hundred monks, all of them arhats, stainless, free from depravity, self controlled, thoroughly emancipated in thought and knowledge.

It is necessary to be emancipated from thought and knowledge. They are "of noble breed, (like unto) great elephants." In India there were strong feelings of class discrimination. "Having done their task"—the task of annihilating evil desires—"done their duty"—their duty to attain emancipation—"acquitted their charge"—acquitted their karmic life charge —"reached the goal"—goal of arhatship—"in whom the ties which bound them to existence were wholly destroyed."

We have buddha-nature, but at the same time, buddha-nature is covered by something— first of all, ignorance. This point should be explained clearly, but I don't think I have enough time. Figuratively speaking, our desires look like a cloud in front of the moon, but it is not actually so. If there is a cloud, it should be destroyed.

Whose minds were thoroughly emancipated by perfect knowledge.

Perfect knowledge is wisdom. Perfect wisdom is different from the wisdom of knowing something. Perfect knowledge is not knowledge in a dualistic sense.

Who had reached the utmost perfection in subduing all their thoughts.

Perfect knowledge is called wisdom. Perfect wisdom is called non-discriminating wisdom or non-judgmental wisdom or non-thinking wisdom. So unless we subdue all our thoughts, we cannot have perfect knowledge.

Who were possessed of the transcendent faculties.

There are many transcendent faculties: clairvoyance, or hearing something from a distance, seeing through some substance; arhats had these kinds of faculties. Those arhats were there when this sutra was told.

The group mentioned next is the eminent disciples, such as the ten disciples of Buddha. I should explain them one by one, but I will only explain the most important ones, the ten eminent disciples or the four eminent sravakas. Sravakas are also Buddha's disciples. They are the most direct disciples of Buddha, so we call them "Theravada." The Theravada are the old disciples or shiniya disciples.

The five disciples, including Kaundinya and the venerable Asvagit were the disciples to whom Buddha spoke his first sermon. Originally those five disciples were Siddhartha's men. When he escaped from the castle, those five men followed him. And as you know, when Shakyamuni Buddha gave up asceticism, they thought, "My master is not strong enough, so he gave up the practice." They continued to practice asceticism, but Buddha started to practice zazen under the Bodhi tree and attained enlightenment. He thought for forty-nine days about how to explain his experience and whom to explain it to. At last Buddha went back to his five men and told the first sermon. Those are the five disciples. And ten more disciples follow those five

When Buddha gave up the practice of asceticism, they continued practicing asceticism at the Deer Park. After Buddha attained enlightenment, he came to the Deer Park. At that time he told them about the four noble truths, dana-prajna-paramita, and shila-prajna-paramita. Instead of saying you will attain enlightenment if you practice shila-paramita, he said you will have a good future life. This means that, at that time, he applied some religious understanding of the common people of India when he taught his own teaching. According to Buddhism, you practice precepts, not to have a good future life, but because we attain enlightenment in this life. This is actually Buddha's teaching.

I think it is better for us to study more about what Buddha taught here about the four noble truths and eight holy paths. The four noble truths are suffering, the cause of suffering, the way to attain liberation from suffering, and nirvana. According to Buddha's teaching, this world is full of suffering. But in the Mahayana teaching which developed from these four noble truths and eight holy paths, this world is the world where we find realization or nirvana within each self. According to the Mahayana, this world is not the world of suffering, but according to the Hinayana, or according to the teaching which Buddha told for the first time to the five disciples, this world is full of suffering.

Actually, this world is full of suffering. Suffering and our life coexist. Where there's life, there's suffering. Suffering and life are synonymous. This teaching is very important, because when you think you have no problem, that is the biggest problem. You know, at first you will have a stomachache, but when your stomach is worse, you have no ache. So having suffering is good, but having no suffering is more serious. As long as you have problems, you have a pretty good stomach, a promising stomach. If you have no suffering, you are hopeless. You say you have no suffering, but that is suffering which is the great problem. In this way, Buddha started his teachings.

Buddha's disciples were very good people, generous and honest and sincere, but they were, I think, very tough guys, and his followers were very strong people. For instance, as you know, the Diamond Sutra was recited at the place called, in Japanese, Giju-gikkodoku-on, the park given to Buddha by Prince Jeta. The story is that when Sudatta wanted to provide Buddha with a place to stay, he looked for some lodging place, and at last he found a beautiful place which was the property of Prince Jeta. So he asked the Prince to give it to the Buddha. The Prince didn't say yes, but said, "If you pay as much money as it takes to pave the land with coins, I will give it to you." Sudatta was also a very wealthy person, so he said, "Okay, I will do that." And he bought a lot of coins and started to pave that land. Prince Jeta was very impressed by him and said, "Okay, okay. I will donate it to your boss."

That was where the Diamond Sutra was told.

That is how we recite the Diamond Sutra in Japan. This is Chinese, actually, not Japanese. We are still reciting the old Chinese pronunciation as people did it, maybe, more than one thousand years ago. Anyway, that park was given to him by Prince Jeta.

Not only his followers, but also his students were very tough people. I didn't talk about Aniruddha yet. Aniruddha was famous for his supernatural power. The way he gained that supernatural power is very interesting. Once he slept when Buddha was giving a lecture. He was one of the seven, or more, priests who belonged to the Shakya family. Maybe Buddha was too familiar to him, so he started to sleep. But Buddha blamed him for drowsiness, so he decided not to sleep anymore. Very tough. He didn't go to bed after that. And, at last, he lost his sight. Giba was a very famous teacher, and Buddha asked him to take care of his eyes. But since he didn't go to bed, he couldn't do anything with him. He lost his physical eyes, but he gained the spiritual eye.

I think Buddha's character was very gentle, but his spirit was very strong. Yesterday morning I told you about the four sufferings or eight sufferings. To come into this world is already suffering, and old age, sickness, death, not to be able to get what we want, not to be able to see who you love most, that you cannot always be with someone you love, and that you will always see someone you don't like. This kind of teaching is very negative, or, at least, it is based on a kind of negative feeling.

But think of why Buddha escaped from the castle. He did not escape because he wanted to seclude himself on a remote mountain. When he saw sick people and poor people and old people having a difficult time in the city around his castle, as their prince, he felt a kind of responsibility for them. His notion was to save them, to find out some way to help them, completely. I think he's a very extraordinary person. Almost all people, even in Buddha's time, must have resigned from the problem of death or sickness. Even though we do not like to die, this comes to everyone. So we think it can't be helped, there is no possibility for us to conquer this kind of problem; there is no possibility of helping people who are going to die. But he didn't give up. He had extraordinary spirit, I think. That was why he gave up his heritage to his father.

So there is no wonder that his disciples were very tough people. They were not afraid of anything, not even death. And their Way-seeking mind even went beyond the suffering of life and death. Buddha did not talk about the problem of birth and death just to make us unhappy, but because we have this kind of problem, and it will help us to have real strength. When our spirit is limited by this kind of problem, we cannot have perfect composure of life. That is why he talked about this kind of teaching from his own very critical standpoint.

So we must see our life completely, and we have to confront all the problems by all means. To confront those sufferings is to develop our religious spirit. And before our spirit is emancipated from this kind of problem, there is no chance to have perfect enlightenment.

Here is a good example: As you know, India at that time (or maybe even now, I don't know), had very strict ideas of class. The highest class was the Brahmans, the religious people or priests. The second was the Ksatriyas, the kings or rulers of the country. Third were the common people who participated in farming or some other work, and the lowest class was the slaves.

Upali was one of the ten disciples of Buddha. Before he joined Buddha's order, he belonged to the Sudra or servant class and served Shakyamuni Buddha's family. Buddha came back to his castle, after saving the five disciples and having been given Giju-gikkodoku-on—I don't know the Sanskrit—that park. And he had more disciples who had belonged to some other teacher or religion, who worshipped fire. There were four brothers who served the god of fire. Their names were the venerable Kasyapa of Uruvilva, the venerable Kasyapa of Nadi, and venerable Kasyapa of Gaya, and there must be one more Kasyapa. They joined Buddha's order with one thousand disciples. So he already had quite a few disciples before he came back to his castle.

And after he came back, all seven members of his family joined his order, including his father's prince, Buddha's son, Rahula, and his cousin Aniruddha—I already talked about the blind disciple Aniruddha—and Devadata. When all those families joined his order, Upali helped them to shave their heads, and at last he wanted to be a priest too. But because he belonged to the Sudra class, he hesitated. But Buddha, knowing that, became very sympathetic with him and let him join. At that time, one more member of his family wanted to join the order, but Buddha said, "Wait. If you join our order, perhaps you will be the last one. And if Upali joins our order after you, he should always be seated in the last seat, and he will not be so happy. So wait and let him join my order before you."

So Ananda gave his tan to Upali. Upali joined the order, and later Ananda joined the order. When all seven members of his family were seated in their own seats and Nanda came, the six disciples saluted him, and he had to take his seat. But when Upali came to his seat, Ananda hesitated to bow to him. He knew Buddha was right, we should not discriminate about this or that class, higher or lower. But when Upali actually came next to him, he couldn't bow. He forgot, or he couldn't do this. Upali had always been his barber, his servant, so it was rather difficult to bow to him. Buddha was very angry with Ananda and gave him a long lecture about not discriminating between classes. These are very famous words: "Whatever their class, when people join our order, they are all of the Shakyamuni family. Just as when all the rivers come into the ocean, there is no name for the rivers, so is our order. There is no family name when people join our order."

You may say Buddha was a strange person. In some way he had a very strange spirit, but his spirit is something unusual. That was why he was called "Buddha," I think. His disciples did not know on what kind of occasions they would be scolded. When they expected to be scolded, Buddha was very gentle, but when the didn't fear anything bad, they were scolded terribly. He had, I think, an unusual spirit which goes beyond our world. So for a Buddhist, this world is one of millions, a small, tiny world. There should be many, many worlds besides this small world. The scheme of this sutra is very big, and there is no wonder why this kind of description came from Buddhas talk.

Upali, who belonged to the Sudra class, is famous for his precepts observation. Not many events are told about him, but after Buddha's death, as you know, they had a synod or compiling conference. At that time, Upali recited the precepts.

I must tell you one more thing about Aniruddha, who became blind from not sleeping. As you know, in India the summertime is the rainy season. When it was difficult to travel around to different parts of India, the members of the order stayed in a certain place with Buddha and practiced with him. But when there was clear weather, they went for a journey. Usually Buddha told them to make the journey alone. He said, "You should always be quiet, trust people, and treat people as your friends wherever you go." This is Buddha's way.

I don't know Christianity, but someone made a comparison on this point. Jesus told his disciples not to travel alone. He said, "You should go in numbers greater than two, because you will have many difficulties and many enemies." But I don't want to compare Buddhism to Christianity in that kind of way. If you try to compare them in some way, you will have the opposite conclusion. So it is not fair to say Buddhism is a more generous teaching and Christianity is more exclusive. But anyway, this is very interesting.

So Aniruddha, the blind priest went for a journey, and he had to stay at a woman's home where there was nobody but her. That woman started to like him too much. She loved him, but as he was a priest, he said, "You shouldn't do that."After he came back to Buddha, he told him what had happened to him. So Buddha set up a precept at that time, that monks should not stay in some woman's home alone. If you want to stay, you should stay with someone else. If there is no one to stay at her home with you, you should always recite the sutra and always think of Buddha. "Buddha, Buddha, Buddha." That is one of the precepts. Aniruddha is famous for helping Buddha to set up one of the precepts.

As Zen Buddhists, it is necessary for us to understand the Second Patriarch Mahakashyapa. He is famous for his zudagyo, or in Sanskrit, dvadasa dhutagunah. We count twelve zudagyo, which are mostly important ways of organizing one's life as a person and as a member of the sangha.

The first zudagyo is to live in a calm place, such as the forest or woods, aranyaka. In India, everyone, after finishing their household or family life, would join the religious life with other people. So to enter the aranya or forest means to start the religious life, not only for priests, but for everyone. That was the Indian custom. Here, to live in aranya means to live like religious people do.

The second zudagyo is to support one's life by begging, yathasam-strarika. This is mostly about food, and there are two more about food.

One is that when you beg, you have to visit houses in order. We should not choose houses. You should not choose someone you know or someone who is wealthy. Whether they are poor or wealthy or you don't know them, you should not change the order. This is the next one.

The fourth one is aikasanika, which means to eat at certain times, not to eat many times. They did not eat supper, just breakfast and lunch.

And you should know how much you should eat, you shouldn't eat too much. That is the fifth one, namatika. This is also important. We should not be greedy.

The next one is also about food. We should not eat or drink except at mealtime. To have tea is our rule; that may be alright. This is a very difficult excuse. Anyway, we should not be greedy, especially when we eat.

The seventh one is about the clothes we wear. We should wear Buddha's robe, which is made from the material people throw away. I think not only clothes, but also furniture and everything should be like this. In America, if you go to a second hand store, you can buy something which you want quite cheaply. So I thought there's no need for us to buy brand new furniture, paying a lot of money, if you can get it for two or three dollars. This is, I think, a kind of attitude we take for our living.

And we should wear only three robes. When we have ordination ceremony, we receive three robes: rakusu, which is made of five pieces, and okesa, which is made of seven pieces, and the third one, which is made of nine pieces. There may be many reasons why they named three kinds. In some scripture it says they wear the simplest kind when it is warm or hot. When it is cold they wear the robe made of nine pieces of material, and in the spring or fall, they wear the robe made of five pieces.

Nowadays we have robes for everyday practice and robes for ceremonies. I think that we should not use as gorgeous robes as we do now, never wore such gorgeous robes. When I gave a funeral service for the first time for a very rich old person, I just wore a black robe with a brown okesa. They were very angry with me. At the time they didn't say anything, but later they said, "Why didn't you wear a more beautiful one like your master had?" They knew what my master wore, so they asked why I didn't wear it that time. But now I think we should not be attached to the material or the outlook of the robes. A gorgeous one is alright, a shabby one is alright. Now that is my attitude, but at that time I was very concerned about what I wore.

Perhaps no one likes to wear robes that are too gorgeous, like an actor or actress on the stage. In Japan we have actresses. In the winter, when they don't have much to do, or during their lunch, they would come out to the city with some gorgeous clothes, hitting drums and bells, and entertaining people with music or a play. So I thought, "We shouldn't be like that." But, I think, this kind of attitude is very important, and we should not forget this point.

So far, all of the zudagyo have been about food and clothing, except the first one, which is about where we should live. And the next three are also about where we should live. We should live someplace where it is appropriate to practice zazen.

One is to live near a cemetery. How about it? An American cemetery is very beautiful, but a Japanese cemetery is not so beautiful. It is supposed to be a very gloomy, monotonous place. A place where there is a shrine or temple or cemetery is supposed to be a very lonely, monotonous place. They live near a cemetery because they will feel more deeply the evanescence of life, and maybe they can eliminate various desires.

The next one is to live under a big tree. Maybe this is because it is cool, especially in India.

But at the same time, we should not be attached to the coolness of the place. So the next one is to live where there are no trees, where everyone can see you, like a common place or square, where nothing will protect you. This is a pretty strict practice.

And the last one is not to sleep in bed, to always sleep in a sitting position. Those are the twelve zudagyo.

You will have various questions, and there are many things to think about in this area. If you see those rules just as rules, in a rigid way, that will not give you right understanding. But if you think about the underlying thought, there are many things to think about.

This is, actually, how to protect people, how to maintain our order, and how to maintain our system of society. If our human life is supported with this kind of spirit, a perfect, peaceful world will be acquired by human beings. It may look rigid and strict, but the underlying thought is very warm and full of mercy. Practicing in those ways, they try to make people happy. Just to have a bare and simple life and to have joy in our life will give a limitless source of spirit to the people. Only when we practice our way, when we live in this way and maintain our order and maintain our joy of life will people be able to know it is possible to have complete joy in various kinds of life. Even in adversity, they may feel, it is possible to have complete composure, and they will have a strong spirit or strong faith in our human life.

On Buddha's nirvana day, at various temples they hang a picture of Buddha lying down on a bed surrounded by many disciples who are very sad. Even various animals and birds came to see how he was. And when they saw that he was critically ill, they all cried. But we cannot find a cat in the picture.

No one explained why there is no cat, but I thought, "Where is the cat?" When I asked them, they said, "I don't know why the cat didn't come."

When I was sixteen or seventeen years old, I found some words expressing a superficial good manner. At that time I didn't like the monk's way or priest's way. They always went like this, and it seemed to me they didn't mean it, they just did it superficially without any feeling. And that kind of way is called a "cat-like manner." Cats look very lovely, and their manner is very gentle, but it is not so deep. There is no strong feeling in it. If we say, "Go away," they will go away. If they think it is all right, they may easily approach you. When we are busy or are observing something else, a cat may come. They are supposed to be very sneaky in some way. In some literature, someone called that "cat-like manner". So I thought that is why the cat did not come to Buddha's last hour.

Why did I start to talk about this? To just do this is not a true expression of respect. To live a humble, bare, and simple life is already an expression of respect. It is the best way to express respect to ourselves and others. Even though we lead a bare life, inside, spiritually, we are rich. Even living the simplest way, we have the possibility of giving good feeling to others.

So I am not concerned about the beatnik style or hippie-like style, but only when they can express respect to others even in those costumes. There is a possibility to express respect to others in the simplest way, even though they may wear rags. But this point is missing in hippie-like living. Of course, I think they have that kind of costume to express some resistance to the old cat-like manner. I can understand their feeling. But instead of being antagonistic or feeling resistance to the cat-like manner, they should express some respect to the truth or to the real religious life. The essential element of religious life is respect. And respect could be expressed in various ways.

Exposing various parts of the body may be an expression of resistance to the cat-like manner. But in that manner, something is missing. Buddhists emphasize being ashamed of our bare, natural, primitive, naive, undefined manner. So to respect Buddha means to be ashamed of not being what we should be when we see how perfect Buddha was or when we see someone who has a very respectable character. Naturally, we become ashamed of our want of practice, want of attainment or acquisition. So to become ashamed of ourselves means to respect Buddha. When we have no idea of religion or Buddha or perfect character, we are not ashamed of anything. So we may enter the Buddha Hall with dirty sandals. When we know who Buddha is, we cannot do that, we will be ashamed of our dirty feet. Naturally, when you want to enter a practice hall or Buddha Hall, you will clean up your clothing and body. That may not be enough, but at least that much we can do. That is an expression of respect.

This kind of attitude maintains our order and supports a warm feeling for our sangha and society. Right now what we have is a cat-like culture and antagonism towards the cat. "Cat, go away. I don't like you at all. Go away." It is so noisy, you know. "Go away, go away, go away," so society. If you go to San Francisco, young people express their antagonism towards the cats. They hit drums and dance with long hair, and, "Go away! Go away, cats!" That is a kind of good feeling, you know. If there are one or two cats, we will feel sorry for them, but nowadays there are too many cats. Even though you use electric sound, they don't go away. The sound is not strong enough, but they have to make as strong a sound as possible. "Go away! Go away! Go away!" I can understand that, but that is too noisy.

So there must be some way to maintain our order, to have some warm feeling in our society. That is why this practice of the twelve zudagyo, in Japanese, or dvadasa dhutagunah in Sanskrit, could maintain our order. When we really make this kind of effort, we will have complete freedom in our society. We should make our effort towards this point.

So instead of being enslaved by antagonism, we should make our effort in right order, with right spirit. This kind of spirit should be established in some place like Tassajara. Someone must do that, or else we have no place to live. And this is why we practice zazen, and in explanation of those twelve zudagyo or zuda practices.

There are many words for zazen, Zen or sitting: eight characters. Two tenths of the characters are sitting. You may understand how the practice of just sitting is so important. We say zazen practice, simple as it is, its meaning is very deep, and spiritual zazen will support, will maintain our order.

Mahakashyapa is famous for his zudagyo, his kind of twelve practices. But he is not famous for his understanding of shunyata or emptiness. Subhuti is the one who is famous for his understanding of emptiness, and Shariputra is the most famous one. Nevertheless, Mahakashyapa is supposed to be a successor to Buddha himself. He devoted himself to Buddha's practice, not only zazen practice, but also the zazen practice which includes everyday life, and to spiritually maintaining the order of our life as a sangha and as human beings. And he became a successor to Buddha. This point should be remembered, I think. We say, "Zen and everyday life," but it does not mean to extend zazen practice to everyday life, but that to have deep understanding of the teaching, of Buddha's spirit, we practice zazen. That is the true way. Actually, there is no Zen or everyday life; Zen or everyday life is the expression of the true spirit of Buddha, the true spirit to help others or to maintain our order or to support this society, this human world. I think this is the reason why Mahakashyapa became the successor of Buddha.

Devadatta. Devadatta is, you know, famous because he tried to kill Buddha. There were also famous King Ajatasattu. His father was King Bimbisara. But his son, he, because he have for a long time no son, a prince; so he asked an old fortune teller—what do you say, "fortune teller"? Not fortune cookie, fortune teller, okay? Asked about his prince. He says, "Yes, you may have prince but he is now in the mountain but soon he may come."

So the king sent someone to kill him, you know, he was so eager to have prince if he is going ... his future life ... next life will ... is ... his prince, it maybe better to kill him. So that he can have his prince earlier. He sent someone to kill him. And he got beautiful boy. And he ... but ... again, the king asked his old fortune teller what will be his next life. And he said, "You killed him, you know, so, he maybe; he may kill you. Because you will him, he is very dangerous." So he wanted to kill him again, and he wanted to throw him from the high tower. But he couldn't kill him so he treated him very well so that he may not have any notion of killing him or he may not give him a chance to kill him. And so another name for him was Michorin. I don't know. A man who has in his mind bad feeling or, not revenge, but what you say ... "grudge?" Yeah. So, as the fortune, the old fortune teller said, when he became quite ... a good use ... he put his father in prison, and made him starve to death. And he took over his father's throne, and became a king.

And Devadatta, the Buddha's disciple, also wanted to take over Buddha's seat. Devadatta was also from the family of Shakya. Shakyamuni Buddha's family. So he wanted to take over Buddha's seat. And Devadatta helped Bimbisara to kill his father, and ... not Bimbasara, Ajatasattu kill Bimbisara, and Bimbisara, after he became king, helped Devadatta to kill Shakyamuni Buddha. But he couldn't do so. Anyway, there is many stories, but he, Buddha get injured, his toe only, when Devadatta and his men throw a stone on the street when Buddha was passing the path. He is anyway famous for his, you know atrociously bad notion to kill Buddha. That is one of the worst violations of the precepts.

Ananda is Buddha's jisha—jisha for more, maybe 20 or more years. Twenty five. Some say twenty five, some say twenty. Anyway, for a long time. One day Buddha asked him—asked jisha, only one jisha without changing, because he was, became so old that he wanted to have someone always help him. And Ananda was—became a jisha at that time when he said, "I will take care of various people who come from remote countries to meet Buddha. I will introduce them without fail if they come from remote country. And I will remember all what Buddha say. If Buddha say something when I was not with him, I will ask him to tell it again."

Buddha was very pleased and he became his jisha. And there were some more things which he told him. "What I get from people is yours; and I will not take anything which was given to Buddha," or something like that. But the most impressive, most important point, maybe two points: he will remember what he said, and that he will be very good for the people who want to meet Buddha.

And Mahaprajapati Buddha's aunt and who after his mother passed away, raised Buddha. Mahaprajapati and Yasodhara, Rahula's mother, along with her train. And this sutra is described as if Buddha himself told this story, but actually it is not so. And this, as I said before, this sutra is told in such a from as Buddha himself told it, but actually two, maybe two, three hundred after

Buddha passed away, this scripture was told by someone, we don't know who. But the thought is based on Mahayana teaching. And Buddha who is telling this story is actually Sambhogakaya Buddha, not Nirmanakaya Buddha. But here it says the are still under training; "along with her train; further, with eighty thousand Bodhisattvas." Bodhisattva is Mahayana, who practice Buddhism with Mahayana spirit, to help others rather than to help themselves. "Bodhisattvas are unable to slide back." Unable to slide back means if you really understand something, you know, you cannot forget it. What you attain, in its true sense, you know, you cannot lose it. Real attainment cannot be lost. So we say, "no slide black." "All unable to slide back, endowed with the spells of supreme, perfect enlightenment." This is so called dharani. Do you know mantra? Dharani. A kind of spell—holy word which has mystic power. Or it means essence of the teaching, essential, you know— essential teaching. Chinese translation of it is sogi. So means "good merit," and gi means "to observe precepts." It means, anyway, the essence: essential teaching.

"Endowed with the spells of supreme, perfect enlightenment," it is translated in this way. Spells, you know, some words which has some important, essential words. "Spells of supreme, perfect enlightenment, firmly standing in wisdom." Wisdom is not knowledge, but more intuitive knowledge, which is his own. Wisdom which is not learned, which should be, could be learned from others but which comes out from himself. "Who moved onward never deviating wheel of the law." Wheel of the law, this idea came from the wheel of the, when the battlefield king, you know, when king turn the wheel of_? It doesn't ... which is very strong and which never be pushed back. It will go always on and on.

Buddha's teaching like a wheel of the_?, or wheel of the horse? So it never deviating wheel of the law; who had propitiated many hundred thousands of Buddhas." Propitiate ... propitiation ... this is a kind of technical term. In Japanese, ku yo. If you consult with dictionary, you will find out the meaning of it. There are three ways of ku yo. One is to give teaching, to offer teaching. Like to recite sutra. One. And to pay respect is the second one. And to offer some materials: food or flowers or incense. Those are the three ways of making propitiation. "Who have propitiated many hundred thousands of Buddhas have planted the roots of goodness." This is Chinese also ... we have technical term. Zenmon. Zenmon—"good root." Zen is "good." Mon is "root." "Who have planted the root of goodness. Had been intimate with many hundred thousands of Buddhas." This is also, you know, technical term.

"Were in body and mind fully penetrated with the feeling of charity." And this is, you know: body and mind, this is ... one is missing here. Body, mind. You know, we say ... when we say body and mind, we usually say body and mind and mouth, you know. Talk. This is also important. Body. Mind ... even though you think something is good, it will be a merit—if you say something, that will also give you merit. And actually by body ... in Japanese or Chinese this is also technical term. Three karmic actions. Good karma or bad karma. Bad karma or good karma will be created by mouth and mind. So here one is missing but in some other translation ... some other origin text, the "word' is also here. "Were in body and mind fully penetrated with the feeling of charity; able in communicating the wisdom of the Tathagatas." Tathagata. Tathagatas is synonymous with Buddha, but this is ... I don't know what. Tathagata is the third person. Buddha himself do not call Tathagata. Tathagata is, you know, the third person. Someone is Tathagata. Or second person ... you maybe Tathagata ... to myself. But anyway, Tathagata. Wisdom of Tathagata.

"Very wise, having reached the perfection of wisdom." This is also technical term, "perfection of wisdom." This is also technical term. "Perfection of wisdom." Anata samya sambhodai in Japanese. "Renowned in many hundred thousands of worlds; having saved many hundred thousand myriads of kotis of beings; such as the Bodhisattva Mahasattva." No we have many names again. This is the ... it means that, you know, Sambhogakaya Buddha, within himself, he includes many things, you know. As he is one with every being. So there should be various names. This is many, those are not enough, but anyway we have here many names such as Bodhisattva Mahasattva Manjushri. Manjushri and Avalokiteshvara Bodhisattva are the most important Bodhisattvas. Those Bodhisattvas like Manjushri appeared two, three thousand ... tow, three hundred years after Buddha passed away, like Manjushri. " Manjushri as a royal prince is: in scripture, he told various teaching for Buddha instead of Buddha. Or, he discussed the holy teaching with Buddha, you know. So he is like a prince for Buddha. So we say prince. Royal prince, Manjushri. And there are many stories how he ... who was his father or mother, where he was born; but so many stories were told about him so we don't know which is right or which is wrong. You know. We don't know whether he is historical person or not. We don't know. But anyway, his character represents the Buddha, one of the Buddha's character. Wisdom. He is very much like Shariputra. And he is sitting on his right, Buddha's right. Here, Manjushri is sitting. And the other side, Fugen Bosatsu is sitting. Manjushri is the symbol of wisdom, and Fugen is the symbol of practice.

"The Bodhisattva Mahasattva Avalokiteshvara." This is the Bodhisattva of Mercy. There is a special chapter for him.

"Mahasthamaprapta."

The Bodhisattva who is always making a great effort. And next one, Nityodyukta. "Nityodyukta." This is Bodhisattva who does not rest. Who make constant effort. "Anikshiptadhura." This is Bodhisattva who make ... treasure in his hands. "Ratnapani." This is seventh one. Oh, excuse me. Ratnapani is the Bodhisattva who always has treasure in his hands. And this is seventh one. By the way, there is, according to the translation of the original text ... they translated, there is some difference in number and order too. Here we have maybe twenty two, twenty three. Should be twenty four. Next one is Pradanasura. Pranadasura is Bodhisattva of to give you courage. Bodhisattva who gives you, who give us courage, or faith, or strong way-seeking mind. And next one, tenth, is Ratchanandra. Ratchanandra means the moon. The round, beautiful moon, Bodhisattva. Ratchanandra Bodhisattva, who gives everything, who is giving always beautiful light. Anantavikramin. Anantavikramin who gives us endless, limitless power. And next one is missing in Chinese translation. Both old translation and new translation ... the original text look like different. But anyway this one is missing in Chinese translation. But his translation very similar to Chinese translation so it is ... for me it is easier. Fifteenth. The next one is Mahapratibhana. This is missing in Chinese translation. And I must find out ... I haven't found out what does it mean. Satanamasuri. He is also missing in Chinese translation. He is translated in other scripture—oh, in other scriptures translated as Bodhisattva who has virtue of flower, lotus. "Nakshatraga." Twenty five. This is also missing in Chinese translation. "Bodhisattva Mahasattva Maitreya." This is Miraku who appears after Buddha fade away. "The Bodhisattva Mahasattva Simha," it says. Bodhisattva Mahasattva Maitreya. And that ... for the first one, Bodhisattva Mahasattva Manjusri. And for the next one there is no respect. But, the escaped, you know, to repeat same title over and over again, instead of giving same title for the first one and the last one. So some people say Bodhisattva Mahasattva Simha was added later. It may be so; I don't know. Simha means, anyway, "lion," so, but—Bodhisattva Mahasattva Maitreya looks like the last one. And Bodhisattva Mahasattva—it maybe same title again, here. I don't know. Anyway, this kind of study is very complicated study, still. But they are studying. They do not feel so good until they have some definite conclusion.

"With them were also the sixteen virtuous men to begin with Bhadrapala." Bhadrapala is the Bodhisattva who we bow, you know. Each time when we take a bath. We have sixteen ... fifteen of his friends all were enlightened in bathroom. I don't say enlightenment but in their previous lives they were good friends. And they took bath together. And this Bodhisattva—Badabara in Japanese—in Sanskrit, Bhadrapala—attained enlightenment in his former life. And under Shakyamuni Buddha they also appeared as good friend and studied under him, under Shakyamuni Buddha, and attained enlightenment.

There is in Blue Cliff Records, then is koan about him. When this Bodhisattva attained enlightenment he said: "Myo jyako zen myo." "Myo jyako zen myo" means: "myo" his mind and body became clear and felt so good. And he realized the water ... he realized that water as well as various beings, has no self-nature. The koan is "What does it mean by "myo jyako zen myo?" How he, this Bodhisattva attained enlightenment? This is the koan in the Blue Cliff Records.

Water has, you know, a boat. Reverend Katagiri's father—teacher or master. I think he is—must be a very good teacher because people in that village—when—I don't remember exactly what Reverend Katagiri said, but, anyway, at that temple, he get water by pipe—by bamboo pipe from a spring pretty far away from the temple, you know. Bamboo pipe. And for that they have a wooden pail. And they sent that pail to get mended. And when they get it back to the temple the pail was still leaking. Still—it was still leaking. And so Reverend Katagiri took it to the store or shop to make it perfect. And the old man who is working on it said, "Maybe water in the temple, in your temple, should be very different if that water—from the water we have in the village. I think if you see Reverend Katagiri—the way he does it is very special, you know. The way he hit mokugyo, the way he recites sutra. His manner is anyway very gentle and precise and gives us good feeling—special, I think, his teacher, in that way. So I think his father, his master should be like him, or must be like him. "So water you use is quite different, must be quite different, from the water we have in our village. That is why it leaks."

Anyway, I think that that kind of enlightenment he may have when he took bath. When Yasutani Roshi came and took his bath, he enjoyed completely the hot spring bath. And he wrote some poem about myo jyko zen myo—about this koan. You know, water penetrate, you know, everything with—with hole or without hole, it doesn't matter. Even through the stone—penetrate into even the hard stone.

Still, why water penetrates to everything is: it has not self-nature. You know. If you have self-nature you cannot penetrate into everything. That is, you know, the koan study about this Bodhisattva.

"Sixteen virtuous men." This is also technical term. Sixteen virtuous men we call, we have to several renderings. Kai shi juroku. When we say juroku, sixteen men means sixteen men—fifteen friends of Bhadrapala. And here we have also many names which I don't know, of which I am not so familiar. But Bhadrapala is the Bodhisattva who is enshrined in our bathroom.

You know here is sitting meditation. And those descriptions describe his self-rejoicing meditation. In his meditation ... his meditation has this kind of quality. Even though he is ... he may not be aware of it, he is absorbed in ... even thought he is absorbed in deep meditation, his meditation has various quality as this. And Maitreya and some Buddhas who has six powers or five powers. When we attain arhatship we have six ... we are supposed to have six powers. Every morning we recite, we say Samyo-rokuso. Samyo-rokuso is arhat's various powers. The power of thinking and remembering the former state of existence. This is ... you may think rather mysterious but mysteriously speaking, it is former being exists, former being. But moment after moment, we reincarnate from one state to the other. Sometimes you will be demon exists with horn on your head. Sometimes you will be asura, in anger. Or sometimes you will be garuda, with big wings, you know, covering whole world. Beautiful golden wing. Sometimes we will be hungry ghosts. If I do not have not much ... not much food we will be hungry ghosts. We reincarnate one state to the other, always.

A man of, you know, powerful ... power of sitting will realize our nature through and through. Then it means thinking and remembering former state of existence, not former but actual state of existence, which transform one state to the other. And capable of seeing everything. Capable of seeing everything. And capable of hearing everything. And insight to the others. And to attain perfect enlightenment ... this is supposed to be Arhat. To attain arhatship. And the power of free activity. It is ... sometimes understood as supernatural ... or mostly maybe. Arhats, for Arhats this is supernatural activity. But for Mahayana Buddhists or Zen Buddhists as you must have studied by various koan or Shobogenzo, those are, you know, our usual ... these kinds of powers of free activity should be always within our life. If your friend wants water, you give him water. "Do you want this?" You know, that is that kind of free activity. That kind of more natural activities. If you have ... if your mind is rigid and stubborn, you cannot have this kind of freedom. You cannot see what is happening around you. Anyway, those are the powers.

And Maitreya see through ... had perfect in Buddha's mediation. "What maybe the cause, what the reason of the Lord producing so great a wonder as this? And such astonishing, prodigious, inconceivable, powerful miracles now appear, although the Lord is absorbed in meditation!" He could see it, but he couldn't figure out what it was . Why such a magnificent event happens.

"Why, let me inquire about this matter; who would be able here to explain it to me? He then thought: Here is Manjushri, the royal prince, who has plied his office under former Ginas and planted the roots of goodness ... Manjushri who has plied his office." This is a kind of, you know, not worship, but kind of, we say "kuyo." "To make office." To give him some office work. And under various, not only Shakyamuni Buddha but various Buddhas, Ginas, "... and planted the roots of goodness, while worshipping many Buddhas. This Manjushri, the royal prince, must have witnessed before such signs of the former Tathagatas." Such omens, you know; good omens of the Tathagatas. "Those Arhats, those perfectly enlightened Buddhas; must have enjoyed the grand conversations on the law. Therefore will I inquire about this matter with Manjushri, the royal prince." And in this, and in this place, important words maybe "the perfectly enlightened Buddhas," Samya sam Buddhas ... perfectly enlightened Buddhas. Those who attained under Samya sam Bodhi. Supreme enlightenment. And "Arhats," you know Arhats. Here it says "grand conversations on the Law." "On the Law," means on the first principle or on the teaching. And the "grand conversations." Grand ... not only just conversations, it means also, it means sermons, you know. Not, in its ... I don't know Sanskrit so well, but "conversations" in its widest sense, the original word means conversations. But it means sermons. Here it maybe better to say sermons. Grand sermons. He must have listened to or enjoyed the grand "sermons" on the Law. Those are the important words. Perfectly enlightened one. Supremely enlightened one. Sambhodi. Samya sam bhodi.

Now, this Manjushri, the royal prince. Royal prince means, Buddha's, you know, maybe Buddha's successor. He passed away, not ... this is not Manjushri but Shariputra passed away before Buddha. And most likely this Manjushri Bodhisattva is characterized by Shariputra. "This Manjushri, the royal prince, must have witnessed before such signs of the former Tathagatas." You see, here, this sutra was told by, supposed to be told or written as if this sutra was told by Buddha himself but actually there is no doubt that this sutra was not told by him. But if we understand Buddha ... if we understand Buddha, not only as Nirmanakaya Buddha, or one Buddha based on the idea on the three bodies of Buddha, then, you know, this sura again and again was taught by many Buddhas before. So Manjushri Bodhisattva must have been it when he attended so many Buddhas in his former life. Do you understand this king of idea of describing the truth. Truth is truth because it exists forever whether Buddha tells about it or not. It exists. But someone must have seen or realized Buddha. So someone like Manjushri. I don't know why, exactly; who exactly; we don't know who, but someone must have, some unknown person before Buddha must have seen those things. Must have attended real Buddha. And Manjushri must be one of them. And he must have seen it before. And he must have, actually, you know, not only seen those six good omens, but also must have listened to, must have heard of those teachings which existed, which appeared before Buddha. And in this way, after those miraculous mysterious omens, Buddha will start his sermon called Lotus Sutra.

So Manjsuri, you know, Bodhisattva Maitreya, inquired about this with Manjushri. And next paragraph is the last paragraph, page eight.

"And the four classes of the audience; monks, nuns, male and female lay devotees, numerous gods, nagas, goblins, gandharvas, demons, garudas, kinnaras, great serpents, men, and beings not human, on seeing the magnificence of this great miracle of the Lord, were struck with astonishment, amazement and curiosity, and thought: Let us inquire why this magnificent miracle has been produced by the great power of the Lord."

The four classes of the audience, namely: monks, nuns, and male and female lay devotees; numerous gods; numerous devas, you know, devas —various, they have various devas since of old. Nagas, dragons—like eight kinds of dragons. Goblins, as I said, goblins means yakshas. There will be evil natured ones and good nature ones. Anyway, they are various spirits. And Ghandarvas. Demons. Demons is asuras. To fight like Asura, you know, with many hands. And mostly painted in his body. Whole his body, red. And his eyes is maybe blue. Mostly Buddha ... Indian gods and Buddhas are blue-eyed. So in all his hands he has arms ... bows and arrows and many arms. And, not arms but he has many arms. He is mostly naked. Asuras. And Ghandarvas are a group of deities since of old. Since the time of the Rig Veda, maybe one thousand years or more before the Lord Buddha. And gandaras is big, big winged bird which is Nagas. Nagas, dragons. Kinnaras as you know, whether he is a man or animal is Kinnara. Man or animal. Great serpents. This is Mangora. Mahora. We say Mangora, but Mahora ... great serpent. This is mystified ... mythological being, of serpent. Men include, to our great astonishment include, hell and celestial beings. Men includes the six states of ... all the beings which exist in six states of world. We will be incarnated in those states. Men includes the six worlds, heaven, and mankind, and Asura. Asura is, you know, Asura here we name Asura, but Asura is included in the men. And some demons too. We will be sometimes demons, like Asura. And animals. Animals is not men you say, but so far as we are, we will be incarnated into men, we count them as men. And those Hungry Ghosts and those who live in hell, too. But this is one interpretation of the six worlds. But there are many interpretations for, about, what is men, and what is not human. But I think it maybe proper to understand men as human being, includes this kind of six states. Which is supposed to be our various states of human existence.

"Men, and beings not human, on seeing the magnificence of this great miracle of the Lord, were struck with astonishment, amazement and curiosity, and thought." This is, you know, why we repeat those words, "were struck with astonishment, amazement and curiosity." This is, you know, gives you some rhythm and make you remember better. And this is the purpose of repeating various synonymous words, one after another. As you will find in the part of verse or poem about this description. In Sanskrit there are, you know, their literature is very rhythmical and a half of it maybe poem style. This sutra also, by the way, has two parts: the gatha parts and what you call ordinary description. Prose. Prose parts and gatha parts. And gatha parts and prose parts do not accord with—there is some difference. And which is first and which was prose part was first, is older or gatha parts is older. No one knows maybe. Maybe they are studying very hard which is older, or they are written at the same time. But it doesn't--they say it does not look like written in the same person at the same time. Because sometimes the content is no the same.

"At the same time," page nine, the second paragraph. "At the same moment, at that very instant, the Bodhisattva Mahasattva Maitreya knew in his mind the thoughts arising in the minds of the four classes of hearers and he spoke to Manjushri, the royal prince: "What. Oh Manjushri, is the cause, what is the reason of this wonderful, prodigious, miraculous shine having being produced by the Lord? Look, how these eighteen thousand Buddha-fields appear variegated, extremely beautiful, directed by Tathagatas and superintended by Tathagatas."

Here I must point out some points. Here it says, "... the Bodhisattva Mahasattva Maitreya knew in his mind the thoughts arising in the minds of the four classes of hearers and he spoke to Manjushri." Here, he knew, but this is also one of the six powers of Arhat or maybe Bodhisattva. And in some version, those names are repeated twice, you know. Those names like "four classes of hearers, and hearers." Not only "four classes of hearers," but also the names of goblins, gods and devas and Nagas and Yakshas ... those various spiritual beings, names of eight spiritual beings again are repeated here. But in this translation, or in the original text, maybe, there is no ... those names are not repeated here. And here again, the third line or second ... third and second from the end of this paragraph:

"Look, how these eighteen thousand Buddha-fields appear variegated and variegated, beautiful   One more word is here, was here, but translator skipped one word here. And the translator translated this sutra from, of course, from Sanskrit, it says here. Original text was the text written on, I don't know where, but old text which is in some museum, you know, in London. So in ... that ... there must be the word "beautiful" here. Why we ... they repeat same word like this, as I said, to give some rhythm to the sentence. But in English it maybe not be so good to repeat so many times. "Variegated, beautiful, extremely beautiful" ... same thing ... same thing happen already six, the earth, whole earth shake in six ways.

Six ways: this way, stronger, this way and more stronger, this way. And this way, trembling, it maybe this way. Don't you think? This way "shake" maybe. This way is to tremble or toss. Toss and toss more harder. This is a repetition of same thing. And here it again ... appeared again--translator skipped. "Beautiful and extremely beautiful, directed by Tathagatas and superintended by Tathagatas. This is also repetition. "Directed by Tathagatas" maybe enough, you know.

This is our way of understanding. The difference between people stick to the sutra and people understand the meaning of the sutra. And for the people who understand the meaning of the sutra, this description is not good enough, even. Must be more fancy. Should be endlessly fancy! One group or two group is not good enough. We understand in that way. Whatever you say, whatever you think, it is already understood by us. Before we understand it. Before we know it, we know it. If you say something, "Yeah. It may be so."   It ... some miracles... "Don't you know something? Don't ... could you tell me something more miracles?" Maybe. We understand in that way. That is rather ... Dogen Zenji's way. He did not say ... he did not ridicule those sutras. He is very serious. Maybe he respected this sutra best. Most. But it is very serious matter. That point is very serious matter.

This sutra titled Saddharma-pundarika Sutra was supposed to be told by Buddha, but actually this sutra appeared maybe after two or three hundred years after Buddha passed away. So historically we cannot say Buddha spoke this sutra. If you ask if all the sutras were spoken by Buddha, the answer may be that only parts of them were spoken by him. And they will not be exactly as he said them. Even the Hinayana sutras were not handed down by Buddha's disciples exactly as he told them. Since even the Hinayana sutras were not told by Buddha, the Mahayana sutras could not have been told by him.

But some aspects of Buddha developed after the historical Buddha passed away. The historical Buddha is not the only Buddha. He is the so-called Nirmanakaya Buddha. We also have the Sambhogakaya Buddha and Dharmakaya Buddha. So Buddha was understood more and more as a perfect one. When Buddha was still alive, this point was not so important because Buddha himself was their friend and teacher and even god. He was a superhuman being even when he was alive. He was their teacher or master, so there was no need for them to have some superhuman being like a god. But after he passed away, because his character was so great, his disciples adored him as a superhuman being. This idea of a superhuman being is a very important element for promoting the understanding of Buddha as the Perfect One.

This sutra was not told by the Nirmanakaya or historical Buddha, but by the Sambhogakaya Buddha. According to this sutra, it was told a long, long time before Buddha. And Buddha, knowing that there was this kind of sutra before him, talked about the sutra which had been told by the Sambhogakaya Buddha. The sutra was attributed to Shakyamuni Buddha, but he told this sutra the way Vairochana Buddha told it a long, long time before.

So it is necessary for us to know first of all what the Nirmanakaya Buddha, the Sambhogakaya Buddha, and the Dharmakaya Buddha are, and how those aspects or understandings of Buddha developed from the historical Buddha. Without this understanding, this sutra does not mean much. It is just a fable, like a fairy tale which is very interesting, but doesn't have much to do with our life. Accordingly, I have to explain the three aspects of Buddha and how the Buddhism which was told by the Nirmanakaya Buddha developed into the Mahayana Buddhism which was told by the Sambhogakaya Buddha.

This may be a difficult thing for you to understand. Do you know of the Nirmanakaya Buddha, Sambhogakaya Buddha, and Dharmakaya Buddha? The Nirmanakaya Buddha is the historical Buddha. But the historical Buddha has two elements. One is a human being, and the other is a superhuman being. These are the two elements of the historical Buddha. Historically, such a character exists. As you know, Buddha was not God Himself, but was a human being. But for his followers, he was a kind of Perfect One. He attained enlightenment and reached to the bottom of our human nature. He was enlightened in human nature, which is universal, true nature. His human nature is universal to everyone and every being. And he subdued all the emotions and the thinking mind. He conquered all of this, and all of the world, and became a World Honored One. He had this confidence when he attained enlightenment, and his followers listened to him as to a teacher who is also the Perfect One.

So the historical Buddha has two elements. The vital element for the idea of Buddha was this superhuman element. If he was just a historical character, or one of the great sages, then Buddhism could not have survived for such a long time. The reason Buddhism could survive for such a long time is this element of superhuman being in the historical Buddha.

This idea of Buddha as a superhuman being was supported by his teaching. One of the most important teachings of Buddha is the teaching of cause and effect, the teaching of causality. If you do something good, naturally you have some good effect. So his disciples wondered how he could have acquired such a lofty character, such a good character. Buddha told them that if you do something good, you will have a good result. If you practice hard, you will acquire good character. Since his character was incredibly high, his former practice must have been an incredibly hard, long one. So, since their adoration for Buddha extended limitlessly, his practice before he attained enlightenment, or Buddhahood, became limitless. It follows that, if Buddha is a limitlessly lofty person, the time he practiced his way must also have been limitlessly long. In this way, the historical Buddha became more and more something like Absolute Being.

It is the same with us. We appeared in this world, but we appeared in this world with a limitless background. We do not appear all of a sudden from nothing. There must be something before we appear in this world. And there must be something before Buddha also. That he was so great means that he had a great practice. This point is very important for the development of the idea of Buddha.

So he was described in various ways as a superhuman being. He had eighteen characteristics and virtues which are completely different from those of a usual person, and he also had the thirty-two physical marks. They say this is just a "big adjective" for the Buddha. That may be so, but there is some reason why they applied such a "big adjective" to the Buddha, to the extent that these kinds of things were even described in the Agamas, which belong to Hinayana Buddhism. This kind of Mahayanistic idea of Buddha is already included in the Hinayana. So it is difficult to say which is the Mahayana teaching and which is the Hinayana teaching, actually. If you read them closely, even Hinayana sutra s have a Mahayanistic description of Buddha.

But actually, he was a human being. When he was 80 years old, he passed away. At this point he was not a supernatural or superhuman being anymore. But how should we understand his death as a superhuman being? If he were a superhuman being, there would not be any need to enter nirvana. Whether to die or to remain alive would have been his choice. For an ordinary person, it is not possible to have this kind of choice. They say that he took Nirvana because he had completely finished giving people a chance to attain enlightenment. He gave a full teaching for helping people to attain enlightenment, so there was no need for him to live any more. That is why he entered Nirvana. They understood his death in this way.

We usual people appear in this world, according to Buddhism, because of karma, and we die because of karma. But Buddha appeared in this world with a vow, the Mahayana vow. The first of the four vows we recite is to "save all human beings." He appeared in this world with this vow instead of karma. Karma and vow are actually the same thing, perhaps, but our attitude changes when our understanding changes. Karma changes into a vow. Instead of living by karma, we live with the vow to help people who live in karma. That is Buddha's teaching. This kind of teaching is supported by what Buddha taught when he was alive, you see? So for them, this is not just a story—this is the actual story we see through the example of the Buddha. In this way, Buddhism survived for a long time.

This kind of Buddha, who made a vow to save people, starting from his training as a bodhisattva, and who appeared in this world as a buddha, is called the "incarnated body" or Nirmanakaya Buddha. So far, all of this kind of teaching is called Hinayana Buddhism. But if you look closely at those teachings, there is already the Mahayanistic understanding of the teaching. I said just now "incarnated body." If there is an incarnated body, there must be an "essential body," the mother of the incarnated body. When our understanding reaches this point, the more profound teaching will be understood as Mahayana teaching.

But some people may be disappointed who believe in historical Buddha. This is not a characteristic of any religion except Buddhism. Only Buddhism went through a long history before having a complete understanding of the historical Buddha. It took a pretty long time for us to understand who he was.

At first his disciples were attached to his character, or to what he said and did. So his teaching became more and more static and solid. His teaching was transmitted by so-called Hinayana Buddhists, or shravakas, because they were the disciples, or followers, who tried to preserve his teaching by memory and discussion or meetings. No one is sure when this kind of meeting was held, but it is said that seventy-five years after his death they had a meeting where they chose various good disciples to compile his teaching.

When they discussed the precepts, Upali was the head of the group, and he recited what Buddha had said. When the Sutras were discussed, Ananda, who was Buddha's jisha, discussed what Buddha said. In that way, they set up some teaching: "This is what Buddha told us, and these are the precepts Buddha set up." Naturally, they became rigidly attached to the teaching, and, of course, those who studied this kind of teaching had a special position among Buddhists. Buddha's disciples were classified in four groups: laymen, laywomen, nuns, and priests. And the distinction between laymen and laywomen and priests and nuns became more and more strict. Buddhism at that time already had become a religion of priests, not ordinary people or laymen.

But when the meeting was held in the big cave, there were many people who did not join it. And there were many good disciples and followers among the people who did not join the meeting. Those people naturally got together and formed a group. That is the origin of the Mahayana School. So Buddha's followers divided themselves into Theravada or Joza-bu and the common followers, called Daishu-bu in Japanese. Daishu means "assembly," a group of people or followers. Among them were many good teachers. One century after Buddha passed away, this group established an understanding of Buddha and his teaching. At that time the difference between the Jozabu and the Daishubu was not so great. But later, after Mahayana Buddhism was established, the other group acknowledged the more traditional and more fundamental teaching of Buddha. That is actually Mahayana Buddhism.

I started this kind of long lecture to explain who spoke this Lotus Sutra. This sutra was supposed to have been spoken by the historical Buddha, but actually, what was recorded here is the Sambhogakaya Buddha, not the historical Buddha. Because this sutra was told by the Sambhogakaya Buddha instead of the historical Buddha, it is valuable.

Last night we had a very interesting lecture and discussion, and I was very interested in your questions and the lecture. How Buddha would feel about the idea of the pratyeka-yana or shravaka-yana is a very interesting question, I think. In my last lecture we explained what the Nirmanakaya Buddha is, and this morning I want to explain the Sambhogakaya Buddha, the one who is actually telling this Lotus Sutra.

The reason I was so interested in the question of how Buddha may have felt about it was because Shakyamuni Buddha, as I told you in the last lecture, has two elements: Buddha as a human being, and Buddha as a superhuman being. The idea of the superhuman nature of Buddha is the result of a more emotional attachment to his character and teaching, which the Sravakas or Hinayana Buddhists had. This Shakyamuni Buddha who has two natures or two elements, the historical Buddha or the Buddha who incarnated to save others, and the more idealized Buddha, who is called the Nirmanakaya Buddha. But the Nirmanakaya Buddha is already not Buddha himself. If you think more about it, the historical Buddha is not Buddha himself. The historical Buddha became Buddha because he was enlightened in his true nature. That is why he became a Buddha. So without being enlightened in his true nature, the historical Buddha is not Buddha.

Here we already have a background for the historical Buddha. And even though that background was idealized so much as to reach the Nirmanakaya Buddha, there is also the incarnated Buddha. In other words, he changed, starting from a Bodhisattva, and became Buddha. So he is not true Buddha; he is always changing. "Who is changing?" is the next thing we should think about when we really want to know who Buddha was. To have, not just an emotional or romantic observation of Buddha, but also to more sincerely and deeply want to accept him as our teacher, it is necessary for us to know why he is Buddha.

If we are to get to this point, we have to have some idea beyond the incarnated Buddha, or Shakyamuni Buddha, or the Nirmanakaya Buddha.

That Buddha is the Sambogakaya Buddha. The Sambogakaya Buddha incarnated into the Nirmanakaya Buddha. So the Sambogakaya Buddha is the Perfect One, and truth itself. When he is seen by people as truth, he may be a teacher. Even plants and animals, mountains or rivers, can also be our teacher when we have eyes to see this. So when the historical Buddha has this kind of background, when he is elevated to this stage, he will be accepted as our teacher in the true sense. Not just in an emotional way, but we can accept him wholeheartedly as our teacher, because he is the one who is enlightened in the eternal truth, who has the strong background of the truth. And he is the one who taught us, who introduced this kind of truth to us. That is why he became Buddha.

He was enlightened in it, and he is the one who teaches us the truth he found out. Without this kind of background, Buddha could not have been remembered by human beings for such a long time. After Buddha was acknowledged as truth itself, then as long as truth exists and as long as we care for truth, we can remain as Buddhists. This Buddha is called the Sambogakaya Buddha.

The Sambogakaya Buddha is not the Buddha who will, or will not, attain enlightenment. He is the truth itself. But people may say the Sambogakaya Buddha is, at the same time, the Nirmanakaya Buddha. People see the truth in many ways, but the truth is always the same. Do you understand? If we understand his background in this way, that understanding is also the Dharmakaya Buddha, truth itself. For the Dharmakaya Buddha there is no need to attain enlightenment. He is already enlightened. From the beginningless beginning to the endless end, he is always enlightened. Only the Nirmanakaya Buddha attains enlightenment and becomes Buddha.

So for Buddha, after he attained enlightenment, to save others, or for others to help themselves, to be enlightened in himself or to cause other people to become enlightened, was the same thing. To help others and to help himself was the same thing.

To be enlightened does not mean to be aware of it. Do you understand? To be aware of it would be for him to observe himself objectively. When he attained enlightenment, that was being aware of himself. But to enlighten himself means to have confidence in himself, to accept himself as he is, to accept "that I am here". And, in this way, when you do not care for anything, you know that "I am here" already. That is the most important point, to stand on your own two feet before you observe yourself objectively. "Who am I, and what am I thinking? What kind of experience did I have? What kind of enlightenment did I have yesterday?" That is not true realization of oneself. To realize oneself is deeper than that kind of superficial observation of oneself. Before we objectively observe ourselves, we should be one with ourselves.

After Buddha discovered his true nature and knew exactly who he was, he attained enlightenment and became the Sambogakaya Buddha. He became truth itself, one with himself and one with the whole universe. And he did not care for anything. He was completely satisfied with himself. And, when he became one with himself and with everything else, whatever he saw, everything had the same nature as he had. Just as he existed under the Bodhi tree as an enlightened one, as a perfect one, so everything existed in the same way. That is why Buddha said, "It is wonderful to see everything has Buddha Nature." Just as he is, so everything is Buddha, we say. But when we say this in its true sense, it means "I am Buddha."

Only when we stand on our own two legs can we help others. Before this, you are observing yourself, thinking, "Who am I? Have I attained enlightenment or not? Am I able to help others?" and you cannot help others. When you become just you yourself, without comparing yourself to others: "I am I. I am here. When you have difficulty, I am with you, and I can manage myself pretty well. If you like, I can help you," that is Buddha.

This kind of Buddha is the Buddha before we attain enlightenment. Without this confidence, you cannot even practice zazen. How can you practice zazen when you doubt, or when you are observing yourself objectively without having any subjectivity? How can you practice zazen? Only when you accept yourself, and when you really know you exist here. You cannot escape from yourself. This is the ultimate fact, that "I am here."

This is very true. Don't you think so? But still you doubt, and still you make a separation from yourself and observe yourself from the outside: "Who am I? What am I doing?" Zazen practice is not this kind of practice. Someone else is practicing zazen, not "you." "You" should practice zazen. That is shikantaza. That is the Sambogakaya Buddha.

Buddha's teaching is not the written teaching or something told by the historical Buddha. When the Sambogakaya Buddha, the true Buddha told it, it was Buddha's teaching—very much so. But when we read, we are trying to figure out what he told us, what was the true teaching, and what was the historical Buddha, Shakyamuni Buddha. We are, in other words, deeply attached to someone else, forgetting all about the ultimate fact that we are here. As long as we try to understand the real Buddha in this way, we cannot understand who he was. Anyway, to help others and to help ourselves is the same thing. To realize myself and to make others realize the truth is the same thing.

So the true Buddha is the Sambhogakaya Buddha, and when the Sambhogakaya Buddha does some activity, or is observed by someone, he may be the Nirmanakaya Buddha. Before the Nirmanakaya Buddha, there must be a Sambhogakaya Buddha. And before a Bodhisattva appears to save others, there must be a Sambhogakaya Buddha as the strong background of the Bodhisattva. So every Bodhisattva and Buddha, and their activity of helping others, comes from this source, from this origin of the Sambhogakaya Buddha. And the Sambhogakaya Buddha is truth itself. So we have Dharmakaya Buddha, Sambhogakaya Buddha, and Nirmanakaya Buddha.

When we understand the Lotus Sutra as the sutra which was spoken by the Sambhogakaya Buddha, or when we understand that, "I am now reading the Lotus Sutra," then the Lotus Sutra makes sense to us. If we lose this point, we will be turned by the Lotus Sutra. If we realize this point, we will turn it. I said, "I am reading," but actually, I meant, "I am telling the Lotus Sutra." So the Sixth Patriarch said, "When we are in delusion, the Lotus Sutra will turn us, and people may be turned by the Lotus Sutra. But when our mind is clear, we will turn the Lotus Sutra, we will speak the Lotus Sutra instead of Buddha." So, to study the Lotus Sutra and to listen to it are not two different things. To read it and to talk about it are the same thing. If there are various materials to talk about, then we can speak the Lotus Sutra.

I have come to the conclusion already, but let us think more calmly and understand clearly what we have been studying in these two lectures. There are several things I want to point out. One is that when we read Buddhist scriptures, it is necessary for us to know at what kind of historical stage each sutra was told—to know, in other words, who spoke the scripture.

For instance, when Westerners started to study Buddhist scriptures, they thought they were a kind of myth. That may be so, a kind of myth, nothing but a myth. If someone studies a scripture literally, without knowing what kind of background the scripture has, and if someone has compiled the scripture in a very emotional way, the description will be very mysterious. So we should know what kind of people described Buddha in this way, and whether this sutra is based on Mahayana or Hinayana teaching. I am not comparing, and I am not saying which is better. But we should know with what feeling, and what kind of attitude, this scripture was presented, or else we will not understand what it is.

The same is true of the way you treat things and people. Without knowing who a person is, we cannot help him; without knowing what things are, we cannot treat them properly. When you know who made this tea bowl and what kind of history this tea bowl has, then you can treat the tea bowl properly. If you handle it without knowing who made it and what kind of tradition it has, it may be just a bowl; it doesn't make any sense.

So it is necessary to know how this tea bowl appeared here, in front of me. And at the same time, it is necessary for you to know whether this tea bowl is suitable for this season or not. Even though it is a very traditional and valuable one, a summer tea bowl cannot be used in winter. So you should know, at the same time, whether this is suitable for this season and suitable for the guest. And you should choose the tea bowl accordingly.

So we should arrange the teaching this way, and, according to the time and occasion, you should choose from the various teachings. But that is not enough. You should also know the history, or tradition, of each teaching. Then you can use the teaching in its true sense.

This way of doing things is, in other words, the four vows. This kind of effort will be continued forever. I am not forcing you to follow our Japanese way at all, but you should know how Buddhism was extended from Buddha to us. This is a very important point. The other point is to understand whether this kind of teaching will be effective enough to use right now, like a tea bowl. To arrange the teachings this way is not good; to arrange the teachings this way is not good enough either. When you arrange the teachings this way and choose one of them, and when you arrange the teachings this way, the historical or traditional way, and understand the characteristic nature of various teachings, then you will find out what kind of teaching you should apply. That is why I am telling you what kind of nature this sutra has and who spoke this scripture.

The point is not whether this Lotus Sutra was told by the historical Buddha, or by some other person. As long as you attach to the historical Buddha too much, you cannot understand Buddhism. Buddha was great because he understood things in this way. How do we know Buddha had this kind of attitude towards things? Even though we do not have very much historical material, we do have quite a bit. We can study Hinayana Buddhism and pre-Buddhistic material and ask how pre-Buddhistic thought became Hinayana teaching.

How did it? It is impossible for pre-Buddhistic teaching to be Hinayana teaching, so what was the bridge? The bridge was Buddha; Buddha made the bridge. When we realize this point, we see that the Hinayana understanding was not perfect enough. The Hinayana Buddhists made Buddha a pre-Buddhistic person. He was pushed backwards to a pre-Buddhistic character.

So Mahayana students found that the Hinayana scriptures cannot be recognized as the main current of Buddhist thought. They are not the main current. This kind of mistake always happens. We do not like sectarianism because that is Hinayanistic. I always say that sectarianism is like having coffee in a coffee shop when you are going to San Francisco. You know, when you have a cup of coffee on the freeway, that is very good. But you shouldn't stay there. You should go on to San Francisco.

Emotionally, we like coffee shops and big banana splits. But that is Hinayana, you know. Even though it is good, we should continue on our trip. This is the Mahayana way—on, and on, and on. Usually people stopped at the coffee shop for many, many days—one or two weeks. But we cannot stay that long, because the coffee shop will not stay open that long. If it is not the main current, it will die, eventually, and only the main current will continue. So we don't have time to stay at the coffee shop very long. Once in a while, when we become sleepy, we must have some coffee. That is our way. With this attitude we should continue our trip. And if we want to continue our trip, the four vows are necessary. At any rate, we should continue our trip as long as our car goes. This is our attitude and our practice.

Delusion

We should establish our practice where there is no practice or no enlightenment. As long as we practice zazen in the area where there is practice and enlightenment there is no chance to make perfect peace for ourselves. In other words we must firmly believe in our true nature. It is beyond our conscious realm.. .conscious experience. There is good or bad or practice or enlightenment only in our conscious experience but whether or not we have experience of it what exists is actually there, exists. In this way we have to establish the foundation of our practice. To.. .even it is good thing to have it in your mind is not so good. You may be.. .it is a kind of burden for you. You do not feel so good. Even you have something good in your mind. So to have something in your conscious realm you do not feel, or you do not have, perfect composure. The best way is to forget everything. Then your mind is calm and your mind always wide enough or clear enough to see things and to feel things as they are without any effort.

To harbor some ill-will is maybe something better than to have something.. .some idea which you should do or you ought to do. The Buddha says, 'You should be like this. You ought to be like this.' And to have what he says in your mind is not so good, but to have mischievous idea in your mind is sometimes very agreeable. That is true. So actually, good or bad is not the point. The point is to stick to it or not is the point whether you make yourself peaceful or not. The best way is not to think or not to have.. .not to retain any idea of things, whatever it is. To forget all about it, or not to leave any trace of thinking, or not to have any shadow of thinking, is the best way.

But if you try to do.. .if you try to be beyond your conscious activity or if you try to stop your mind that will be another burden for your mind. "I have to stop my mind in our practice but I cannot. My practice is not so good." That is also wrong way of practice. So don't try to stop it but leave everything as it is. Then there will.. .things will not stay in your mind so long. Things go as they go. Things come as they come. That is.. .this kind of things will go in your mind in that way. Then your clear, empty mind eventually last pretty long. So to have a firm conviction of empty mind in your practice is the most important thing. That is why in Buddhist scripture we use some astrological description. We describe the empty mind in various ways. Most of the time we calculate the big mind is some astrologically great number.. .so great that we cannot count. It means to give up calculating. If it is so many you will lose your interest in counting it and you will eventually give up counting. But still the good thing for this kind of calculation.. .you have some kind of help, a kind of adoration of the innumerable number will help you to stop the thinking of your small mind. But actually when you sit you will have the most pure, genuine experience of the state of mind.. .that is not even a state of mind.. .original or essence of mind which Buddha meant, or the 6th patriarch meant. Essence of mind or original mind or original face or Buddha nature, emptiness.

Those words mean the absolute calmness of our mind. There is, you know how to take physical rest. You don't know how to take mental rest. Even though you lie in your bed your mind is still busy. Even though you sleep your mind is pretty busy in dreaming something. Your mind is always in intense activity. This is not so good. So we should know how to give up thinking or busy mind and firmly believe in the perfect rest of our mind and resume to our pure mind. So we should know how to go beyond our thinking faculty. Dogen-zenji said, "You should establish your practice in your delusion." Even though you think you are in delusion but there is your pure mind. So, if you realize the pure mind in your delusion that is practice. If your have the pure mind, the essential mind, in your delusion - delusion will vanish. It cannot stay when you say, this is delusion. He will be very much ashamed of it. He will run away. So you should establish your practice in your delusion. To have delusion is practice. "To attain enlightenment before you realize it." So you will attain enlightenment before you realize it. Even though you do not realize it, you have it. So, when you say 'This is delusion' that is enlightenment. But when you try to expel the delusion it will stay and your mind will become busier and busier to cope with the delusion you have. That is not so good.

Just say, 'this is delusion'. That is enough and don't be bothered by it - 'oh, this is just delusion'. When you see delusion you have your true mind - calm, peaceful mind. When you start to cope with it you will be involved in delusion. So, when you sit, whether you attain enlightenment or not - just to sit is enough. When you try to attain enlightenment, then you have big burden in your mind. So your mind will not be clear enough to see things as they are. Moreover we always exist with two sides—things as they are and things as they should be. So we should attain enlightenment. That is one thing. But as long as we have physical, as we are physical beings it is pretty hard in reality. That is how we are actually in this moment. Even though we are not good right now we want to be better. That is another side. We exist here in that way, as everything exists in that way. So if we start to attain something, the other side of our nature will be brought up as they are and as they should be. But if we have transcendental mind beyond the things as they are and the things as they should be there we have perfect, peaceful mind. Usually religion develops itself in realm of consciousness by beautiful building, by wonderful music or by perfect organization. Those are in realm, those are religious activities in conscious world. But Buddhism emphasizes the world of unconsciousness.

So how to study Buddhism is how to sit, or how to join the practice or to live in good Buddhist is the way to study. It is much better than to read some book or to study some philosophy of Buddhism. Of course it is necessary to study our philosophy because by studying it you will have a firm conviction in your religion but our philosophy is not only philosophy of Buddhism. It is philosophy in general. Those practices were built up to protect the true teaching. In the way people may discuss about Buddhism is the most common way, the most understandable way, for everyone. So the purpose of Buddhist philosophy is not to propagate Buddhism in some wonderful, mystic way, but to protect our way so when we discuss something about religion we should discuss the problem in the most common and universal way, so that is why Buddhist philosophy is so universal, so logical, but it does not mean to expand our way, to propagate our way by some wonderful philosophy—philosophical thought.

So in some way Buddhism is rather polemical and some feeling of controversy is in it because the Buddhist has to protect their way from some mystical or some magic understanding..

.magical understanding of religion. So philosophical will not be so good unless we have some particular interest in discussion with some other religious people. If you want to be a sincere Buddhist the best way is to have some place to sit, or to see some Buddhist culture, heritage, may be the best way. Anyway, when we sit we have to sit. That's how to study Buddhism. We are very fortunate to have a place to sit in this way. So, I want you to have firm, wide, imperturbable conviction in your zazen of just to sit. Just to sit. That's enough.

Topsy Turvy Views

I want to still continue to speak about topsy-turvy views. When your understanding of life is based on some concrete concept of material or spiritual, this view is called topsy-turvy idea. When your understanding is based on your true nature or your true inmost request, this aspect is the right aspect. Dogen Zenji, founder of our sect , he says, "Practice should be established in our topsy-turvy idea. Practice should he established in our defilement or delusion. We should attain enlightenment before, we should attain identity before we attain enlightenment." This is very subtle understanding of Zen. Usually we say enlightenment and your practice is quite different thing. After you practice zazen you will attain enlightenment, but Dogen Zenji said, "You should study your practice in your defilement." If your understanding of your life which is always dualistic, which is always based on the idea of right or wrong, good or bad, this is our usual -- how we live in this world. Wherever you go there is a problem, good or bad, right or wrong, but this problem itself is, if your understanding of the problem is right, it is the practice itself. Because of your poor understanding of the problem, you cannot establish your practice in defilement. You have problem now. You have many problems I think, and some of the problems is pretty hard to control. Why it is difficult to control your problem is your orientation of the practice is wrong. If the - your orientation of the practice is right, your problem itself is a kind of practice.

If you try to control yourself, and, by controlling yourself to attain enlightenment is, this kind of practice, orientation of the practice, is wrong.

Why you have, if you think why you have problem you will understand the problem itself is ... why you have problem is because your inmost request is working on your difficulty you have.

Because you want to live, you have problem. If you give up to live in this world, there is no problem. Because you want to remain, because you want to develop your life, there is problem. So problem itself is well orientated, and so, if you should have problem this understanding is right. If you think I... we should get out of the problem... this understanding is wrong. This is topsy-turvy view.

You may say it is impossible for me to accept this problem, but even though you think you cannot accept this problem right now you are accepting... you have accepted the problem, because you have accepted the problem you suffer. It is not matter accept problem or not accent problem. Problem is right there, and already well orientated, and your effort is always right. If you have this kind of... this understanding of the problem, to have problem is to have right practice. The right practice is nothing more than to accept problem. That you have problem is that you have right practice too. This is right view or right understanding of practice. So he says the right practice should be where you have problem, where you have problem there is right practice. And right enlightenment is where you have problem... to have problem is already enlightenment. There is no enlightenment without problem. There is no awareness of the problem... enlightenment without problem. The perfect enlightenment is something unintelligible, but the awareness of the enlightenment is... should be or is, actually is where you have problem. So he says, "Right practice should be in the problem, and. right enlightenment should be before you attain enlightenment." It means on everyday life there is right practice and right enlightenment. If you seek enlightenment outside of everyday life, that is wrong attitude. Enlightenment is there, always, in your reach, you know, not outside of your house. Enlightenment is in your house already. This is right practice and right awareness of enlightenment.

Dogen Zenji, Dogen Zen master rather emphasized enlightenment, rather emphasized awareness of the enlightenment than the concept of perfect enlightenment, the enlightenment which will be attained when you suppress all the evil desires and thinking and emotional activity. This kind of enlightenment is not for everyone. The enlightenment for everybody should be awareness of the enlightenment. The awareness of enlightenment will be attained when you have right understanding of your problem, and when your effort is, when your effort has, right orientation. This ... usually, but usually, when we have problem we like to escape from it. This is wrong, you know. It is not impossible to escape from the problem. Why... we have... we should think... why we have problem, because we want to sustain our life, because we want to extend our life, that is why we have problem. So we should be rather grateful for having problems. This is right understanding, and right effort.

When you try to escape the problem you create many, you know, excuse, or you create many dualistic idea to escape from the problem, and to make some excuse to escape from this problem. You have You will have... you will create the idea of yourself and the idea of the problem. But when... that you have problem is because you accepted the problem, because you have the problem. The problem is already a part of you, so there is... actually there is no problem or there is... there is no problem beside you, and there is no you beside problem. Problem and you are one. You create L.concept of I and concept of problem. So, it looks like it is possible... you know this is problem. This is I. so it is possible to escape from the problem. This is mere, an excuse. it is riot, possible, actually, but when you create the idea of you yourself and problem, you yourself decide the problem, the idea of problem, concept of problem beside you yourself. It looks like possible to escape from the problem, but actually it is not possible. This is so called delusion, and this is just an excuse. So if you determined to accept your life, there is enlightenment and awareness of the enlightenment, and gratitude for your life, having your life.

You may say, "That is impossible!" This is... it means your lack of understanding and lack of your determination, and lack of sincerity to live. But if you have this determination, you can think, and you can analyze and you can find out how to solve the problem. This is... but only when you have completely accepted. the problem, this kind of effort will work, but before you have this kind of understanding, even. though you will try to escape from it, that is Just a mere excuse. This point is very important, to live in this world.

Last right San Francisco Zen Center had a guest speaker, who is nuclear, who is studying nuclear physics, and. he said, "In science, in physics, the matter we study matter, but the matter is quite different from our mind, and when we study matter we should clear our mind so that we can observe matter exactly as it is." From the scientific viewpoint, it should be so, or else, that is not science, but when, but if you do not know that the matter and you yourself is one, on the other hand, if you do not know the truth, the matter and your mind is one, the science will not serve it's own purpose. It should always help our life. But scientific truth should be always true and under some condition. it should be always... it should be accepted as a truth under some conditions. What I think is true should be accepted as truth by you, too. This is science, but the conclusion science will give us will not help us if we do not know the matter and mind is one. Actually there is no matter, without our mind. There is no mind without matter. The matter and I is actually the same. But science is... will give us some certain knowledge on the condition that matter and I, mind, is completely different. So, scientific knowledge can exist. Without this hypothetical, hypothesis, science cannot be... scientific research is not possible. To divide the mind and matter is... means to ignore the various conditions, but actually some scientific conclusion will be given when the other condition was ignored. You may say, when it is cold you will. the water will freeze into ice... when it is cold. It is so, but actually, even, if it is cold, inside of your room will not... ice will not get... will not freeze, because there is some other conditions in your room. Only when the conditions all over the world. only when it is cold all over the world, ice will become... water become ice. But actually such condition will not be... will not exist in this world. Somewhere it will be warm, somewhere it will be cold. So, the scientific truth is true only when the other... the rest of the conditions was ignored, but actually it is not possible to ignore various conditions in our actual life. So, if you want to serve, if a scientist... if... when science serves our purpose the oneness of the all the conditions should be put into consideration. To put various considerations... to put various conditions into consideration means to become one with the rest of existence. It means to become one with problem. Only when you become one with problem, you can. the scientific knowledge will serve it's own purpose. Because we can use the scientific knowledge under some conditions.

Not for... to escape from problem, but for... to get along with the problem. So, the attitude of science is not the same as the attitude of Buddhism, but if we understand what is science, what is Buddhism, then you can use the scientific knowledge. But when you are caught by the scientific knowledge, or when you use your scientific knowledge to get away from the problem, or to entertain some idle idea of... towards your life, science will make our life idle and the science will not serve its true purpose. So, it is necessary to understand what is the basic attitude towards our life, and basic attitude toward our life, is to accept our life and to become with the surrounding. This is very important point. And this is why we practice zazen.

Last night he emphasized that in science I myself and the scientific truth is completely different. That he emphasized this point is not to mix up religious... religion and science. He gave us the kind of warning. Science is some research based on dualistic idea. If so, we must be careful in using the scientific knowledge. That was his warning. When we take his statement in our consideration... when you use scientific knowledge the science will serve its own purpose. This is right understanding. From, our viewpoint, science is a kind of... scientific knowledge is... although it is true, but it is a kind of delusion. But, true practice should be established in delusion, in delusion. The true... so he says, I am science. scientist, so to work in his laboratory is my practice. That is right. True practice should be established in delusion, knowing this is delusion. This is very important point. You should not try to escape from scientific truth or you should not abuse the science to make some excuse for escaping from the problem. This is very important point. The purpose of science is to give perfect interpretation to our life as much as possible, to give some interpretation of our life, as much as possible is purpose of science. But it is not... it is the interpretation of our life, not life itself. Our purpose is to accept our life, and use the scientific truth, because it gives us the clear interpretation of our life, within the possibility in the most perfect way possible. So, scientific truth will help us a lot, but we should know that it is not perfect, and perfect knowledge of our life is already... already we have, but we don't know. It is difficult to give some interpretation of our life, so we should study science... not to escape from the difficulty we have. So, in our study, the most important point is self-confidence to live in this world, to survive in this world as a human being. This is most important point. Not as a... as some supernatural being, but just as human being. This is the most important thing to practice right zazen, transmitted from Buddha to us.

Buddhisms

As you know, in Buddhism there are many schools. But you can classify Buddhism into Mahayana and Hinayana schools. Almost all schools in Japan belong to Mahayana school. Mahayana people called original Buddhists, old Buddhists or direct disciples of Buddha, called Hinayana Buddhists. It means small vehicle while Mahayana is big or large vehicle. But Mahayana school originated from Hinayana school. Development of Buddhism take place and Mahayana school is supposed to be more advanced school. But it is not exactly so. Even in the time of Buddha there were many Maayanistic disciples. And it is pretty difficult to say which is better, Mahayana or Hinayana. So in Soto school we do not say Mahayana is good or Hinayana is good. Just the same, and from standpoint of zen Buddha practiced zen, and Hinayana Buddhists and Mahayana Buddhists have been practicing zazen. So, if we become...if we discriminate the teaching which was told by him, or forms which he set up at the time of Buddha, or the rules which were set by some other disciples is based on his character, and his character is based on his practice. And so, from this standpoint, for zen Buddhists, there is no need to say Mahayana Buddhism or Hinayana Buddhism.

But original, direct disciples of Buddha were to0 much attached to the form and teaching which was set up by Buddha. But Mahayana Buddhists emphasized his speech rather than teaching or precepts (observing precepts) or form of rituals. And Hinayana Buddhists emphasized to save themselves, but Mahayana emphasized to save others as well as to save themselves. To save themselves and to save others is principle of Mahayana Buddhists. For Hinayana Buddhists zen practice is to save themselves, but Mahayana Buddhists practice is to save others. In this practice we are supposed to save ourselves and others. This practice is not just for ourselves. It is actually to save others. When we practice zazen, when we become one with others, there we have enlightenment. When we have this enlightenment, this practice is for others too.

You may say you are just sitting on your cushion but that is just form. But spiritually our practice is to save ourselves and at the same time to save others. And save all the living beings (animate and inanimate beings) this is our practice. So, in understanding of zen there is a slight difference between Hinayana practice and Mahayana practice. But even Hinayana practice cannot be just egocentric practice. To save themselves is at the same time to save others. At least by their hard practice they will encourage people. To do something for yourself and to be happy by yourself is at the same time to make the others happy. So there is no practice just for themselves. 'Every practice will help others. So it is not necessary to classify our activity - this is for myself and this is for others. Whatever you do that is for yourself and for others too. And strictly speaking we cannot be separated from others. We exist with others. So, when you become happy your mother will be happy and you family will be happy, your boys and girls will be happy.

When you are distressed your family will be distressed and your friend will be distressed. So, actually, especially mentally, we cannot be separated from others. It is impossible to live alone.

So to say this is for others or this is for myself is poor understanding of our life. Because of poor understanding we uselessly discriminate our activity. Here the most important thing is to do something from the bottom of our heart. That is the most important point for purity our impetus of doing something. Straightforwardness is wanted, as the sixth patriarch emphasized. Whatever you do, if you do it with straightforwardness that is the most important point we emphasize. In this way Mahayana Buddhism developed after the Hinayana Buddhism became more formal and rigid. When Buddha was teaching them there were no need to be so spiritual or just because they were spiritually supported by him. But after Buddha was no more they become more and more concerned about what is Buddha and how to attain Buddhahood like him. This kind of study resulted in Mahayana Buddhism two or three hundred years after Buddha passed away, and between two hundred and three hundred Mahayana Buddhism completely formed by famous scholars like Nyaraguna(?) or Seshin(?). That is of course, how zen Buddhism arose.

And then Zen Buddhism became more and more - Zen Buddhists became more and more powerful and zen practice became more and more popular in India, until Bodhidharma came to China. And in China Zen Buddhism developed in various ways under the influence of Chinese civilization. By Chinese civilization I mean Toaist or Confucionism -anyway more practical culture. Zen Buddhism became more and more practical in China. And on the other hand, Zen Buddhism became more and more popular. And how they propagated Zen Buddhism was very interesting. They applied various ways in propagating Zen Buddhism, not just by practice, by art, poem or painting. And this kind of civilization based on Zen Buddhism was introduced to Japan in the twelfth century, and in Japan Zen Buddhism became more and more aesthetic and simple, and on the other hand, Zen Buddhism organized in more philosophical way because Japanese people are interested in simplicity of the teaching. How to simplify zen philosophy or Zen Buddhism was their main effort, especially by Dogen, Zen Buddhism became one teaching with the other teaching.

As long as we have some idea of attaining Buddhahood or enlightenment by practice, it is not possible to understand what Zen is. But when you just whip the horse, the cart will go. When you just practice zazen, enlightenment is there. But when you start to intellectualize or start to understand the value of Zen in terms of some gaining idea, zazen, you cannot value zazen, because you are trying to figure out what is Zen in a worldly sense. Thus you will get no answer to your question. There is no answer to that. We don't know why we practice zazen, why we have been practicing for such a long time, thousand of times practicing zazen in this way. No one knows, but we just did. There must be some meaning. That is why we practice zazen. But while you are doing it, you will find out for yourself, you cannot stop the practice of zazen. This is the so-called true practice from Buddha to us.

In China there were many families but in Japan Soto and Rinzai was most outstanding schools. Actually Dogen studied Rinzai school. I think, nowadays they become more and more (even Rinzai masters) more and more became Soto-like. And Soto masters also studied Rinzai. Maybe for fifty or seventy years we are studying Rinzai way too, and the philosophical interpretation of zen is mostly Soto way, according to Shobogenzo which was written by Dogen.

So, if you want to understand what is zen, it is better to understand it by Dogen. Intellectually, it is better to understand by Dogen. Of course, intellectual understanding is not enough, or intellectual understanding is not zen. Zen should be understood by practice, but because we are so intellectual, intellectual interpretation of zen is necessary. But why Dogen worked so hard, was because we will be involved in intellectual study completely, forgetting all about our actual practice. That is why Dogen worked so hard. Unfortunately, for us, our publication is not so good. We have many things to do, and we have to translate Dogen's work in English and this is pretty hard job. Even for Dogen, Japanese language was not good enough. He found it very difficult to express his way in Japanese language so he made many technical terms for himself to express his idea, and he used some special grammar. His writing, you know, is very difficult because his grammar is very special—not usual, you know, Japanese grammar. He wanted to express it as much as he can, in words. That was, that is why it is so difficult to understand, even for a Japanese. Until we get accustomed to his way of putting his idea in his word. But it is lucky we have Dogen in our civilization, and his idea will help the Western world a lot, because his thought transcend Japanese way of thinking.

So, if you have time (I think you have already been through D. T. Suzuki's work and you are through already D. T. Suzuki's work, but his zen is, for you especially you who are very much interested in psychology, so his work is concentrated on psychological interpretation of zen, but that is not perfect, you know.) Of course he knows about it—not perfect. Zen is not just psychological state of mind. Zen is based on, the most important thing, for zen is the way-seeking mind or our sincerity or constant effort.

Our constant effort will result some, you know, psychological state of mind, but the most important thing is transmitted spirit from Buddha to us. Our constant effort which will last forever. So the most important point for us is to acquire the spirit of practicing zen, or to realize your true nature, or to make your effort to appease your inmost request, or to attain vital freedom is our—the most important point. If you want to attain vital freedom- to attain vital freedom is to realize our inmost request - to realize our inmost request is to make your mind peace. Without realizing your true nature, it is impossible to make yourself peace. So by peaceful mind we mean to have eternal practice based on our inmost nature. So far, zen practice is the most, is the best way to appease our inmost request. That is why we practice zazen. Zen practice is not for sake of attaining some state of mind. It is rather....to practice it to appease ourselves. So when you realize that whatever you do, you cannot satisfy it with what you do, then you will find out zen practice is the only practice we have. This is why we practice zazen. So zen practice is to find yourself. By practice you will find yourself and your...when you realize your nature, when you realize what is your life, that will encourage your practice. In this way, once you start zen, little by little you will realize how important it is to sit, in this way, and to continue this practice. This is not only a kind of religion. In its larger sense zen practice is something more than religion in its narrow sense.

Ananda

Here we recite the sutra just once but in Zen Center we recite three times. The first one is for direct disciples of Buddha. We call them arhat. Arhat means the disciples who completed their way. Arhat. But Mahayana Buddhists called them Hinayana which means small vehicle. Small vehicle means Hinayana. They called themselves great vehicle while direct disciples of Buddha was called Hinayana or small vehicle. That is not so fair but actually they called themselves great and called other Buddhists small vehicle. But in Soto way we respect the direct disciples. So first of all we recite the sutra for the Hinayana Buddhists. This is one of the characteristics of Soto way. And our way is not Hinayana or Mahayana. Our way is Buddha's way - not small vehicle or great vehicle. There's no vehicle in Buddha's way. Our way is not only Buddha's way, but also it is, maybe, we, human beings way. So before Buddha we count seven Buddhas. Buddha is the seventh one. Buddha is not the first one. But this is another characteristic of our way. So teachers of Buddha is also...we should respect them, but....so Dogen Zenji did not like to call Zen...to call themselves Zen. He says, 'We are just disciples of Buddha". So some people say Soto zen..zen which transcend zen is Soto zen.

But to attain this kind of Big Mind is our way and why we practice zen. Without this Big Mind various practice of Buddhism will not work. When various schools based on this practice.this great practice.every school has its own meaning, but if we have no background which is...which will cover every school, all the schools of Buddhism, the Buddhism will divide into various schools without any connection, or without any mutual understanding. So we have to acknowledge that we are Soto school.we are students of Soto school but that does not mean we are one independent school from Buddhism. We are all Buddhists but as we are raised in some particular family, Buddhism also has many families in which many people will be raised. It is difficult to raise all the boys and girls in only in kindergarten or in grammar school. So we have to have some families. So we are Soto family but we are also...we have to go to school....public school or private schooL.whatever it is...we have to join some institute of human being.

That is Buddhism. This kind of understanding is not only Soto way of understanding. This is original understanding of Buddhism. The most learned and bright student of Buddha, called Ananda....Ananda was the most learned and bright student. But unfortunately, or fortunately, he well in love with some girl....a beautiful girl____he was enchanted by her. And Buddha once told him.Buddha became very sympathetic with him.and told him...once Buddha told him, watching incense table in front of him...in front of Buddha.and he said, 'I see the incense table right here". Ananda said, "Yes, I see the table with you, and I see you too. I think I have seen you. I have acknowledged you."...he said...Ananda said. You know this is.this means."I see something. I see something and Buddha sees something, too and.in the same way." And Ananda thought the way I see something should be the same with the way of.with same as Buddha's way to see something.some special thing. That was, you know, hidden meaning. But Buddha said.Ananda said I see the same thing as you see, in the same way, and I know how you feel about it. He didn't say so, but it means I see the same thing and I see you too. And Buddha said that you see the table or the stool...stand.incense stand which I see is all right but if I don't see anything, what will you see?. He said now I see something..some particular thing, and you see some particular thing.maybe the same way.that is all right. But what will you do...what will you see if I don't see anything...when I don't see anything... when I shut my eyes?

What will you do? What will you see? But Ananda said, I see you when there is no table. When there is nothing. I see you. But Buddha did not acknowledge him. When I see something.when my not-doing something is known only by me.you know.when my not doing or inactivity I, myself know, but that inactivity will not be known to anyone else and your known activity or inactivity will be known just by you. No one knows it, so if I don't do anything, what will you do, he says. Ananda was impressed by his kind teaching, so he found out how to detach from some special experience. It is impossible....some teaching is impossible to teach you but some teaching is not possible. To stay in activity and find composure in it is also the.based on.should be based on the same understanding of teaching.or same.should be the same. Our way should not be divided two or three. Our way should be always same whether we are in activity or we are not in activity.our way.our fundamental way should be the same.

So Ananda found out that his love was not deep enough so he rather became ashamed of it. And he thought 'I understand Buddha completely' but he did not understand him completely. So our activity is various schools_various_our activity will form various schools of Buddhism, and various religious_it is the expression of deep religious experience, but when we do not express any thing.when we resume to our true nature and don't do anything_who are you? We are all the followers of the religion should be the same_But if we do not realize this fact, Buddha will point out something which is not deep enough. So Buddhism is not just religion. It is based on our_it is based on reality_how we_.who you are, and who I am_who else exist. So he found out how everything exists. That is Buddha's enlightenment. How everything exists just not mean just superficially the difference between A and B. We should acknowledge the differences but at the same time we should acknowledge the universality_the same background. This is how we understand our life. Our life is different; each one's life is different from others but at the same time each ones life is the same. Same but different. One but two. Two but one is so called middle way_Narajunas' middle way. Different but same. It is not just different but also same. So we can say A is B_.just A is B. A is B is allright but at the same time A is not B. So perfect... .according to Tendai school_each existence can be understood from idea of nonexistence. And it will be understood at the same time_.the idea of existence_we are existent_we exist here but we don't. We don't exist but we exist. We are not permanent so we don't exist, but at the same time, in the smallest particle of time, we exist. So we are existent and not existent. This is Tendai School_.true intellectual understanding of our life.

If we take the viewpoint of time_idea of time_continuity, we don't exist. But in the smallest particle of time, in the discontinuity of the time, we exist. If we could change the universe for a moment, we exist, but it is not possible. So those ideas_intellectual understanding of existence is not perfect. So we have to have superior viewpoint, which is middle way. The middle way accepts the truth_everything exists and everything does not exist. The understanding, or the viewpoint which accepts those paradox is middle way. Those paradoxical_there is no way to understand those paradoxical way of understanding. The only way is to resume to direct experience of our life, or to practice zen in_just by zen you can accept this teaching.

Intellectually you cannot.intellectual understanding will be the understanding of existence or non-existence, but in actual experience... .actual experience will accept the truth that everything is permanent and not permanent. And we are different and we are.this kind of paradox will be accepted by actual practice. This practice is the basic practice, and actually there are many ways of practice. Someone was sitting in front of fire this morning but some people ....some Buddhas who use to practice zen in front of fire, dwelling on the idea of being burned by fire, and in the midst of burning fire, I am burning. You are burning when you sit in front of burning fire. But that is not the only practice. There are many kinds of practice. To practice zazen in front of water, you are water itself and when you sit in front of fire you become fire and if you sit in front of water you become water - you become one with water is a kind of practice. But those kind of practice is based on our way transmitted from Buddha. This practice is basic practice. So without this basic practice each practice will not work. So, when you practice it is necessary to be encouraged by.to encourage with each other and it is also necessary to be independent in your practice. This is the way how you practice zen. We cannot say which is better. Actually it should be the same. It should not be different to practice zen just by yourself should be the same as to be encouraged by people, or your teacher, but to be encouraged by your teacher does not mean.. .is not the only way. Just to sit by yourself is also.. ..should be also to practice. We should not be caught by the idea of difference only.

So as Buddha suggested, 'what will you do if I do not exist?' He didn't say so, but 'If I don't see anything.... If I don't do anything, what will you do? And he was enlightened. So love someone is not only to do.to have something to do is not the only way. Not to do.not to have anything to do with her is also love. This is pretty important point. There are two ways. Not to love, you may say you would go away. You maybe say that is cruel. That is not the way to love people. You should go away if the word is different.expression is different, but love is the same. should be the same. If it is different your love is not deep enough. When the love reach to this stage we call it mercy, or great love. That is the mercy we mean.

The Two Zens

Between Rinzai Zen and Soto Zen there—there must be some clear understanding of—of the two, or relationship of the two. Dogen Zenji's, you know, problem of, or koan was, "If we have buddha-nature," you know, "why we should practice zazen?" That was his, you know—that is why he went to China. All—all—in all the scriptures say that everyone has buddha-nature. If so, why we should practice zazen?

And Soto more put emphasis on the statement that we have buddha-nature. And Rinzai put emphasis on practice to attain enlightenment, you know. If we have buddha-nature, like Soto student says, why is it necessary to attain enlightenment? And usually, you know, people understand that "we have buddha-nature" means that potentially we have buddha-nature. We have buddha-nature within ourselves, but that nature—buddha-nature is covered by many things: many evil desires. Or because of the bad karma we cannot, you know, reveal—we cannot realize buddha-nature. But if we practice zazen, or if we get rid of evil nature, the buddha-nature, which is innate nature, will reveal itself. Usually people understand in that way. But, as the Sixth Patriarch said, that is nihilism. But anyway, people understand in that way to explain why we must practice zazen.

But this understanding is not true understanding, even according to usual understanding of sutra. There are many, you know—we try to understand Buddhism just our ordinary way of thinking ordinary way. That is maybe why we cannot understand what—why Dogen has to go to China to understand that point. If he understand in that way, you know, it is—for him it was not—there was no need for him to go to China. You know, if—by practice, by our practice, by stopping all sort of evil desires, and we will attain enlightenment, and we will have no trouble, you know, and our buddha-nature reveal itself because there is no evil desires which covers our innate nature. If he understand in that way, there was no need for him to go to China.

But that was not, you know—that kind of understanding is just, you know, usual understanding which you can accept it intellectually, but you cannot accept it emotionally in its true sense, you know. Your mind says you are —you think, you know, or you can explain why we should understand—we should practice zazen intellectually. But actually if you try to attain enlightenment in that way, you will be discouraged, you know, because it is not possible to annihilate all evil desires you have. One student out of thousand, you know, can attain enlightenment in that way. So naturally Dogen Zenji, you know, didn't—couldn't satisfied that kind of answer. So he actually went to China, not because of study of philosophy of Buddhism. He wanted to have complete—he wanted to accept Buddhism as his own teaching. He was very sincere person. He couldn't satisfy—he couldn't be satisfied with the usual, you know, intellectual, philosophical understanding of Buddhism. Although he was the eminent philosopher, he was—he is actually very profound—established very profound philosophy—Buddhist philosophy. But even so, he couldn't satisfy with his philosophy of—philosophy—Buddhist philosophy, and he went to

China. And after he received transmission from Nyojo Zenji, he, you know, described this point from various point.

So he is the one who, you know, understand—understood what is enlightenment and what is real practice. What do we mean by—what does the Sixth Patriarch or old Zen masters mean by practice and by enlightenment? This is the point he—Dogen Zenji strived for to explain. And he thought people of his age—of his time will not understand this point fully. And he wrote his understanding for his descendant, who may understand his point.

This morning I want to briefly, you know, explain this point: enlightenment and practice, you know. What is enlightenment and what is practice? The enlightenment—according to Dogen Zenji, enlightenment equal practice. We use, you know, soku. Soku means, you know, "equal," but not just equal. When you say "equal," you know, although—two side of the equal, you know. Although it looks—there looks like different, but if you change, you know, form, two things is equal as, you know, as you solve the problem of algebra, you know. If you change the form, both side is equal. But when we say equal without changing , you know, anything, that is equal. If, you know, practice and enlightenment is same if, you know, if you attain enlightenment, that is equal. Practice and enlightenment is—are equal, same.

But when we say soku, "equal," it means that without changing — without changing form it is equal. They are same. This is rather difficult to understand. Practice equal enlightenment. It means that the other side of, you know, practice is enlightenment, and the other side of the enlightenment is practice. He understood in that way. So there is no need to change the practice into enlightenment, or there is no need to change enlightenment into practice. Without changing, practice and enlightenment are same. That is his understanding of our practice.

Now, as I said last time, in Rinzai Zen they put the emphasis on—on kensho. To put emphasis on kensho means actually to put emphasis on our practice. To encourage our practice, they put emphasis on kensho. But actually, kensho is not the actual goal of practice. Practice itself is important. Kensho is just candy. You strive for candy, and you make good practice. That is why Rinzai put the emphasis on kensho.

Soto put emphasis on practice, you know. Forgetting all about our practice is shikantaza, as you know. We, you know, forget all about kensho and fully devote ourselves to practice. So actually both Rinzai and Soto put emphasis on—in actual practice. And if you talk about, you know, kensho in Rinzai school said, small enlightenment— numberless small enlightenment and several big enlightenment. What does it mean? Small, you know, numberless enlightenment , and big, several enlightenment. If, you know, enlightenment is a goal of practice, one enlightenment will be enough . Why do they want so many, numberless, numerous enlightenment? And several big ones? You know, it is, you know—it is just words, just means of encouraging people to follow Buddha's way, to continue our practice forever, from beginningless beginning to endless end, we should follow Buddha's way because Buddha's way is the true way. And for Buddhists, there is no time to stop our effort to save people and subjectively to save ourselves. That is why we decide, you know, we have four vow.

I think it is necessary both for Rinzai and Soto to have this kind of clear understanding of our practice or Buddhism. Forgetting all about the fundamental teaching of Buddha, just to put emphasis on Rinzai or Soto means nothing. As you know, in all religion the most important point is to have conviction to follow the truth. That is, in other word, faith, or to believe in, or to trust in the truth whatever happen to us. That is our basic attitude of—basic attitude for human life.

So for Rinzai or Soto—for Rinzai because, you know—Rinzai people— because we are not sincere enough, you know, they put emphasis on kensho. But Soto put emphasis in attitude or belief. So naturally Soto is more rigid in our practice, or more formal, you know. If you, you know, if you—to have strong conviction to follow the truth means try to have strong faith or to— in our buddha-nature, and to have determination [to] try to follow the truth or try to help people. So naturally, instead of putting emphasis on kensho, we Soto students should follow rules of monastery or rules of our life.

So for Soto students, it—we put—it is necessary for you to organize your life so that you can practice zazen well. For Rinzai students, it is necessary to realize, to reach the point where you don't mind your everyday problem so much, so that you can easily follow the Buddha's way. That is more Rinzai way.

Soto way—nowadays we have, you know, many Soto followers in Japan and many priests. But originally Dogen Zenji try to—tried to have just several sincere students. We say "one by one," or "half by half" . He said one or half by one or half . Half by half. Half is enough if he is sincere.

So, you know, the relationship between teacher and student should be very close. We say if one is someone's disciple one should, you know, make calligraphy exactly the same as his teacher, you know. You sign, you know—in America you have signature. By your handwriting is your signature, but it doesn't work so well in Japan. We put the emphasis—we practice calligraphy so hard that one can imitate someone's calligraphy exactly the same as your friend does or your teachers—your teachers does.

That much, you know, close relationship is necessary, but not by imitation but from bottom of your heart. So how you, you know, learn Oriental— Japanese—Oriental culture is to imitate, you know, his teacher's way. And when you are able to, you know, imitate his way, like his own calligraphy or way, you can, you know, establish your own way after you are able to imitate his teacher's way. And after you acquired fully his teacher's way then, if necessary, you know, you should create your own form of calligraphy. But not before you can fully—you can imitate his way exactly the same.

My teacher is not, you know, my father—was not my father. But people said when I laugh, you know : "You must be," you know, "your teacher's," you know, "secret boy" , because the way you do something, way you laugh, way you speak, and way you make your voice [are] exactly the same as your teacher. So your teacher must be your father," they said—some—not every one of them, but some people said. That is more Soto way.

But the point is to give up selfish, you know, way as much as possible. Not completely, because it is not possible to give up our selfish idea. And we know that is impossible. We continue our practice forever. But you may say if it is not complete—if it is not possible to complete it, it does not mean to try to, you know, try to annihilate evil desires. But it is not so. That is not Buddhist understanding, Buddhist effort. Even though it is not possible, if it is right we should follow the way. It is not a matter of possible or impossible. Even though it is impossible, if it is right, or if we want to do it, we should do it. We should try to—at least we should try to do it.

Maybe both Rinzai way and Soto way is necessary, I think. If, you know, I want you to be completely Soto students or Soto disciples, I will not allow you to have long hair . I wouldn't. At first even, you know, that much, you know, confidence is necessary. If you want to follow Buddhist way from the starting point, that is more Soto way. "Even though you don't like it, you should do it!" Do you understand? That is Soto way. Rinzai way [is]: "Practice zazen! Practice hard until you have kensho! Whether you have long hair or dirty shoes, it doesn't matter. Practice zazen hard!" That is more Rinzai way. If he attains enlightenment, he will not matter whether his hair is long or not. Whatever costume—in whatever costume he is, he [it] doesn't matter.

But Soto way is: "WHY DO YOU—DON'T YOU SHAVE YOUR HAIR if you are Soto student?! That is difference. So whether you like it or not, we will force you to —we will put you in square box! Instead of, you know, putting emphasis on enlightenment or kensho. Same thing, you know.

So in Rinzai way there is more freedom, maybe. In Soto way we don't have freedom until you have complete freedom, until you feel freedom in your everyday life.

So we should not, I think, be—we shouldn't be too much attached to Rinzai, or idea of Rinzai or Soto. But we should know that—we should know the point. I think this is, in this sense—when we understand this point, I am very much grateful for Dogen Zenji who found—who was sincere enough to found out this point clearly. And, according to him, there is no Soto or Rinzai or no Zen even. We are all Buddha's disciple. That is enough, he said. He is—he was a person who [was] sincerely devoted [to] Buddhism and wanted to be a good Buddha's disciple. Fame or rank was not his point, or how many students he has, that was not his point. To be a good disciple even, you know, he—no one knows where he is, who he is. That is not his point. And he wanted to be a good disciple. And he want—but he wanted to help real disciple. He doesn't mind how much, you know, student he has. If he—if he has one good disciple, that was enough for him. Or even though he hasn't no disciple, maybe that was—he will not regret for that, because he wrote so many things for his descendants, who may understand his way. Usually even priest—even a priest are very much attached to his achievement, in its worldly sense. Because of him, I think, we came to this kind of understanding of Zen.

We say, you know—last year at Tassajara, Peter Schneider] asked me to speak about non-sectarianism . And after I gave lecture, he said: "That is sectarianism!" Maybe our sectarianism is non-sectarianism: sectarianism of non-sectarianism.

And he says, also—people may say, you know, "Zen," but no patriarchs said—called themselves Zen master. Even though people said "Zen," there is no need to—to be or to call ourselves Zen. We are not Zen Buddhist. We are just Buddha's disciple. If you, if—to understand Buddhism in that way, or to understand Zen in that way is sectarianism, we are very sectarian. But it is not so, actually. At least we have sincere enough or honest enough to accept his teaching, giving up our selfish viewpoint or criticism.

True Happiness and Renewal of Practice

Everyone seeks for true happiness, but happiness cannot be true happiness if the happiness is not followed by perfect composure. The— usually happiness does not stay long. Happiness is mostly just very short time and it will be lost in next moment when you have it. So, sometimes we will think rather not to have it because after happiness usually followed by sorrow and this is, I think, everyone experiences it in our everyday life.

Buddha, when he escaped—can you hear me?—when he escaped from his castle, he felt this kind of—he had this kind of happiness in his luxurious life in the castle, he at last forsake all of those, this kind of life, so we say he started his religious trip because of evanescence, because he felt evanescence of life. That is why he started study of Buddhism. I think we have to think about this point more. I think everyone seeks for happiness, that is all right, but the point is what kind of—how to seek for happiness is the point. But whether our way, whether the happiness we seek for is something which we can...it is something which is possible to have it.

Surely there is—we have to seek his teaching more carefully. He taught us the Four Noble Truths and first of all he taught us this world is world of suffering. When we seek for suffering— happiness—to say this world is world of suffering is very, you know—you may be very much disappointed with your teacher. World of suffering. This world anyway is world of suffering, he says. And he continues.

Why we suffer is this world is world of fantasy, everything changes. When everything changes we seek for some permanent thing, we want everything to be permanent. Especially when we have something good or when we see something beautiful or we want it to be always in that way. But actually everything changes. So that is why we suffer. So if we seek for happiness even though we seek for happiness it is not possible to have it because we are expecting something to be always constant when everything changes. So naturally we must have suffering. So far, according to this teaching, we are—there is no other way for us to live in the world of suffering—that is the only way to exist in this world. Then it is not possible to obtain eternal happiness, or eternal composure of life. Though we have some way to have eternal composure of life or happiness of life, but first of all if we want to composure of life, we have to change our view, our way of observing things. To observe things as it is, we say, but to observe things as it is for usual sense and to observe things as it is in our way is not the same. This point is not truly realized by even Buddhists. Things as it is, way as it is. What is way as it is. Usually things as it is means to observe things as if something exists in that way, constantly, forever. We say—here in incense bowl. But this is already mistake. There is no such thing exists. This is always changing. This is bronze, but even so this is changing, and you sense in it always changing. In ten minutes there will be no more incense, but if it is very good incense you will think as if something exists—not forever—you may not think in that way, but at least you think this incense exists and fire exists in that way, but the fire is not exactly the same fire as you observe this fire.

This is actually, you know—instead of combustion, it is not red—red fire as you —as you see it. It is constant repetition of combustion—like this—there is electricity, but that light is always—current back and forth, this way, and doesn't exist in that way, but we see there constantly electric light, like so. But that is not true. So we Buddhists call this kind of naive way of looking —observing things is aspect of being because we think everything exists in this way. Aspect of being. And when you understand everything changes and everything is changing, like electric light or fire, we call this kind of view, is view of non-being. No such thing exists, so non-being. And for Buddhists, for you maybe if you seek for happiness, if someone who has view of seeking for happiness, it means that he is seeking for something which is impossible and if you have the view of non-being you will not care for anything. If you accept things in that way, you will be very — your way of life is very empty. And you will not find out any meaning of life at all. And our way of observing things is based on view of being and non-being, both. And we know that view of being is too naive, and view of non-being is too—logical. Or too critical. Or view of—true view of life should be both. View of being and view of non-being. This is our way.

But view of being and view of non-being is not—is not possible to accept. We can accept one of the two, but we cannot accept two of those viewpoints. And here there is another problem for us. But when you face —when you face this second problem, you will be said to be Buddhist. And you will give up to rely on your intellectual understanding of teaching and you will start our practice—to accept this kind of paradox.

Recently I ask you and I want you to reflect on why you seek for—why you study Buddhism. Because I think this point is—if this point is not fully understood, it may be difficult— to put whole physical and spiritual power in our practice. Usually maybe in your practice without thinking about our life more deeply and you try to if you have problem you will try to solve it by means of practice or teaching, but if you really think about whether your view of life is right or wrong, whether you are trying to obtain something which is possible to obtain or you are doing— you are trying to accomplish something which is not possible to accomplish. Then you will not be sincere enough to practice our way because you are always fascinated by some teaching or chanting. We don't know—what we study in intellectual way is very shallow, but what we actually experience is very deep.

When—after—when I came to America, I found very, you know—I found— special, some special food for me and I enjoyed it, I enjoyed it very much —that was potato. Potato was delicious to me, but I don't know if it is so for you or not. I don't know what kind of nourishment potato has, I haven't studied anything about potato, but I like it very much. The reason why I like it is—I don't know why—when I was in Japan, of course, I liked it, but I didn't think I liked potatoes so much!

But after I came to America, having very—various foods and I haven't not much chance to eat potatoes: maybe once a month or so. When I was invited for Thanksgiving, I had mashed potatoes—that was delicious. But usually I haven't mashed potatoes, or even baked potato. At Tassajara I told Ed I like potato . Sometimes, as we have various food— various kinds of food, so Ed cannot give me always potato. So only once in a while I had potato.

As soon as I come back from Tassajara I go to the grocery store and buy three or four potatoes. And as it takes pretty long time to cook it, I cut it and fry it. My boy doesn't like it, but I like it. My wife doesn't like it much. So I cook it just for myself. Do you know why? Potato was— when I was young I—my hometown produced a lot of potatoes, so I was eating potatoes always when I was a boy. So that is why I like it. When I was eating I didn't like it so much because I had it almost not everyday, but four times or more a week.

This kind of experience characterized our character. I think you may not like zazen so much, but you think this is good, so you may practice it. But you may not realize how much progress you made in your zazen practice. Some may do, but most of you don't, I am afraid. But that is all right. This kind of experience which is not just reading or listening to lecture and something which you experience, both physically and spiritually, without thinking about it. Without trying to find out the meaning of it, beyond our intellectual understanding, to practice our way without any gaining idea. To practice our way is valuable and you will have real power of digesting things.

In Lotus Sutra, as you know, Chapter Three, Buddha told Shariputra:

You may not know what you have done before. You will not remember what you did in your former life or even in this life. You may not remember all of it, but," he said, "you have been practicing our way for so long time. That is why now—you have been practicing our way for so long time, that is why now you have attained enlightenment. I know that, but you may not know it—why you have attained enlightenment. I ask you why you came here so many times. I think you don't know why you came here, but there is some reason why you came here. You didn't come here just by curiosity. Why you came here is, I don't think possible to figure out. But there must be some reason.

This kind of reason—you practice your way is so-called-it—there is no other way to say so we say—your buddha-nature seeks for buddha. Buddha seek for buddha. This is very mystic way of putting it, but there is no other way to say it. So we say buddha-nature seeks buddha-nature.

We have various Buddhist philosophy, and we have a lot of teaching to study, but Buddhism is not actually philosophy or teaching. Buddhism is always within ourselves and always helping us. But we do not—when we are not—when we don't realize it, then that is so called it suffering. Or when we live in the realm of good or bad, right or wrong, we lose our meaning of life. Only when we do something we practice, with right understanding, whatever you do that is our practice. Because we are so intellectual being, it is necessary to—to be free from our reasoning or our intellect. That is necessary. And instead of being caught by intellectual mind, we should seek for something more or we have to rely on way things goes and the way we live without— without every reason—why we are practicing—Indian way or Chinese way or Japanese way—you may feel in that way. But actually there is no special way. Our way is not just for Japanese or Chinese or Indian people. This is for everyone. We sit in cross-legged position, but if you think just cross-legged position is just Zen, that is a big mistake.

If you want to practice our way, we should free our mind from intellectual or conscious activity in term of right or wrong, or good or bad. Whatever it is we should try it and we should have taste of it through direct experience. Not just feeling or thinking, but direct experience. That is zazen practice.

So many people here practicing our way. I feel a great responsibility as a teacher. If I am not here maybe you will not come here. If I am here you come here and spend all day in our practice. But if you misunderstand—if you have misunderstanding in our practice it will not work at all. It is quite natural for us to think some result or effect as long as you do something, but our practice is something different from that kind of activity.

The People in Hell

It's been a pretty long time since I saw you. I am still studying hard to find out what is our way. Recently I reached the conclusion that there is no Buddhism or there is no Zen or anything. And I thought of the story which I was told in Obun Festival when I was young. The story is about the water or the story is about the people in Hell. Although they have water, the people in Hell cannot drink it because the water burns like a fire, or water which they want to drink looks like blood, so they cannot take it. While the celestial beings...for the celestial beings it is jewel and for the fish it is their home and for the human being it is water. You may think, if you think water is water (if you understand that water is water, as we do) is right understanding the water sometimes looks like.although water sometimes looks like jewel or house or blood or fire that is not real water.you may think in this way. As you think that zazen practice is real practice and the rest of the everyday activities is the application of zazen, but this (zazen) is fundamental practice. But Dogen zenji, amazingly said, 'Water is not water'. If you think water is water your understanding is not much different from the understanding of fish's understanding, and hungry ghost's understanding of water, or angel's understanding of water. There is not much difference between our understanding and their understanding.

Then what is our zazen? Or what is water?

This may be another...the next question you will have; if zazen is not zazen, what is that which we are practicing everyday? This will be the next question. Here Dogen Zenji says, 'This is Buddha's activity, some activity which was given to you.' Tentatively the water is not water actually; it is something which was given to you. Our practice is not something which you can understand because it is something which is given to you. You didn't make it; you did not invent it; you did not practice zazen through and through. But the reason why you can practice it is just because it was something which was given to you. So this practice is possible because Buddha gave this practice to us. So there is no reason why we do not know what it is, but because it was given to us we have to receive it, we have to accept it. That is just why we practice zazen. Now, if you understand our way in this way whatever you do that is the gift for you, something which was given to you, and which is something, which you should accept; because you cannot accept anything, and you cannot chose anything you have no chance to accept things when it was given to you. Even though there are various treasures, if they are not given to you, you cannot accept them.

And the way to accept it is to accept it when it is given to you. You cannot say, 'I will accept it tomorrow". You cannot say, 'I can accept it yesterday'. The only way is to accept it right now, when it was given to you, then tomorrow something new will be given to you. So, day by day, we practice our way, as a gift. And we accept it when it is given to us. So there is no wonder that the same gift Buddha gives us everything according to the people and the situation.when they are in Hell the gift will be fire. For celestial beings the gift will be the jewel. For fish gift will be the house. And there may be many kinds of gifts from Buddha, according to the people, according to the nature of people. In this way, when you understand our way in this way there is no problem and this is the way to practice our way. This is the real gift from Buddha; not only water but also mountain is a gift. So that mountain is not always mountain. To us it is mountain but to a bird it is their home. There may be various merits or virtues of the mountain, so (Fuyo Dokei zenji?) says, 'The east mountain flowing and the river stays.' Water stays and mountain flows. We think mountain is something which is always staying in some certain place, but there may be some who understand the mountain...that there may be some person who sees the mountain flowing and water staying. Because it is something which was given to us, that gift is not something, is not only just something which we see. It looks like something like mountain, or water, or cake, or something else. It looks like so. But we don't know exactly what it is. So before we understand what it is, the only way is to accept it and to practice it. That is actually true practice, or else you cannot practice our way. Even though you have complete Zendo you cannot practice.

At Tassajara we have a very difficult time to practice our way. For almost one year we are trying very seriously to practice our way and the more we make our effort to practice our way, we are involved in big problems. You can see what we are doing at Tassajara. There are more than forty people and they each have their own understanding of Zen, ore or less. "This is Zen". "This is Zen". That is the trouble. Because you practice zazen you cannot practice; you cannot have Tassajara. Even though they are there they cannot do it. Why? Because they practice zazen. So I think the best way is not to practice zazen....(laughter). Just to live in Tassajara, like a bird. Then you can practice zazen. Birds or badgers know what is zazen better than students in Tassajara. This happens, actually, because we understand water is something to drink, the water is not something to live in, this kind of one-sided understanding of our way creates many problems. So, at Tassajara, there is Tassajara's way; here in Los Altos there is your own way; as a gift. And the only way to practice it is to receive it, just to receive it when it is given to you.

This is very important point. Even though I say so to have..to make our effort to find out what is real practice is not in vain and I am so grateful for students in Tassajara, and the students who practice in Los Altos, in the Bay Area, and recently at Mill Valley, too. They are making a big effort. And we are now in the state to find out the real meaning of our practice. After making a big effort to find out what is zazen we are finding out what is.we almost find out what is true zazen. And why we should practice our way in this cross-legged position like Buddha did, and the understanding of our practice which was given to us by Buddha.

From Present to Past

To live in the realm of Buddha Nature means to die as a small being, moment after moment. When we lose our balance we die, and at the same time, to lose our balance, sometimes, means to develop ourselves, or to grow. If we are in perfect balance we cannot live as a small being. So whatever we see the things are changing, losing their balance. Why everything looks beautiful is because it is something out of balance, but it is background is always in perfect harmony and on this perfect harmony everything exists, losing its balance. This is how everything exists in the realm of big Buddha Nature. So if you see things without knowing, without realizing Buddha Nature everything is in the form of suffering. But if you understand the background of everything, which looks like suffering, suffering itself is how we live, how we extend our life. So in Zen we, sometimes we emphasize the "out of balance" or disorder. Nowadays our Japanese painting which was developed by the spirit of Zen became pretty formulated; became formal. That is why nowadays we have more that is why we have modern art.

The painters in old time practice how to put dots out of order. Even though you try to do it what you did is always in some order. This is a kind of practice. And how to take care of things is the same thing. If you try to make them—even though you try to put them under some control, it is impossible. You cannot do that. So sometimes, if you want to control people the best way is to encourage them to be mischievous. Then they will be in control in its wider sense. So to observe —to put things—to put large, spacious meadow for your sheep, or cow is how you control people. So let them do what they want, first, and watch them, is the best policy. But let alone policy is not good. That is worst. The second worst is trying to control them. The best one is to watch them— just to watch them, without trying to control. As you practice zazen if you obtain the perfect calmness in your practice don't be bothered various images you have in your mind. Let them come and let them go out. Then they will be under control.

But his policy is not so easy. It looks easy, but it needs some different, special effort. How to make this kind of effort is the secret of practice. Suppose you are sitting under some extraordinary circumstances. If you try to calm down your mind you cannot sit, and if you try to ...try not to be disturbed by it, your effort will not be right effort. If you have to make some effort, the only effort you can do is to count your breathing or to be concentrated on your inhaling or exhaling. Why this kind of effort is necessary is that this kind of effort will help right effort in your practice. We say concentration but to concentrate your mind on something is not the purpose...is not the true purpose of Zen.

True purpose of Zen is to see things as they are, to observe things as they are, to let everything go as it goes, and to put everything under control in it's widest sense. In other words, to open up our small mind, is Zen practice. So to control your mind is just an aid to obtain the big mind. So if you want to find out the true meaning of Zen in your everyday life, some...you have to study, or you have to find out the meaning of controlling your mind...them meaning of keeping your mind on your breathing, the meaning of keeping your body in right posture. This is rather difficult to explain, but your study should be more subtle and careful. And we have to find out the true meaning of Zen.

Dogen Zenji said, "Time elapses from present to past." This is absurd, but in our practice it is true (sometimes it is true). From present to past, times goes from present to past. So as Dogen Zenji said, "Time elapses from present to past." This is not true in our logical mind, but in our actual life, when we make past time present we have...there we have poem, there we have human life.

So when we find out this kind of truth it means we have found the true meaning of the time which constantly elapses from past to present and present to future. If this is true, at the same time, the time elapses from future to present and from present to past is also true. As some Zen master said, "To go Eastward one mile is to go Westward one mile." This is the vital freedom. We have to acquire this kind of vital freedom, perfect freedom.

So perfect freedom is in—is under some rules. If there are no rules, there is no freedom. As long as you have rules you have freedom. Without being aware of the rules to try to obtain freedom means nothing. This kind of freedom is...I don't know what to say. It means nothing. In Japanese we say, muchacha. Muchacha means nothing. That is why we practice zazen. We are aiming at the same thing but it looks like there is no need for us to practice anything; there is no need for us to have any rules, as some young people may say, but it is absolutely for us to have some rules. But it does not mean always to be under control. This is the secret of our life.

Complications

When we sit in this way our mind is calm and quite simple. But usually our mind is not so calm and our mind is very complicated. When we do something it is difficult to be concentrated on what we do and because, before we do (something) we think and when we think the thinking leaves some trace, and the thinking not only leave some trace but also it will give us some particular notion to do something. That notion makes our activity very complicated. When we do something quite simple we have no notion, but when we do something difficult, or when we do something in relation to others...other people, or in society, we will have many convenient idea for ourselves, and that makes activity very complicated.

In America. American people in this point, I think are very good. You are much simpler in your way of.when you do something you have very good attitude in what you so, but usually we have double or triple notion in one activity. That makes it very difficult to be concentrated on one activity because we have.you know.to be concentrated on one activity because we have.you know.we want to catch too many birds. So you will catch any bird because you want to try to catch too many birds. We say, to catch two birds by one stone. That is usual activity. That kind of thinking, we say, is to have shadow of thinking. Shadow is not...you are not thinking actually. Your thinking is divided in many ways that means you have shadow of the activity or the thinking or you will have trace of the thinking.

We have to think but we should not have the trace of the thinking. Trace of the thinking— even if it is one trace, it is not good because you will be attached to the trace. This is what you may say, "This is what I have done", but actually it is not so. When we...in our recollection you may say, "I did such and such thing in some certain way" but actually it is not so, and when you think in that way you limit the actual experience of what you have done. So if you attach to the idea about what you have done that will create some selfish idea. So usually what you have done is always good but it is not actually so.

When we become old we are very proud of what we have done. That is. when others listen to us saying something proudly; others will feel funny or may not feel so good because his interpretation...his recollection is onesided. They know that is not actually what he did. Moreover, he, himself will be proud of what he did and that pride will create some problem for him while he is repeating what his idea is. His personality will be twisted more and more until he becomes quite a disagreeable person. It means to leave trace of the thinking or activity. We should not forget what we did but we should not have trace. It is a different matter to leave trace, what I mean, and to remember something in its true sense is quite different matter. It is necessary to remember what we did but we should not have.we should not attach to what we have done in some special sense. That is so-called attachment or trace of activity. So we should not have any trace of the activity or we should not have any shadow of the activity.

When we do something we should do it with our whole body and mind. You should be concentrated on what you do and when you do something you should do it completely -like a good bonfire. It should not be smoky. You should burn yourself completely. You should not be smoky fire. That is one thing. If you do not burn yourself completely you will have trace of yourself in what you did. It means you do not change it into ashes completely. You have something remaining without completely burned down or burned out. That is so-called 'zen activity'. This is the goal of our practice. That is what it means by 'ash does not come back to firewood'. Ash is ash. Ash should be completely ash. The firewood should be firewood. If this kind of activity takes place, one activity covers everything. This is the goal of our practice.

So our practice is not matter of one hour or two hours; or one day or one year. Even for a moment you practice zazen with your whole body and mind. That is zazen. So moment after moment you should devote yourself to your practice. You should not have any remains after you do something; but it does not mean to forget all about it. If you understand this point all the dualistic thinking or all the problems in you life will be vanished because you have no idea of duality. When you practice zen you become one with zen. There's no 'you' or no 'zazen'. When you bow there is no Buddha or no you. One complete bow.bowing takes place, that's all. That is Nirvana, or attainment, perfect attainment.

When Buddha transmitted our practice to Mahajuna he picked up a flower. He just picked up a flower with smiling.with a smile. And all the.only Mahajuna understood what he meant but the rest of the people didn't understand. We don't know if this is historical event or not but it means something. It means our traditional way. Some activity which covers everything is true activity and that activity, that secret of this activity, is transmitted from Buddha to us. That is zen school not some teaching taught by him but not rules of life which was set up by Buddha. This teaching, or the rules, should be changed according to the country or according to the place or according to the people who observe it, but this secret of the practice cannot be changed. It is always so and we should live in this way always because in Buddhism we have no idea of the world which is completely different from this world. The old world is the extension of this world. The future world should be extension of our present world and our past life should result in this present life. That is how we believe in truth. Truth is not something which is beyond our reach. Truth should be always here.

So there is, for us there is no other way to live in this world and I think this is quite true and this is at least more acceptable.easy to accept.easy to understand and easy to practice it. In comparison to this kind of life, if you think what is happening to this world, or to human society you will find out how true the truth Buddha left us. The truth is quite simple and practice is quite simple, but even though it is quite simple we should not ignore it. If you...we should find out great value in this simple truth. Usually, if it is too simple."Oh, I know that. It is quite simple. Everyone knows that." But if you do not find its value it means nothing. It is the same thing as not knowing. The more you understand our culture, the more you understand how true our teaching is. So for the people who are attached to our culture too much it is better to be critical of our culture. It means you are coming back to the simple truth left by Buddha. But our approach is just concentrated on simple practice and simple understanding of life, but for someone it is necessary to criticize our culture. There are two approaches. But anyway, we should not attach to some fancy idea to beautiful things. We should not seek for something good. The truth is always near at hand, within your reach

Appreciate Your Practice

The purpose of my talk is not to give you some intellectual understanding but just to express appreciation of our practice. To sit with you in this way —very unusual. Of course whatever we do in this life should be unusual; it is so unusual anyway. As Buddha said, "To appreciate our human life is as rare as soil on your nail." You know, soil on your nail is so little. Our human life is so rare, and so wonderful, and when I sit I want to remain in this way forever, but I encourage myself to have another practice, for instance, to recite sutra or to make bow. And when we make bow, I think, "this is wonderful", but we have to change our practice for reciting sutra. And when I recite sutra I don't feel to talk after reciting sutra _. So the purpose of my talk is to express my appreciation, that's all. Our way is not to sit for something; it is to express our true nature. That is our practice.

So if you want to express yourself there should be some natural and appropriate way to express. Even when you sway yourself, right and left, after you sit, is also to express yourself. It is not relaxation or preparation for the practice. It is a part of the practice. So we should not do it as if you are preparing for something. It is part of your practice, not preparation. To cook, to fix some food, is not preparation, according to Dogen's idea. It is practice. It is the expression of our sincerity. To cook is not to prepare food for someone or for yourself. It is the expression of your sincerity. So when you cook, you should express yourselves in your activity in the kitchen. So you should take plenty of time to do it and you should work on it without expecting something, or without something in your mind. You should just cook. Even cleaning is not preparation for rituals. Cleaning itself is practice; and then we observe rituals; and then we clean up again. That is also expression of our sincerity; that is a part of practice; that is our way. So we should appreciate what we are doing always. There's no preparation for something else.

So, Bodhisattva's way is called 'single-minded way' or 'one railway track thousand miles_.thousands of miles_.one railway track thousands of miles, we say, one railway track. The railway track is always, you know, the same. If the railway track became wider, or narrower, it may be awful. Wherever you go the railway track is always the same. That is Bodhisattva's way. So even though the sun were to rise from west, the Boddhisattva's way is only one. There is no other way. To express his nature, his sincerity, is his way. And there's no other way. But, we say 'railway track', but actually there's no railway track. The sincerity is the railway track. And the sight you see from the train will be different, but we are running always on same track. This is Boddhisattva's way. And there's....for the track there's no beginning or no end. Beginningless and endless track. This is Bodhisattva's way; and this is the nature of our zen practice. So there is no beginning , or no attainment, no starting point or no goaL.no attainment....nothing to attain.

Our purpose is just to run on the track is our way. But when you become curious about what is zen, what is railway track, danger is there. You should not see the railway track. If you see it you will become dizzy. You should appreciate the sight you will have on your train. That is our way. There's no need to be curious about the railway track..for the passenger. Someone will take care of it. Buddha will take care of it. But sometime we have to explain what is railway track, because we are so curious..we become so curious if something is always same. "How is it possible for him to be always same, like that? What is the secret?" But there's no secret. Everyone has same nature as railway track. This is our way of practice. So it is necessary to sit in this way. But just to sit is not our way. Whatever you do, it should be the same activity.

There were good....two good friends, Chokai and Shi Fu Ku. They started some talk about the Boddhisattva's way and Chokai said, "If the Arahat were to have evil desires, the Boddhisattva has no two ways." Shi Fu Ku said, "Even though you say so, your comment is not perfect." Chokai said, "What is your interpretation....what is the actual Boddhisattva's way?" Shi Fu Ku said, "Now I found out that you did not understand Boddhisattva's way." Chokai said, "What is your understanding of Boddhisattva's way?" Shi Fu Ku said, "We have had enough discussion. So let's have a cup of tea." They are good friends you know. Let's have a cup of tea. He didn't give any answer to him. It is impossible, you now, to give some interpretation to our way, but as a part of practice, they discuss something....they try to discuss, but they didn't want to find out something new, so, "Our discussion is over, let's have a cup of tea." That's very good isn't it? So, I should say, "I am hungry enough to have breakfast, so let's have some breakfast.....my practice is over....I mean your listening is over." That is our way. There's no problem, and there's no need to remember what I say. There's no need for you to understand what I say. You understood. You have full understanding in....within yourself. But something must go on the track. We have to have some passengers. If we have railway track we have to have train..so, train track for dining room.

Group Zazen

Back East they find pretty difficult to have good students. Of course there are many people who are interested in Buddhism, but quite few people are interested in pure form of Buddhism. They are interested in studying the teaching of Buddhism, or philosophy of Buddhism and they are comparing our Buddhism to another religion and they understand intellectually how Buddhism is good for intellectual mind. But whether Buddhism is philosophically deep or good or perfect is not our point. To keep our practice in its pure form is our purpose. When I felt something even blasphemous when they talk about how Buddhism is perfect as a philosophy or teaching without actually knowing what it is.

To practice zazen in this way, with group, is the most important thing for Buddhism and for us. There is nothing so important than this practice for us because this practice is the original way of life. Without knowing the origin of things we cannot appreciate the result of our effort. Our efforts must have some meaning. To find meaning of our effort is to find our original source of effort. We should not be concerned about the result of our effort so much, before we know the original source of our effort. If the origin is not clear and pure all our effort will not be pure and so the result of our effort will not satisfy you. When we resume to our original nature, and starting from the original nature, making our effort incessantly, we will find out, we will appreciate the result of our effort, moment after moment, day by day, year by year. This is how we should appreciate our life.

Those who attach to the result of our effort only will not have any chance to appreciate our effort because the result of our effort will not come forever. But if your original intention is good all what you do is good and you will satisfy with whatever you do. Zazen practice is the practice to resume to our pure way of life, beyond gaining idea, or beyond fame and profit. By practice we just keep our original nature as it is, for the pure original nature, there is no need to intellectualize what it is, because it is beyond our intellectual understanding and there is no need to say, to appreciate because it is beyond our appreciation. So just to sit, without any gaining idea, with purest intention to remain quiet, as quiet as our original nature is, is our practice. Here in this zendo there is no fancy idea. Once in a week we just come and sit, and after communicating with each other we go home and resume to our own everyday activity as a continuity of our pure practice, enjoying our true way of life. This is very unusual.

What you study...what you...wherever you go people may ask you what is Buddhism.(with notebook). You may imagine how I feel. But here we just practice zazen, that's all what we do. And we are happy in this practice. For us there is no need to understand what is zen. We are practicing zazen. So, for us, there is no need to know what is zen, intellectually. This is, I think, very very unusual....unusual for American society. As you know, back East there are many way of, many patterns of life, according to their religion. So, it is maybe, it is quite natural to talk about what the difference is between various religions and to compare one religion to the other religion. But for us, there is no need to compare Buddhism to Christianity. Buddhism is Buddhism and

Buddhism is our practice. So we don't know even what we are doing when we just practice pure mind. So we cannot compare our way to some other religion, but we don't know how to compare our religion. Some people may say Zen Buddhism is not religion. Maybe so. Anyway, Zen Buddhism is religion before religion. So it might not be religion in usual sense. But it is wonderful, even though we do not study religion, what it is intellectually, or without any cathedral or any ornament, it is possible to appreciate our original nature. This is quite unusual. This kind of unusual experience will be found out when you practice it without any gaining idea. I feel the practice of zazen is enough but if I should say something, I think what I shall talk will be how wonderful it is to practice zazen in this way.

Our purpose is just to keep this practice forever. This practice is started from beginningless time and it will continue for endless future. Strictly speaking, for human being there is no other practice than this practice. There is no other way of life than this way of life, because zen practice is direct expression of our true nature. Of course, whatever you do, it is the expression of our true nature, but without this practice it is difficult to realize what is our life. As long as you think, 'I am doing this. I have to do this', or 'I must attain something special', actually you are not doing anything. When you give up, or when you do not want to, when you do not do anything, you do something. When you do not do anything with some gaining idea, you do something. Actually what you are doing is not for sake of something. You feel as if you are doing something special but actually it is the expression of true nature, or that is the activity to appease you inmost desire.

It is our human nature to be active always. To do something is our human nature and it is universal nature for everyone, every existence. So, in this way, just practice of zen is enough. But so long as you think you are practicing zazen for sake of something that is not true practice. If you continue this simple practice every day you will obtain some wonderful power. But before you attain it, it is some wonderful power but after you attain it, it is just power. It is not something special. It is just you yourself. Nothing special. As Chinese poem says there is nothing special. If you visit there, there is nothing special. However Losan is famous for its misty mountains. And Seko is famous for its water. This is zen. There is nothing special.

If you go there there is nothing special. But people think Losan is wonderful. It is wonderful to see the range of mountains covered by mist; to see the misty mountains in Losan is wonderful. And people say it is wonderful to see the water covers all the earth. It is wonderful they may say but if you go there you see just water and you see just mountains. There is nothing special. But it is a kind of mystery that for the people who has no experience of enlightenment, enlightenment is something wonderful, but if you attain it that is nothing. Although it is nothing, it is not nothing. Do you understand? For some person, for the mother who has children to have children is nothing special, nothing special. But if she lose her children what she will feel? That is zazen.

So if you continue this practice we don't know when you will acquire the power, but more and more you will acquire something. Not special, but something. You may say, universal nature, or Buddha nature, enlightenment. You may call it by many names but for the person who owns it, it is nothing. And it is something. So I cannot express my joy to practice zazen with you here once a week. And while you are continuing this practice, week after week, year after year, you will.your experience becomes more and more deeper and the experience you have you obtain, will cover everything you do in your everyday life. The most important thing is when you practice zazen it is necessary to forget all gaining idea, all dualistic idea. In other words just practice zazen in certain posture. This is very good point. Don't think about anything. Just remain on your cushion without thinking, without expecting anything. Then your true nature will resume its own nature and eventually you will resume to your own nature. You resume your true nature when the true nature resumes to its own nature.

The monk, the disciple of the sixth patriarch, told Basho, 'when a vehicle or cart does not go, which do you hit a horse or the cart.?' Which do you hit? He couldn't answer and Nanga said, "If you think, if you try to hit your cart, your cart will not go. If you hit the horse, the horse will be angry. What will you do?" he said. When you resume to your true nature, when your true nature resumes to its true nature, you resume to your true nature. Do you understand? When horse becomes horse, cart will go. When cart becomes cart, horse will go. The horse and cart is not two. Horse and cart is one. So when horse start to pull the cart the cart will go. Usually, but usually we think our true nature and you yourself are something different. So there is problem always. But actually you are cart itself. Horse is cart and cart is horse. Without horse there is no cart. Without cart there is no horse. Horse is something to pull cart. If there is no cart, horse may be a wild beast. He is not a horse. Because he pulls the cart, horse is horse.

When we express our true nature, we are human being. When we don't, we don't know what we are. We are not animal because we walk by two legs. We are something different from animal. But if we are not human being what are we? We may be ghost, or we don't know what to say. There is no such thing exists. That is delusion. We are not any more human being. So, we say, when zen becomes zen, we become human being. We exist. When zen is not zen, nothing exists. What I am talking about is not intellectual understanding. Intellectually it makes my talk makes no sense, but you will understand what I mean so in ????? Nirvana Sutra Buddha says, everything has Buddha nature. That is Chinese rendering. Everything has Buddha nature. But Dogen reads this way, "Everything is Buddha nature". There is difference. There is, "Everything has Buddha nature". If you say 'Everything has Buddha nature", in everything is Buddha nature. So Buddha nature and everything is different. But 'everything is Buddha nature' is everything is Buddha nature itself. When there is no Buddha nature, everything is not everything. It is just delusion, which do not exist. It may exist in you mind but actually such thing does not exist. So even though you do not do anything you are actually doing something. You are expressing yourself. You are expressing your true nature. Your eyes will express. Your voice will express. Your demeanor will express. So the most important thing is to express our true nature in the most simple way, in the most adequate way, and to appreciate the true nature in smallest existence. This is the most important thing. So truth is.the most valuable truth.

Made in United States
Troutdale, OR
02/20/2025